Remembering Revell Model Kits

COLLECTOR'S SET 2 BATTLE OF BRITAIN FIGHTERS

Revell *Authentic Kits*

1/32 Scale 11" long ready to assemble
plastic models loaded with realism and detail!

Cement included

Messerschmitt Bf-109F

Spitfire MK-I

**Revised &
Expanded
3rd Edition**

Thomas Graham

Schiffer Publishing Ltd ®

4880 Lower Valley Road, Atglen, PA 19310 USA

To Lewis H. Glaser

Published by Schiffer Publishing Ltd.
4880 Lower Valley Road
Atglen, PA 19310
Phone: (610) 593-1777; Fax: (610) 593-2002
E-mail: Info@schifferbooks.com

For the largest selection of fine reference books on this and related subjects, please visit our web site at
www.schifferbooks.com
We are always looking for people to write books on new and related subjects. If you have an idea for a book please contact us at the above address.

This book may be purchased from the publisher.
Include $3.95 for shipping.
Please try your bookstore first.
You may write for a free catalog.

In Europe, Schiffer books are distributed by
Bushwood Books
6 Marksbury Ave.
Kew Gardens
Surrey TW9 4JF England
Phone: 44 (0) 20 8392-8585; Fax: 44 (0) 20 8392-9876
E-mail: info@bushwoodbooks.co.uk
Website: www.bushwoodbooks.co.uk
Free postage in the U.K., Europe; air mail at cost.

Revised price guide: 2004
Copyright © 2008 by Thomas Graham
Previous copyright © 2002 & 2004 by Thomas Graham
Library of Congress Control Number: 2008922198

Designed by Joseph M. Riggio Jr.
Type set in Futura Hv BT/Humanist 521 BT

ISBN: 978-0-7643-2992-0
Printed in China
1234

Contents

Revell created a record in plastic of the epic of Modern America. Scott Eidson painted this illustration for the Let's Take a Trip gift set. *G-335*

Introduction

"We were making history. As history was being made, we were making models of it. It was terribly exciting."

—*Royle Glaser Freund*

America and the world underwent a transformation in the decades of the 1950s, '60s, and '70s. The era began in the shadow of World War II and the Great Depression. All things military stood out prominently in European and American cultures, especially when the Cold War followed so closely upon the epic events of the World War. Army surplus jeeps were as common a sight on American streets as the Air Force jets that left contrails overhead. During a typical week the evening television news might carry grainy newsreel photos of the launching of the first nuclear powered submarine, and *LIFE* magazine could do a several page-spread photo essay on the Navy's most powerful aircraft carrier, named after recently deceased President Franklin D. Roosevelt.

Revell's model houses for electric train sets harkened back to a simpler, rural America that was passing away in the 1950s. *T-9009*

Most Americans still lived in medium-size towns or in the new suburbs that were creeping out into the countryside. Cars sprouted bulbous fenders, and there was no such thing as an interstate highway. Sears Roebuck, J. C. Penny, and Woolworth were the major retail stores on Main Street where housewives shopped. As she shopped, Mrs. Modern American discovered more and more consumer items in the stores made of plastic, a material she probably associated with inferior quality. If she bought a toy for Junior, it might be a cheap plastic item, but a nice gift would be made of wood or tin. The companies that made America's toys—and there were thousands of them—operated, for the most part, out of garages and small rustic workshops. Mostly they made old-fashioned toys in old-fashioned ways.

Thirty years later a transformation had taken place, World War II had lost its immediacy and was rapidly fading into the pages of history. The Cold War remained a continuing threat, but familiarity had diminished some of its edgy power to intimidate. The evening news was likely to cover plans for routine launchings of the Space Shuttle. Mega stores like K-Mart dotted the suburbs that now spread far across the landscape. Mom very likely drove a van or perhaps an import compact from Japan to save money on gas fill-ups. Business transactions were now done by credit card and computers kept track of all the debits and payments. Plastic toys littered American homes, and a toy made of wood or tin looked like an antique.

During these three decades plastic model kits played a central role as the preferred pastime for millions of boys in America and around the world. Revell, Inc. began operations in the 1940s in very modest rented space and grew in thirty years to occupy a manufacturing complex of several buildings in Venice, California, with factories in Great Britain and Germany, and subsidiaries in Mexico, Brazil, and Japan. The models produced by Revell so dominated the world market in hobby kits that the name "Revell" became synonymous with plastic models.

Revell first brought the all-plastic model kit to the public's attention in the early fifties, and then proceeded to capture the great, wide real world with its miniature versions of almost everything that flew, floated, or rolled. Revell models became a record in styrene of world history.

Whenever a new Air Force jet like the Lockheed F-104 took to the skies, a new Revell model took boys' imaginations into the skies with it. *H-199*

The streamline nuclear-powered freighter *Savannah* portended revolutionary changes. *H-366*

Boys growing up in the 1950s, '60s, or '70s built models simply as part of being adolescents. Everyone made at least a couple of models, but for many boys it became something more. Building whole collections of aircraft, ships, or cars was a sort of prologue to the larger universe of adulthood. Youngsters could, in a highly tactual way, imagine participating in the great events of history and the vast modern world of cars, ships, and aircraft.

Revell models, like the X-15, pointed to space exploration. *H-198*

Revell's models introduced several generations of boys to the basic principles of design, form, and construction. Many an engineer, architect, dentist, and auto mechanic began honing his skills, both mental and manual, by assembling model kits as a boy. Many of today's leading artists and illustrators will testify that their first introduction to the thrill of artistic creation came when they gazed at the rows of model kit boxes lining hobby shop shelves. The dramatic, colorful paintings on Revell's packaging sent creative imaginations soaring.

World War II provided a vast array of subject matter for Revell models, like the humble Jeep. *H-525*

The modern woman in the 1950s drove a VW Microbus. *H-1228*

This book is a record of Revell and its role during an epochal period of world history. Today Revell, as a part of Revell-Monogram, Inc., continues to lead the world in the model hobby field and marked its fiftieth year of model making in the year 2001. But this book will focus on just Revell's first three decades. There are two specific reasons for this. First, the company passed from the hands of the founding Glaser family in 1979, signaling the end of an era in company history. Secondly, in that same year Revell ceased marking its model kits with the "H" designation, and today's hobby enthusiasts recognize the "H" series kits as having a special place in modeling history. With their passing a chapter in history closed.

This book is also a tribute to the men and women who made Revell the innovative, accomplished company that it was and remains. First among these stands Lewis H. Glaser. He started Revell from scratch; he had the vision of what it could become and led it to world leadership in its field. His wife and successor as president, Royle Glaser, contributed to the success of Revell from the day in 1950 that she married Lew, but she would be the first to add that Revell could not have achieved greatness without the contributions of many very talented persons. "The greatness of the company was its people," she once declared. For most of the individuals who worked at Revell, it was much more than just a job. Mrs. Glaser once joked: "We paid people to work for Revell, when they would just have easily paid us for the chance to work there!"

This book would not have been possible without the contributions of many veteran Revell individuals who furnished research material to the author and consented to be interviewed. First among these is Mrs. Royle Glaser Freund. Equally valuable were the contributions of Derek Brand, Ernest Brown, Anthony Bulone, Ronald Campbell, Roma Coe, Clare Darden, Dave Deal, John Deegan, Allan Erickson, Donald Ernst, Paul Escoe, David Fisher, Lillian Furtivo, Howard Goldstein, Charles Gretz, Lloyd Jones, Jim Keeler, Sol Kramer, Ben Lench, Dottie Leschenko, Robert Paeth, Richard Palmer, Bernard Ramos, Howard Rieder, Betty Tomeo, Al Trendle, Dan Westbrook, and Darrell Zipp.

I would especially like to thank the artists who created most of the illustrations first used on Revell's boxes and now reproduced in this book. Nixon Galloway did only a few pieces for Revell, but has long been one of America's premier aviation artists. Richard Kishady and Jack Leynnwood (and Jack's widow Joanne) were happy to recall their days at Revell. Mike Boss and Mike Machat—both students of Jack Leynnwood—furnished some great stories about their mentor. Boss generously supplied photographs of Leynnwood's work. Scott Eidson told me about his father's years at Revell and career in illustration. Carole Steel furnished me with both some examples of her husband's box art and stories of his career as an artist.

Revell's fabulous box art, like the Air Borne Marines gift set, inspired a generation of American artists. *G-271*

Dean Milano shepherded me through the Revell-Monogram plant in Morton Grove for an all-day photo shoot of the marvelous framed box art hanging on office walls.

Nor would this book have been possible without help from some of the world's most dedicated and enthusiastic hobbyists. I would especially like to thank the following men who opened their homes and model kit collections for some daylong photography sessions: Dennis Bowman, Craig Clements, Rusty Cowart, and Vince Paulauskis. Pete Gitzel furnished photos from his collection. Some photographs were taken at the Don Garlits Museum of Drag Racing, Ocala, Florida.

Some of the biggest Revell model fans in the world contributed their knowledge to this book. They include: Michael Boileau, Alejandro Botello, Rod Carri, Bob Ferguson, Jim Gonyier, Mark Gustavson, Stephen Knight, Hal Sanford, Carlton Shank, Bob Shelton, Dean Sills, James Sniffen, Fred Sterns, Randy Vandraiss, and Scott Virgo.

The publications of John Burns, Brad Hansen, and Robert and Beth Halberg proved invaluable.

The staff of the periodicals room of the Library of Congress was most helpful in retrieving the bound volumes of hobby trade journals that chronicle the development of the industry.

Most importantly, an infinite debt of gratitude is due my longsuffering, helpful wife Susan.

Lastly, I would especially like to give thanks and an apology to that person who generously helped with this book, but whom I have slipped-up and neglected to mention by name.

Chapter 1 –
Birth of an Industry

One day in the Hard Times of the 1930s, Baltimore teenager Lou Kramer paid $2.95 for a stick-and-tissue model airplane kit. When his mother found out what he had done, she became furious. The Kramers were an immigrant family from Eastern Europe scraping together a living in the needle trade, and such extravagance seemed totally irresponsible. But Lou loved to build and fly model airplanes, and he couldn't resist temptation. "Lou was the spender," explained his younger brother Sol, "and I was the saver." (Unless otherwise noted, all direct quotations come from interviews with the author.)

In the months that followed the family explosion over the expensive model airplane, the Kramer brothers teamed-up and found ways to turn their hobby into a making-money venture. They organized model airplane flying clubs for their fellow teenagers. "In those years there was a certain enchantment about flying," recalled Sol. The fantasy of flight allowed youngsters to rise above and escape the problems of the era. Economists would later note that two industries grew during the Depression: the movies and hobbies. Both were relatively inexpensive and both were escapist. The Kramer brothers started selling the flying club members materials they needed to build planes: bamboo, rubber, tissue, and wire. "I was a good locater," explained Sol. He went to a yeast-manufacturing factory and found that tins of yeast were insulated for shipping in trucks lined with balsa wood, and he turned this scrap balsa into parts for model airplanes.

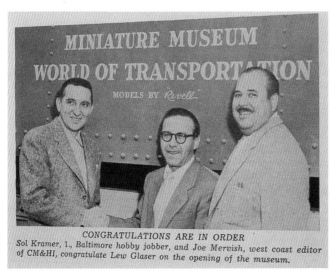

CONGRATULATIONS ARE IN ORDER
Sol Kramer, l., Baltimore hobby jobber, and Joe Mervish, west coast editor of CM&HI, congratulate Lew Glaser on the opening of the museum.

Sol Kramer and Lew Glaser appeared at the opening of a Revell model exhibit in a Los Angeles park with hobby magazine editor Joe Mervish.

A local department store allowed Lou to come in on Saturday mornings and demonstrate flying models to customers—and sell packets of materials and instruction sheets. The kits sold for 75 cents, and the Kramer boys

got to keep 45 cents. One day an order came in for $100 worth of kits. Sol took the $45 from this sale, added his $7 in life savings and opened a hobby shop on the backside of a Chinese laundry on West Mulberry Street in downtown Baltimore. From this humble beginning grew Burd Model Airplane Company.

By the end of the 1930s Burd Models employed four designers and kept a staff of workers busy operating machines for die-cutting balsa wood into the pieces needed for model kits. Burd eventually issued two hundred different kinds of flying models, some with gas-powered engines. The Kramers learned that in the hobby business you had to pay very close attention to every detail of a product, because, in their case, the product always had to fly. The Kramer brothers also became distributors of kits from larger companies like Megow and Comet and also hobby supplies such as dope and cement.

The American hobby industry slowly emerged out of the efforts of distributors like the Kramers and their counterparts in New York City, the Polk brothers, who helped small retailers set up garage and basement shops in thousands of cities and towns across the country. In 1940 distributors, manufacturers, and retailers joined together to establish the Model Industry Association and began holding annual meetings to exchange ideas and show new products. Then World War II struck and dealt a body blow to the fledgling industry. Materials like balsa wood become impossible to find, manufacturers converted to making products for the war effort, and young men went off into the armed forces. When Sol Kramer joined the service, Burd Model Company disappeared.

Yet the war promoted model building, too. Thousands of school kids built wooden identification models of Allied, German, and Japanese airplanes for use by the armed forces in military training. The government also hired companies to mold solid plastic ID models. Such "solids" or shelf models had not been very popular before the war because most boys wanted models that would fly. But with the war on and materials needed to build flying models scarce, non-flying models started to become more popular. Besides, every boy became fascinated with the machines fighting the war in the Pacific or in the skies over Europe: planes, battleships, tanks, and submarines. Building models of these went right along with collecting military uniform patches and souvenirs of the war. Even before peace arrived new hobby shops were popping-up to sell kits and supplies. The Polks started selling surplus ID solids. When the war ended some returning GI's turned to hobby shops as a relatively low-budget way to start a new business.

However, the years right after the war turned out to be disastrous for the hobby industry, as business slumped and many companies—new and old—went bankrupt. But this proved to be only a temporary setback, and by 1948 the country had pulled out of its post-war recession and things were looking much brighter for hobby businesses. Interest in solid models continued to be strong. Jack Besser, who had co-founded Monogram Models with Bob Reder in 1945, urged his fellow manufacturers to bring out low-cost wooden models with more prefabricated parts so that younger, less skilled boys could enjoy making them.

Monogram's Hot Shot Jet Racer from 1946 typified the model kit of the period: partly shaped wood body, sheet balsa wood stamped with parts to be cut out, rubber wheels, metal axles, and a vacuum-formed canopy.

The man who most successfully answered this challenge was Anthony Koveleski, an ex-grocer from Scranton, Pennsylvania. He was an old-time auto fanatic who drove a Stutz Bearcat. In 1948 he introduced Hudson Miniatures, a collection of 1/16 scale wooden antique cars. The first car in his line was a 1911 Maxwell—the car driven by America's best-known radio comedian, Jack Benny. The coughing, wheezing, honking car appeared as one of the "characters" in the radio show.

Koveleski proved to be a consummate promoter, and his models became well known across the country. In the 1953 movie *Niagara* actor Joseph Cotton builds a Hudson Miniature car and neglects his wife, Marilyn Monroe (showing that some hobbyists are *really* absorbed in their craft!). The big problem with the Hudson kits was that they required a lot of scratch building from the modeler. A hobbyist had to be able to shape and sand a wooden block into the car body, and then add wire, pipe cleaners, metal, paper, and plastic accessories in order to have a decent looking model. The kits also sold for the fairly high price of $2.50.

A model made up totally of plastic parts would be easier to build and have greater detail, but such all-plastic models had never caught on with hobbyists. The English company Frog had introduced them in England back in the 1930s, and Hawk Models of Chicago had been selling a handful of plastic model airplanes since 1946, but nobody paid much attention. Monsanto Chemicals spoke to the Model Industry Association and tried to promote its product, saying that plentiful, inexpensive plastic would solve the problem of scarce materials and high prices. Yet the hobby industry clung to the old-fashioned craftsman ethic that models had to be made of wood and intrinsically challenging so that model makers would be required to develop high level sculpting and fabricating skills. The virtues of plastic were apparent, but most companies thought they had done enough when they just added some plastic detail parts to their wooden model kits.

In the meantime, after the war Sol and Lou Kramer had re-established themselves in the hobby business, but this time only as distributors. Although the Kramers handled just hobby products, Sol was interested in new items being brought out by the toy industry. Thus in February 1951, he traveled to New York City for the Toy Fair to see what the toy industry was up to. This once-a-year extravaganza brought together all the toy manufacturers in America, from giants like Ideal to little mom-and-pop back room operations. Convention headquarters and showrooms filled the twin-tower Fifth Avenue Toy Center, where companies maintained year-round sales offices. The beginnings of America's 1950s economic boom manifested itself in a crowd of exhibitors that forced the show to spill over into rooms in the adjacent New Yorker Hotel.

Kramer had heard rumors among hobby dealers that one of the toy companies, Precision Specialties of Los Angeles, was showing some all-plastic model car kits. Although he had never even heard of the little West Coast toy company before, Kramer was intrigued. At the door to the Precision Specialties parlor he was greeted by a short, smiling, bespectacled fellow, Lew Glaser, who proudly showed him a collection of plastic toy cars on metal leashes and model kit versions of the same cars. Kramer later remembered, "I saw what they had done, and I thought it was very clever." He placed an order for some of the model car kits, which were called "Highway Pioneers" and marketed under the brand name "Revell."

The Maxwell first appeared as a toy car; then its disassembled parts became Revell's first model kit.

Kramer went back to his hotel room to think some more about the Revell model cars. It was Kramer's business to know what merchandise was in demand by the public. He knew that the Hudson Miniatures had been very successful, and he had a hunch that all-plastic cars would find much greater acceptance from the general public because the cutting, sanding, and scratch-building involved in wood construction would be eliminated. Also, plastic allowed for much greater detail and authenticity than wood. Kramer calculated that he could "force" this new product into hobby shops simply because of the large number of customers he served across the country. "I've always been a person who will support my feelings with everything I've got," he later said. "If I believed in something, I'd bet the company bankroll on it." He had a gut feeling about the Revell Highway Pioneers and decided to bet the bankroll on them.

The following day found Kramer back in the Precision Specialties exhibit room. He later described his initial encounters with Glaser: "The first day he was ebullient when I placed an order. When I came back the next day to talk some more, I explained that my order was not for pieces, but for grosses. It increased the order from $1,500 to $15,000. He started jumping up and down." Kramer offered some suggestions for packaging the Highway Pioneers, and he had one demand: every store order had to include a built-up display model to show potential customers what the plastic parts in the box would eventually look like. (Revell would create small display cases by fixing the cars to wooden shingles, then covering them with the clear acetate boxes florists used to hold corsages.)

The 1951 Toy Fair brought together two kindred spirits. Visionary, optimistic, enterprising Sol Kramer encountered a man of like temperament in Lew Glaser. The future course of Revell was set from that moment on, although that would not become apparent until another year had passed.

Lew Glaser had been born in Brooklyn, New York, in 1917, the same year as Kramer, but when Glaser was five years old, he and his mother moved to Los Angeles, California—the city of golden possibilities. From an early age Lew demonstrated two of the defining aspects of his character: an enormous capacity for hard work and an absorbing curiosity. While in elementary school he sold newspapers to supplement his mother's income, and by his junior high years he was doing chemistry and electronics experiments in a makeshift home lab. He got a ham radio license at age thirteen. Years later Kramer recalled that Glaser was fascinated by innovations and could digest and understand anything that captured his imagination.

Glaser's formal education ended when he graduated from Roosevelt High School in 1934—straight into the Great Depression. He made his way by working in a "hole-in-the-wall" radio repair shop, which, in 1938, the owner sold to his young apprentice for $100: $25 down and $5 a week. Quickly Glaser expanded the shop to include retail sales of radios, phonograph records, and home appliances. "It was quite successful in a small way," Glaser later recalled, "but I was looking around for other things, and I got intrigued with plastics. I found somebody that had had an unsuccessful experience in the business and had a few hundred dollars worth of machine tools that he wanted to sell. One weekend I bought them for $750—and I was in the plastics business." (*Toys & Novelties* 1967, 43) Glaser's money bought him a drill press, a table saw, and a stack of Lucite plastic sheets. He set up shop in a small space on Washington Boulevard in Los Angeles. Later he added an injection-molding machine and moved to slightly more spacious quarters on Western Avenue.

Precision Specialties, as Glaser named his new company, opened just weeks before the bombing of Pearl Harbor. If the war caused problems for Glaser's company, it also presented opportunities. As the military effort consumed raw materials normally used in consumer products, it opened the way for plastic to display its value as an alternative component in a variety of items. Precision Specialties showed that picture frames could be made of plastic as well as wood. Glaser's company became essentially a job shop, making assorted items for many customers, including the armed forces. "We did a little bit of everything," remembered one employee. That included fabrication of aircraft parts and radio accessories. However, the product that became the core of company business was a lady's cosmetic compact. Glaser marketed the compact under his own trademark: "Revell." The name was suggested by an employee, who won a twenty-five dollar war bond in a "name the company contest." It derived from the French word *reveil*—"awaken." But Glaser just liked the sound of it. (It also sounded a lot like the name of cosmetics giant Revlon.)

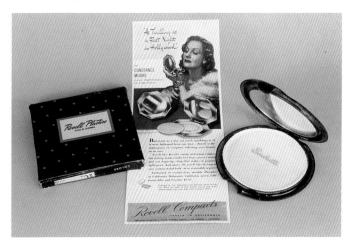

During the Second World War Revell released its first brand name product—a lady's compact.

The ladies compacts and a companion product, cigarette cases, were fabricated from sheet Lucite. Revell also sold an injection-molded plastic cigarette holder and acetate plastic photo holders that went into wallets, but none of these items satisfied Glaser. He disposed of his surplus stock of compact mirrors to Mattel Toys, which found them just the right scale to make into doll hand mirrors.

In 1946, with the war over, Glaser ventured a gamble in the toy business. He borrowed a lot of money to set-up production. "That was a rough year," he later declared. (*Playthings* 1950, 152) Revell's very first product previewed things to come. It was an injection-molded plastic washing machine that little girls could use to wash doll clothes. Although an oddity compared to Revell's later model kits, the washing machine embodied qualities that would become hallmarks of Revell products: well made, priced a shade above the competition, with an attention to detail unusual in toys. Even at this early date Glaser believed in the educational value of his product and advertised the "play-planned" toy as a valuable learning tools for young children. Unfortunately, sales of the washer quickly sagged.

The Walt Disney Minnie Mouse washing machine and Pluto flashlight were among the first Revell toys.

Glaser attempted to perk-up interest in his toy by making an alliance with Southern California's giant Walt Disney Productions. The washing machine changed colors to pink plastic and became the "Minnie Mouse™" and "Snow White™" washer. A second Disney licensed product drew on Glaser's interest in electronics. The Pluto™ flashlight featured a light bulb held in Pluto's mouth that could be switched on by pushing-in his tail. Glaser's assembly line manager Ben Lench described it as "less than an engineering marvel, but interesting."

Lew Glaser was a radio enthusiast from his boyhood.

Lench was another Brooklyn-born boy who had moved West to seek his fortune. He had experience running a production line; so Glaser had made him assistant plant manager. He went to work assembling a Mickey Mouse bank telephone and a Mickey Mouse radio that utilized surplus World War II components. The Woody Woodpecker Laugh Harmonica received a test blow from workers as it came off the assembly line—filling the packaging area with offbeat sound effects.

Revell put a great deal of effort into its cleverly designed Circus play set, but it never quite caught the buying public's imagination.

However, none of these items paid their way, and Glaser found his company even deeper in financial trouble. He had to reduce his work force to just ten people, and—too soft-hearted to do it himself—Glaser asked Lench to deliver the bad news to those who had to be let go. Then Glaser told Lench that he could not afford him either, but said it would be OK if Lench wanted to set up his own company on the premises. So for a while Lench stayed on and assembled house wares in a section of the Precision Specialties facility.

By the summer of 1948 Glaser was ready to renew his efforts in the toy business. On the 4th of July he hired a man to set up an in-house toy design department. As it turned out, the new employee, Charles Gretz, would become an invaluable part of the company and guide Revell's engineering department for the next crucial decade of the company's history. Born in Germany in 1918, Gretz learned the art of metal engraving, tool making, and plastic molding as an apprentice in his home country. By 1937 he was in New York making molds for a toy company, and his path crossed Lew Glaser's. He told Glaser that he would like to move to California if Revell ever had a spot for him, and in 1948 the time arrived.

Gretz was expected to do more than simply come up with designs for new products. Glaser wanted to be able to control the whole process of toy development internally at Revell from the concept stage, through tool making, to manufacturing, and then sales. Thus Gretz was given the task of setting up a whole design and engineering department. At first he did not have much to work with. The Revell plant—if it could be called that—encompassed a couple of storefronts in a business block at 212 Western Avenue, Los Angeles. The engineering department occupied a wooden shed on the roof. Dust covered everything in summer, and in the winter rain came right through the roof.

Gretz's first designed a set of circus animals and characters, together with all the equipment required for a three-ring circus act. His inspiration came from the Schoenhut Circus he had played with as a child back in Germany. The Schoenhut animals were wooden and held together with flexible fabric joints, while Gretz's animals were smaller in size, made of plastic, and held together with rubber tendons. It took some time to get them into production and into stores. They first appeared one at a time in dime stores in 1949, and then later packaged together as sets in department stores.

Charles Gretz and Lew Glaser look over blue-prints for the Revell Circus elephant toy.

About the same time Gretz joined Revell, Glaser met John Gowland, a British-born toy designer, who asked if Revell would like to sell some toys developed by Gowland's company. Glaser thought this a great idea because it would extend Revell's toy offerings without any capital outlay by Revell for design and tooling.

Jack Gowland, as a young man, had been an observer in the English balloon corps during World War I, and then worked as an art instructor, and, finally, a toy designer. He and his son Kelvin emigrated to America after the Second World War and settled in California because everyone told them that was the best place in the US to live.

They set up a company in Santa Barbara staffed with several other British expatriates. Jack led the team and ran the show. Kelvin was one of the designers and did some of the prototype sculpting. The chief engineer and sculptor was Derek Brand, a short, chipper fellow with lots of ideas and artistic talent. (He later would invent the HO electric slot car.) The Gowland trademark was a balloon with three men in the gondola—a plump man, and tall man, and a short man: Jack, Kelvin, and Derek.

In 1949 Gowland gave Revell a license to manufacture one of their toy designs in exchange for a five percent royalty. "Champ," a toy dog on wheels, could be led by a metal leash, and with a pull on its trigger-handle he would bark and jump. The toy was a hit, and the Revell/Gowland partnership launched a whole line of pull toys. Unfortunately, as Glaser already had learned from the rapid demise of his washing machine, the toy market is extremely volatile. None of the follow-on Gowland toys made the hit enjoyed by Champ. Revell again found itself in debt and losing money.

Revell worked hard to get publicity for its new product. LOOK magazine featured them in a one-page story on the 4th of July, 1950. A special boxed set came out in conjunction with Cecil B. DeMille's movie *The Greatest Show on Earth*, and Revell issued a news release saying DeMille used the toy animals and people to plot out scenes for the movie. Despite the ballyhoo, and although the Revell circus toys were truly charming, they never caught the public's imagination and would be abandoned a year later.

Revell teamed-up with Gowland to produce and market Champ, a pull-toy that came in two sizes.

The Woody Woodpecker Laff Harmonica reproduces Woody's "Ha-ha-ha-HA-ha" call. Cap'n Noah and Polly can be wound-up to sail either the floor or bathtub. Jolly Polly flaps his wings, closes his beak, and squawks when you lift his tail.

Gowland designed some unique pull toys for Revell: Buckaroo Bill and Chu Chu jump when you pull the trigger on the leash. Quacky Wacky lays a marble egg.

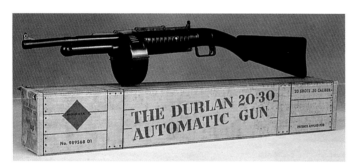

Gowland's chief engineer Derek Brand, a transplanted Englishman, named his semi-automatic machine gun after the counties of Durham and Lancaster.

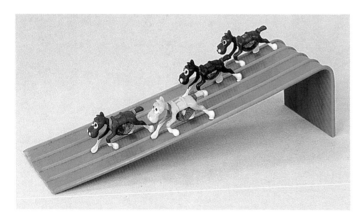

It seemed like a good idea. Phony Ponies were powered by Mexican jumping beans strapped to their bellies.

However, at the 1950 New York Toy Fair luck swung Revell's way when it unveiled the latest Gowland pull toy: a 1911 Maxwell—a toy that, like Hudson Miniatures' wooden model kit, was inspired by the Jack Benny radio show. Revell promoted it as "the car made famous by America's top radio star." Glaser had been turned down when he asked to use Jack Benny's name, but everybody recognized the Maxwell.

This product struck a magic chord in the minds of buyers from the large chain stores. The big 1/16 scale car was molded in bright red acetate plastic, and when you pulled the cable trigger it emitted a comic honk and bucked the jaunty driver out of his seat. Every store in America wanted the Maxwell. "The company received so many orders that it was difficult to fill them," said Glaser. "Production of the Maxwells reached 10,000 a day, and we still had a back-log of 800,000 on order." (*Toys & Novelties,* January 1, 1967, 43)

Jack Gowland next came up with the bright idea of a Model T Ford in 1/32 scale—half the size of the Maxwell. It also came on a pull cable with a trigger to make it jump. When sales of the Model T seemed promising, a Packard, Cadillac, and Stanley Steamer joined the "Action Miniatures" line. Soon the 1903 Model A Ford was added to the others—but it was just the Cadillac, molded in a different color plastic with the rear seat left off. These pull toys came with an intriguing suggestion: if you wanted to display the little car on your bookshelf or mantle, you could easily disconnect the pull cable. By this simple process the toy car might be transformed into a model car—something that would appeal to hobbyists.

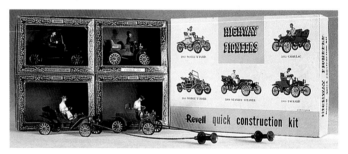

Two gift sets: The Action Miniature toy cars became the Highway Pioneers ready-to-assemble model kits. *H-37*

Some of the leading men in the hobby industry looked at the unusually good detail in the toy Maxwell and the Action Miniatures and realized that the unassembled parts of these toys might be sold as ready-to-assemble hobby kits. New York City distributor Nat Polk explained it this way: "We hobby guys all had our eyes out for product to sell. So Lew had his great model car, but he was selling it as a cockamamie jumping toy. All us hobby guys ganged-up on him and said he had to sell it disassembled as a model kit."

Glaser was not convinced: "Why would anybody want to buy something that was not put together?" (*Toys & Novelties,* January 1, 1967, 43) But Glaser was curious. He took Philadelphia hobby distributor Bernie Paul out to lunch and learned something about the hobby and craft industry. Still, Revell was having trouble keeping up with the demand for the Maxwell toy, and launching a new product seemed like more than his company could handle at the time. Yet Glaser knew from experience that toys had a brief shelf life in stores. "The trouble with most toy novelties is that they will go over big one year—and the next year they go blooie. It's a fleeting business. You live on the edge of a cliff." (Boyle 1954) Maybe the hobby field was worth a try. Turning the antique car toys into a hobby item seemed something easy to do. All that would be required to market them as model kits was new packaging. The same molds that made parts for the toys could be used to make parts for kits.

The first Ford Model A came from the Action Miniature mold and still retained the plastic ring that held the cable of the pull toy. The second Model A was produced from a new mold, with finer detail and a driver closer to 1/32 scale. *H-36*

Advertising by Woolworth's played a key role in making Highway Pioneers a national sensation in the early 1950s.

Thus in February 1951, Glaser headed to New York for the Toy Fair and his fateful rendezvous with Sol Kramer. Two men from opposite sides of the country met and brought together two threads of history—one from the hobby industry and one from the toy industry. Big things were about to happen.

Later that summer Glaser scored another business coup when Woolworth agreed to begin carrying Highway Pioneers in its national chain of dime stores. Woolworth's management was already familiar with Revell toys, and Glaser convinced them that the model car kits were revolutionarily different from old-fashioned wooden model kits. All-plastic kits were so easy to build that even a ten-year-old could successfully complete the model and then play with it like a toy. Yet the level of detail in the models satisfied adult hobbyists. Woolworth bit and, in August 1951, began displaying the inexpensive 69 cent kits as quick pick-up items that mom or dad could buy on a whim and take home as a novelty. It worked. Ordinary people who didn't think of themselves as hobbyists took one or two home just to see what they were. Pretty soon customers were coming back for more of the nifty little car models.

It created a sensation; nobody had ever seen anything quite like them. Highway Pioneers became one of the first fads that swept the country during the 1950s, contributing their part to the rise of mass consumer culture. Eminent sociologists like David Riesman and Paul Goodman noted the trend and felt such handicrafts represented a creative way for Americans to fill modern society's increased leisure time.

Orders for tens of thousands of Highway Pioneers began pouring into Los Angeles. Since Revell's own modest plant was busy manufacturing toys, production of the Highway Pioneers was done by Gowland's own plant up the coast in Santa Barbara. Parts for the models would be molded by Gowland, sealed in cellophane bags, and then sent to Revell for packaging and shipment to customers.

The 1/16 scale Maxwell model kit went into an orange and white box labeled "Revell Quick Construction Kit." The 1/32 scale cars were packaged in a generic yellow box with pictures of all five cars on the top. A rubber stamp on one end panel indicated which car was inside. The parts were just like the pull toys and still bore the "Action Miniatures" imprint on the bottom of each car body. The models were so simple that Kelvin Gowland did not bother to include assembly steps on the instruction sheet he drafted for each car. "We'll make them so any silly beggar can put 'em together." The most intriguing part of the construction process was mounting the wheels: builders would slip the wheels on the axles, then press a red hot screwdriver head against the end of each axle to melt the plastic into a mushroom that would hold the wheels in place.

Revell launched a major advertising and promotion effort for Highway Pioneers to encourage the budding fad for model building. "Antique Car Craze Sweeping the Country!" read one hobby trade journal article. Revell sent out window banners to hobby shops and display racks for boxes of kits. Revell jumped to the head of the hobby industry in promoting its product and in self-promotion. It advertised in *LIFE* and *LOOK* magazines. All this made Revell seem bigger than it really was. Yet, the success of Highway Pioneers was undeniable.

In Santa Barbara, Jack Gowland prepared to launch a second series of Highway Pioneers. Kelvin Gowland researched old antique car books for photographs and then drafted blueprints for the models. Derek sculpted the parts for the cars, working in wood and carving his patterns in the same 1/32 scale as the final model. Kelvin created slightly oversized comic characters to sit in the driver's seats. When the prototypes were finished, the parts would be sent off to Arrow Tool and Engineering in Inglewood where steel production molds would be cut. In those days die cutting was an art in itself, and Brand acknowledged that oftentimes the finished mold was more a reflection of Arrow's craftsmanship than his own.

When molds were completed they went back to Santa Barbara where eight injection molding machines in Gowland's plant ran round-the-clock banging-out Highway Pioneer parts. "We couldn't make enough of them," said Brand. In ten months Gowland made and Revell sold an astonishing million kits. A new industry was born that epic year.

The production backlog at Gowland became so great that the Series Two kits took until the summer of 1952 to reach stores. Revell turned a negative into a positive by promoting each new model as it became available as "The Car of the Month." The Series Two models were a little more sophisticated and a little more expensive—89 cents—than their predecessors. Each of the five models came in the same kind of generic box (orange this time) as 1951-issue kits, which now bore the designation Series One.

Despite the fabulous success of Highway Pioneers, neither Jack Gowland nor Lew Glaser wanted to give up on toys just yet. In fact, Revell still earned about forty percent of its revenues from the sale of toys. In 1952 Revell released a 1/16 scale 1917 Ford Model T pull-toy as a companion to the Maxwell. This car was another Derek Brand creation, and it incorporated an ingenious feature: when you pulled the trigger on the cable handle, the car backfired! Brand had simply taken a cap-gun mechanism, turned it on its side beneath the chassis, and attached a trip-wire to the trigger. The Model T also came out as a hobby kit—with an unsightly parting seam down the middle of the roof.

Revell's own chief engineer, Charles Gretz, chipped-in his contribution to the 1952 new toy offerings with a set of three Caterpillar earth movers: a wagon, a scraper, and a grader. These sturdy yellow metal and styrene plastic toys were designed for rough handling—yet with Revell's standard regard for accuracy and detail. The Caterpillar road-building equipment enjoyed immediate popularity.

Lew Glaser's years of hard work finally paid off, and Revell stood with two feet firmly planted in both the toy and hobby industries. He had shown that plastic worked in both fields. Indeed, he had opened up a whole new territory in all-plastic model kits. Yet his model cars hearkened back to olden times, while the whole modern world lay open for exploitation.

Charles Gretz's sturdy sand box toys epitomized the rugged
qualities of the real Caterpillar road construction equipment.

Chapter 2 –
"Authentic Kits"

During the summer of 1952 Lew Glaser arrived at a critical turning point in his thinking. He was accustomed to seeing demand for even the most successful toy dropping-off after the first year in the market, but orders for Highway Pioneers continued to rise month after month. They also were selling steadily year-round, unlike toys that enjoyed peak sales at Christmas time, then tailed off the rest of the year. As Glaser later explained it, the antique car models "were selling better the second year than they were the first, and at that point I knew that I had found my niche in business life." But, he added, "I decided that I really wanted to go beyond the old-time car business." (*Toys & Novelties,* January 1, 1967, 44)

Glaser felt Revell should create a diversified line of all kinds of high-quality model kits with enduring market appeal. When Sol Kramer visited Los Angeles in June 1952 Glaser told him about his plan to expand further into the hobby field, but said that he lacked two essential ingredients: investment capital and knowledge of the hobby industry. He asked Kramer if he wanted to put some money into Revell, but Kramer declined, saying that he didn't have that kind of money and had his own business to look after. However, Kramer agreed to become consultant to Revell in exchange for part ownership of the production tooling for whatever new models he recommended to Revell.

They shook hands on a deal making Kramer close business consultant to Glaser. Kramer stayed in contact by way of frequent long distance telephone calls, and from time to time he stayed as a guest in Glaser's home, talking business with Lew long into the early hours of the morning. His position as a national distributor allowed him to feel the pulse of the industry. He knew what products were being reordered and which products were resting unsold on store shelves. "We knew where the vacuums were and where the niches were." He would recommend new subjects for models and then, as they were developed, inspect every step of the development process.

However, Kramer's relationship with Revell had to be kept secret because his distributorship served all hobby companies, and he couldn't be seen favoring one. "I was the mystic who didn't exist," recalled Kramer. But his deal with Glaser would eventually give him almost twenty percent ownership of Revell.

With Kramer on board as expert advisor, Glaser and chief engineer Gretz sat down to plan Revell's own model design and mold making shop. They began looking for a craftsman who could create the hand-made prototypes (often called patterns or masters) for new models. About that time a young man named Anthony Bulone walked in the front door carrying a sample case filled with examples of his sculpture work. Gretz liked what he saw and offered Bulone a job on a one-month trial basis. Bulone accepted.

Tony Bulone had grown up in Cleveland, Ohio, in an Italian-American family of craftsmen. His first job had been shaping plaster figures and making molds for ceramic companies. He did flower planters, lamp stands, black panthers to crouch atop TV sets, and a diverse assembly of both realistic and cartoon subjects. He made enough money to buy the Chevy convertible that brought him to Los Angeles, where he went to work for Douglas Aircraft making clay and plaster patterns for airplane parts. When he first went to work for Revell in December 1952, he did not give up his job with Douglas—he continued to work the graveyard shift there and then showed up for work at Revell the next morning at 8:30.

After painting the box art for the motorized *Missouri*, Richard Kishady decided not to attempt any more ship illustrations. *HM-30*

Bulone's first assignment turned out to be the most important modeling work he, or anyone, would ever do for Revell because it truly launched Revell into the wide world of plastic models. Sol Kramer's very first suggestion for a new kit proved to be a stroke of genius. Kramer had long known the demand for authentic models of modern ships and that it was impossible to put fine details into a ship model made of wood. Injection molded plastic models opened-up intriguing possibilities for incorporating even the minutest

The USS *Missouri*, Revell's first model produced in-house, is also its most enduringly popular kit. *H-301*

parts into a ship model. But what ship? Kramer thought that the battleship USS *Missouri* would make a very dramatic looking model. It had gained world fame when the leaders of Japan signed the surrender ending World War II on its deck, and during 1952 American television audiences thrilled to the story of U. S. Navy's wartime exploits in *Victory at Sea*, a documentary accompanied by the stirring music of Richard Rogers.

The first problem for Gretz, Bulone, and the three or four other men who constituted the design and engineering department was finding accurate information about the *Missouri*. "The military wouldn't give us the time of day," recalled Bulone. Security attitudes held-over from World War II and reinforced by the Cold War blocked access to even the most mundane information. So Revell went to *Jane's* international warship reference books and other books and magazines, where they collected photographs. Using these they made three-view drawings. The underwater configuration of the Missouri remained classified; so they gave the model a basic shape below the waterline. Bulone then set about sculpting the parts for the pattern from blocks of plastic, working in exactly the same scale as that intended for the finished model. Carving in exact size made it easy to calculate the cost of plastic that would go into the finished model kit, but it demanded a high degree of exactness from the sculptor. Gretz devised the layout of the parts for the mold, arranging it so that molten plastic would fill all the cavities of the mold at precisely the same time.

The original *Missouri* mold was modified to manufacture the *New Jersey*, while a second new mold took over production of the *Missouri*. H-301, H-316

After Kramer had given his OK to the work, the completed pattern was taken to Ted Neward's tool and die shop in Pomona. Neward often did contract work for regional model and toy companies—and would continue to do state-of-the-art custom molding right through the 1960s. The cost of the model's tooling represented a huge up-front expense and thus a terrific gamble. If the model failed in the marketplace, Revell would find itself right back on the edge of bankruptcy. Even if it turned out to be a success, it would be years before Revell could amortize the cost of the production tooling.

Meanwhile, Glaser had been busy preparing for great new things. On December 8, 1952, he changed the name of his company from Precision Specialties to Revell, Inc. Glaser's advertising agency, the Sudler Company (just down the way on Western Avenue) devised a new trademark: a play on the American flag with red and white stripes and a blue field with "Revell" in the same style lettering that had been used for several years on toy boxes. The catchwords "Authentic Kit" emphasized that these were accurate scale models—very different from toys.

To make room for expansion, in February 1953, Revell moved from its home on Western Avenue to a brand new facility near the ocean front at 4223 Ocean Park (soon to become Glencoe) Avenue, Venice. To celebrate its grand opening, Revell invited hobby industry leaders to a big bash at the plant, with old-time autos as the theme. Men received straw hats and fake cardboard mustaches for the occasion. The stars of the day were Lew Glaser and his wife of three years, Royle Ebert Glaser.

Lew and Royle Glaser arrive in style for the opening of the Venice plant.

Many people in attendance got their first chance to meet the charming, petite Mrs. Glaser. She, like so many Californians, started life in the Midwest, but landed in San Francisco right in the middle of World War II. After the war she enrolled at Berkley, but on a blind date in 1950 she met Lew Glaser and married him three weeks later. By the time the new Venice plant opened Royle was tending two young daughters, but she still took an active part in her husband's business affairs. "Lew was the kind of man who wanted his wife to share all his thoughts," she later explained. "He had no business partner—I was his sounding board. He talked constantly about his activities and plans. I was getting all the atmosphere, learning the business from intimate contact with all that was happening." As time passed, Royle Glaser's place in the company steadily evolved into a more active role.

The new Revell plant lay near the huge Marina del Rey boat basin among boat-building shops and marine supply stores. A dairy and greenhouse stood next door and, beyond that, fields where Japanese-American farmers grew celery. In the rainy season the streets flooded. The building itself was constructed of concrete slabs, tilted into place to form the walls. Production equipment went into the ground floor, while the offices occupied the upstairs. Gretz could now set up an in-house tool and die shop so that Revell could make its own molds with its own quality standards.

plush Hotel Belvedere for a trade show displaying every product the hobby industry had to offer—but his wife Doris stole the show when she unveiled Revell's *Missouri*.

Whether it was a stroke of genius or of luck, the *Missouri* turned out to be in the money right from the start, and as late as the 1970s it remained one of the top dozen sellers in the Revell inventory and might rank as Revell's all-time best selling model.

The heavy cruiser *Los Angeles* added another capital ship to the Revell line. *H-306*

To promote its new line of models, Glaser hired Milt Grey, a tall dynamic man who had made his living selling kitchen appliances in the Midwest and had come to California for its warm climate. As it turned out, his tenure at Revell lasted only a little more than two years, but while he was on board Revell had the most aggressive advertising and promotion program in the hobby industry. He became an expert at getting Revell's press releases into all sorts of national publications as human interest items—but it counted as free advertising. He also promoted a free-standing metal display rack so that Revell kits could be sold in any kind of store—a pharmacy, candy store, bicycle shop, or even a grocery store.

By the summer of 1953 Revell's USS *Missouri* kit was ready for launching, and Grey saw to it that much ballyhoo attended the occasion. For the first time, declared Revell's advertisements, the average person could have a beautifully built ship model on his mantle that would exceed anything the best craftsman might make by hand. On the other side of the country Sol Kramer rented two floors of Baltimore's

Soon Revell introduced its first model airplane: the Lockheed F-94 Starfire. However, unlike the *Missouri*, this kit failed to rise above ordinary industry standards of the day. The packaging was uninspired: a one-piece, thin cardboard box with a not-very-colorful illustration on the front and the assembly instructions printed on the back. The model kit inside had very few parts, and these showed not much detail. The pilot and co-pilot figures were represented by just heads-and-shoulders molded into the fuselage parts. The completed model rested on a simple stand, and the plane had no landing gear.

Revell's earliest aircraft model first appeared in a drab, one-piece box and then reappeared with blazing, full color art. *H-201, H-210*

Bulone remembered that he had worked from photographs to create the model (although Revell's release announcement proclaimed it: "produced from official prints.") Kramer recalled later that since the plane rested on a stand, Revell's development team decided that no landing gear parts were necessary. The F7U Cutlass and F9F Cougar followed later in 1953 with the same mediocre style and features as the Starfire. Gretz later passed his judgment on the first airplane models: "It was an evolutionary process. The first ones were good enough, and we got better as we went on."

From the start Revell sent paper window banners to hobby shops to call attention to their latest kit releases.

Revell's first aircraft gift set united its first three fighter plane models. *H-204*

Richard Kishady painted the box illustrations for the F-94, Cutlass, and Cougar. *H-210, H-211, H-212*

The second issue of Three Jet Fighters carried much improved box art by Kishady. *G-204*

Meanwhile, the Navy's first atomic-powered submarine, USS *Nautilus*, under construction all through 1953, generated a great deal of public interest, and Revell wished to exploit that fascination by having a model of the *Nautilus* in stores before the real vessel was launched. However, secrecy cloaked the atom sub project, and nobody knew what it looked like. Sol Kramer tried to help by visiting Navy officials in Washington, D.C. They let him confer with a Navy submarine captain who had no connection with or special knowledge of the *Nautilus*. The Navy man drew sketches of what he guessed the *Nautilus* might look like.

The Glaser family at home with daughters Leslie and Kim.

The original issue *Nautilus* had an inaccurate glassed-in observation station that was corrected in the second issue—which added an inaccurate deck missile. *H-303, H-308*

Back in Venice, model sculptor Tony Bulone went to work on the basis of an article that had appeared in a December 1952 issue of *Colliers* magazine. The article had been written with the cooperation of the Navy, and, as it turned out, contained several generally accurate drawings of the *Nautilus*. (Aurora and Lindberg also followed the *Colliers* article in designing their models.) Revell deviated from the *Colliers* rendition by giving its *Nautilus* a tapered bow section, and this turned out to be a major inaccuracy since the real sub had a simple cigar shape. The propellers and tail section Revell put on its model must have been too accurate to suit the Navy, because a couple of Federal agents later stopped by the Venice plant to quiz Gretz and Bulone on their sources.

The Victory at Sea gift set capitalized on the popular TV documentary series. *G-311*

While Bulone worked on these early models in the Venice plant during the day, at home in the evenings he started playing around with an idea for improving Revell's models. Behind his apartment house stood a tool shed, where he set up a work bench. After dinner he would sit in his shed, listen to classical music—and carve tiny human figures in wax and plastic. After he had created a few, he took them to show Gretz and then Glaser. These human figures, he explained, would add life and interest to models, and also would clearly illustrate the scale of a model. Glaser liked the idea and paid Bulone a bonus for his creativity.

Meanwhile Bulone and Gretz had been busy with another project. Glaser was afraid that a large toy company—like Mattel or Ideal—would see the success Revell was enjoying with hobby kits and jump into plastic models in a big way. To discourage competition, or to be better prepared to meet it, Glaser wanted to grow as big as possible as quickly as possible. Investment capital for new tooling always presented the biggest obstacle to expansion. So in May 1953, Glaser made another partnership with an outside investor. Steve Adams (and his sons Robert, James, and Jerry) owned a tool and die company, and Adams agreed to cut the molds for a new line of plastic models at his own expense, if Revell would design them. The series would be models of historic horse-drawn carriages and wagons: "Miniature Masterpieces."

Scott Eidson painted a Christmas Card image for the Miniature Masterpieces Tally Ho Coach. H-513

Ben Lench, Glaser's former assembly manager, became president of the new Miniature Masterpieces company. To the public the company appeared to have no connection whatsoever to Revell, but behind the scenes it was virtually a branch of Revell. Gretz researched the models and then designed their part breakdown and assembly configuration. The prototypes for new models were sculpted by Gretz and Bulone at the Revell plant; then they sent them to Adams where molds would be made and the kits manufactured. After that, the kits would be distributed from Lench's own company, Romalite, in Culver City. Lench also assembled the store display models for Miniature Masterpieces and soon also for Revell's own models. He designed a new domed acetate display case for Revell's display models that was more attractive than the square florist boxes that Revell had been using. By 1955 Lench molded Revell's own kits at his plant during the busy fall production season when stores were stocking-up on products for Christmas sales.

Miniature Masterpieces turned out to be some of the most cleverly-designed, finely-sculpted models ever made. The State Coach of England, famous for its appearance in the coronation of Elizabeth II in 1953, opened the line. The coach came without horses or human figures because the pattern was completed while Bulone was still working on his proposal to add figures to Revell's kits. A few months later, however, the second kit in the series—the Wells Fargo Stage Coach—included four horses, a driver, and a shotgun-toting guard. Gretz, who lived in the country and owned several fine horses, sculpted the horses, while Bulone handled the humans. The succeeding models—all in constant 1/48

scale—included an obscure coach used by the Marquis de Lafayette in 1820 and a Roman Chariot, before settling down to Western subjects like the Covered Wagon.

You could view filmstrips on the battery powered Philco TV set or play Tiddily Winks Baseball with a game Revell sold through the mail.

Three Miniature Masterpieces kits could be slipped into the cardboard sleeve of the Collector's Editions gift set. G-518

After a year of operating Miniature Masterpieces as an "independent" company, Glaser announced in the fall of 1954 that Revell had taken over the Miniature Masterpieces line. The existing kits retained their old packaging, but subsequent additions to the line went into boxes with the Revell trademark. The first of these, the revised State Coach of England, now came with eight horses, four mounted riders, and figures of Elizabeth and Philip—"so perfect they are immediately recognizable." Bulone later observed that it was fairly easy to capture likeness of the queen and prince because he sculpted the patterns five times the size of the production model. When the model's steel mold was made, a pantograph machine would reduced the original master model to 1/48 scale at the same time that it cut the mold.

Most of the Miniature Masterpieces depicted horse-drawn transport from the Wild West—natural subjects for a time when cowboy shows dominated both movie and television screens. The neat little Miniature Masterpieces attracted the attention of executives at United States Borax Corporation, sponsors of the popular TV series "Death Valley Days" (hosted for a while by popular actor Ronald Reagan). They approached Revell to ask about making a model of their famous 20 Mule Team wagon. Gretz traveled to Death Valley to inspect and photograph the wagons and equipment, and he talked with an old timer about how the mules were hitched to the wagons. Then he and Bulone designed and sculpted the model according to the same standards as the Miniature Masterpieces. Adams made the molds and handled production. Later Borax offered several of the Miniature Masterpieces wagons along with the 20 Mule Team kit as premiums customers could get by mailing in a Boraxo cleanser box top and 50 cents.

Unfortunately, Miniature Masterpieces just did not catch on with the public. They came out of the old-fashioned 1930s crafts tradition and, despite all their excellent qualities, just couldn't compete in the stores with modern jet planes, battleships, and rockets. Later in the fifties, Steve Adams, who owned the tooling he had made, brought them out in his own Adams Action Models line.

Back in the summer of 1953, shortly after Glaser began work on Miniature Masterpieces, he made another agreement with yet another outside company to sell a similar product: models of old-time, horse-drawn fire engines—American Firefighters. Marlin Toy Company of New York City had launched the series in the fall of 1952, but by the summer of 1953 Marlin decided that it would be advantageous to let Revell handle distribution of its kits. Glaser set up Collectors Kits, Inc. in Closter, New Jersey, to warehouse and ship both the Firefighters kits and also Revell's own kits. The Firefighters were switched from their original Marlin packaging to boxes with the Revell trademark. All three kits came in the same generic box that showed the three fire units rushing to a turn-of-the-century fire. Originally the kits had been sold without horses or fireman figures, but when the kits came out under the Revell label they included horses, firemen, and even a Dalmatian dog.

This printer's proof of the Miniature Masterpieces Western Collection gift set was used by the graphics staff in planning lettering and package design. *G-511*

The Steamer was one of three kits that used the same American Firefighters box. *H-700*

Although Revell's input was not acknowledged, Boraxo's Twenty Mule Team mail-away premium model shows that it was made by the same hands that created the Miniature Masterpieces.

Scott Eidson's talents as an illustrator nicely fit the needs of the Firefighter Water Tower. *H-706*

Unlike Miniature Masterpieces, Revell's craftsmen had nothing to do with the development and production of these models. The collection started with just three kits: the Steamer, Chemical and Ladder, and Hose Reel. These models were typical of many early-1950s kits in that they had not quite evolved out of the "toy-like" stage. They also included some metal and string parts. Yet they built into interesting and unusual display models.

Revell issued just a couple of Gowland's ship-in-a-bottle kits under the Revell label. Revell brought out the Morgan and Flying Cloud in versions both with and without the bottle. H-415, HB-415, H-416, HB-416.

Early in 1954 Revell announced three new Firefighter models: the Hook and Ladder, Water Tower, and Aerial Ladder. However, something disrupted the plan. Production of the line shifted from New Jersey to Revell's Venice plant. The Hook and Ladder never appeared and the Aerial Ladder made it to stores only late in the year. It was the first Firefighter kit to appear in its own individualized box. Then in 1955 the American LaFrance Water Tower finally debuted as the only Firefighter model developed by Revell's own staff.

Unfortunately, the American Firefighters were doomed to go the way of the Miniature Masterpieces. They simply did not sell, and Revell lost money on the line. Years later the molds for the first three kits were shipped to Brazil for use by Revell's licensee there. These Brazilian-made kits are still commonly found on the collectors market today. Rumor has it that the freighter bringing the tooling back to the United States sank, carrying these molds to the bottom of the sea.

While all this hobby activity went on, Revell continued to make toys, although toys generated only about ten percent of Revell's revenues by this time. (Revell added the distinct "H" prefix to the product numbers of its hobby items to distinguish them from its toys.) Early in 1953 Glaser set up three new corporations with outside investors to create tooling for three new toy lines: a set of "Young Gardener, Young Plumber, and Young TV Serviceman" play trucks; a Shooting Gallery hand-held game; and a pull-toy 1932 Ford Hot Rod. The trucks had been designed by Gretz and the Revell staff.

The Young Plumber truck had a jack for lifting it up so kids could use the plastic wrench to remove a wheel.

The 1932 Ford Hot Rod employed the same Gowland metal cable-and-backfiring mechanism used in the 1/16 scale Model T, but the body had not been designed by Gowland, and it had a distinctly toy-like appearance. Yet Glaser thought that the Hot Rod might be made into a model kit like the Maxwell and Model T. It was—but it turned out to be the worst model kit Revell would ever issue. Glaser quickly realized that this model violated his own standards for both toys and models. It was too simple and unauthentic. Model builders needed something that satisfied their sense of craftsmanship and that they would be proud to display once they had completed it.

The backfiring Hot Rod worked just like a cap gun.

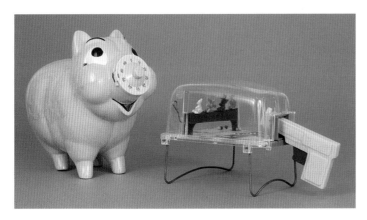

Revell continued to make toys like the Pig Bank and Shooting Gallery for several years after it began making model kits.

As time went by Highway Pioneers models like the Deusenberg became more sophisticated. *H-72*

The Speedy Sportsters showed that the Highway Pioneers series had entered modern times by the mid-50s. *G-79*

Meanwhile, the Highway Pioneers continued to hum along in 1953 with the arrival of the Series Three kits. This time the box was green, and a new feature came with these cars: hubcaps. No longer would model builders have the mess, smell, burnt fingers—and intrigue—of securing the wheels by melting the axle ends.

The Series Four kits arrived in 1954 in blue packaging, with another twist: each car had its own distinctive set of wheels. Up to then all the cars had used the same wheels produced from the same forty-cavity mold. The Series Four cars were all European. There was a French Renault, a German Mercedes-Benz, an Italian Fiat, and two English cars: a Jaguar and an MG-TD. The English cars were the first modern autos in what had been a line of antique cars up to then.

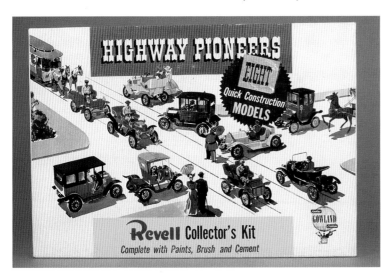

To make its low cost Highway Pioneers kits more appealing to department store retailers, Revell created a wide variety of gift sets with higher sticker prices. *P-695*

About this time Gowland switched from molding its kits in acetate plastic to modern styrene. In the beginning acetate had been the plastic of choice because it molded well and had dark, rich colors. But acetate tended to warp. The newer formulas of styrene had better color and stability. It was the plastic of the future—and Gowland made the switch.

Some of the molds received makeovers. The Series One cars lost their "Action Miniatures" moveable rear axles and front ends where the pull cables had once fit in. Kelvin Gowland's oversize comic drivers were replaced with smaller, more realistic figures created by Revell's staff. A whole new mold was created for the 1903 Ford Model A; thus it was no longer the Cadillac under an assumed identity. Details like floor mat texture appeared on some of the other models. The simple Highway Pioneers became more sophisticated models. Between 1951 and 1954 the plastic model field underwent a revolution, and the Highway Pioneers were in danger of being left behind.

The clearest revolution in Revell's model kit line in 1954 appeared as a dramatic improvement in the quality of its box art. The packaging for the Highway Pioneers had been pedestrian from the start, and the first three aircraft kits likewise came with washed-out three-color illustrations on flimsy cardboard boxes. The first ships—the *Missouri*, PT Boat, and Chris Craft Cruiser—looked a lot better because they came in boxes constructed of thick cardboard with a shiny, varnished paper wrap glued to the box—but there wasn't much room on their narrow box tops for inspiring illustrations. In 1954 this all changed. Revell went to a flat rectangular box for its aircraft and ship kits, and it put dramatic, colorful, highly detailed original paintings on the box lids. The transformation was stunning, advancing Revell far ahead of all the other model companies in the quality of its packaging.

The PT-212 torpedo boat was manned by a tiny crew of figures created by sculptor Tony Bulone. *H-304*

The freighter *Hawaiian Pilot* and tanker *J. L. Hanna* both used Eidson box art. *H-315, H-322*

If you look closely, you can see tiny crew figures in the rigging of the *Flying Cloud* clipper ship. *H-344*

The box wrap for the tug *Long Beach* shows Scott Eidson's eye for color and detail. *H-314*

One of the men responsible for the revolution in the company's box art was Andrew Scott Eidson, a veteran commercial illustrator and also World War II veteran. "Scottie" Eidson had been born in 1908 and received his training at Chicago's prestigious Art Institute. As a young man he did illustrations for newspapers and magazines—when the World War started he developed advertisements for Lockheed aircraft. During the war he served as a signal man with the U. S. Army in Europe, getting caught right in the middle of the Battle of the Bulge. Returning to California he found plenty of demand for his skills, and Sudler Advertising steered him to one of its clients, Revell. Eidson worked for Revell on a freelance basis, although he stayed in close touch with his client to meet their needs and demands. Like most illustrators of that day, he simply sold his paintings to Revell for the going rate of $500 or $600 dollars each and lost all legal rights to his creations. Most of the time Revell wouldn't even allow him to sign his art.

As color illustration became more important in the early 1950s, Eidson started experimenting with all sorts of blends of paints. When he sat down to do a painting his palate consisted of an array of paper Dixie Cups containing his own concoctions of opaque watercolors—the favorite medium of commercial artists since it is easy to work with, dries quickly, and reproduces well because it reflects a lot of light. The other elements of his style were a high degree of realism and such extreme attention to detail that his fellow artists sometimes accused him of painting with a one-hair brush. Eidson was an excellent photographer, and it showed in his paintings; yet no one would mistake his colorful compositions for photographs.

The hospital ship *Haven* made for colorful box art. *H-320*

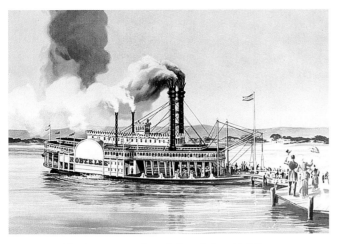

The famous riverboat *Robert E. Lee. H-323*

The Boeing B-47 was reissued in 2006 to celebrate Revell's 50th Anniversary. H-206

A second player in Revell's art renaissance was another veteran of World War II who had found himself on the other side of the fighting. Richard Kishady started life in Hungary at the end of World War I and grew to be a man just in time for the Second World War. After graduating from Hungary's Air Force Academy, he flew Stukas and Focke-Wulf 190s against the Russians on the eastern front. After a brief stay in a POW camp at the end of the war, he traveled to Munich, Germany, to study art, earning his tuition by helping to paint the walls of the recently rebuilt art academy buildings. After a few years he applied to immigrate to the United States, but was rejected when he listed his occupation as "artist." When he changed his answer to "sign painter," immigration said, come right in!

Richard Kishady, and his brother Charles, ended up in Detroit, where Richard went to work for the New Center Studio across the street from General Motors doing commercial illustration for car company catalogs. This was a learning experience for someone who had studied to be a sculptor and painter of fine art. Here he learned to slice the photograph of a car into two dozen vertical strips, then reassemble them to create a slightly stretched image of the car. A painting done from the new image showed a subtly longer, lower, more exciting car than the original photo. Later at Revell Kishady would apply such "cheating" to the box-top images of model airplanes. "It was fun."

Finally, one bone-chilling Detroit Christmas, the Kishady brothers held a family conference, decided they were tired of Michigan's snow and slush, and caught a Greyhound for Southern California. After a year of working in an art studio, Richard spotted an ad in the newspaper for an artist, "trained in the European style." When he showed up at Revell for an interview, he found that they wanted someone to design paint-by-numbers sets!

Art director Richard Kishady sits amid his creations, wearing the USS *Missouri* tie tack that Revell handed out as a promotional item.

The American Airlines DC-7. *H-219*

Each shipping case of United Flight 707 kits sent to hobby shops contained one with the parts sealed in plastic for display. *H-220*

Kishady sketched-out several paint-by-numbers designs that were shown at the Hobby Industry Association annual convention in Chicago in January 1954, but the competition in the paint-by-numbers field was just too formidable; so Revell dropped the project. Kishady then suggested to Gretz that he could paint aircraft and ship illustrations for Revell's kit boxes, and he was given the assignment of doing the illustration for the new B-52 kit. Gretz and Glaser liked that one so much that Kishady got a permanent job and soon became in-house art director.

Kishady admired the work Eidson already had done for Revell, and the two men split assignments between them as they came in. After trying his hand at a few ship box covers, Kishady decided that nautical scenes were best left to Eidson, while he concentrated on aircraft. They both did cars. The result of this partnership was a collection of model kit box art that many of today's hobby connoisseurs think has never been surpassed. A lot of collectors value Revell's 1950s box art more highly than the kits that came in the boxes.

Landing an F-89 on snow may not be safe runway practice, but it sure makes for great art. *H-221*

The SS *United States* is an early, rare ship painting by Kishady. *H-312*

Whenever Revell's new product evaluating committee decided on another model to add to the catalog, Kishady or Eidson would be given photographs to work from. Gretz and Bulone would talk with the artist about how the box art might be composed to highlight the most interesting or dramatic features of the model. Kishady or Eidson would then paint two or three preliminary color sketches, called comprehensives or "comps." These would be shown to all those involved (including mailing them to Kramer back East for his opinion), and the artist would then paint the final box art.

New aircraft like the Piasecki YH-16 were Revell's bread-and-butter subjects. *H-223*

Both Kishady and Eidson painted their compositions twenty to fifty percent larger than the size of the box it was intended for. This made it easier to include fine details. The illustration had to be faithful to the real aircraft, but also needed to accurately portray the Revell model, including what Kishady called the "silly nicknames" on the decal sheet. To sketch-in the outline of an aircraft on his artist's board, Kishady used the old-fashioned technique of penciling a grid over a photograph of the plane he wanted to paint—then he measured-in the same grid on his art board. After that he would carefully copy the image in each small square of the grid from the photo on to the board—just as Michelangelo had done in the Renaissance. Most paintings took only about ten days to complete. Commercial artists had to work fast.

Kishady's Air Power gift set art just knocks your socks off. *G-240*

The world's smallest models: An F-89 Scorpion
encased in a promo cigarette lighter and two tiny kits
produced in 1960 by the Merry Company of Cincinnati
for inclusion in several of its miniature toy sets.

The "Buffalo Bill" B-24's nose art endeared
it to a generation of boys. *H-218*

Once the painting was done, it would go to Revell's art department where the layout for the box graphics—the "mechanics"—would be designed. The finished paste-up went to Western Lithographers in downtown Los Angeles where four-color lithographic proofs would be shot for Kishady's approval. Then Revell's box wraps would be "gang printed" two or three on the same sheet—along with soup can labels or whatever other printing jobs Western had at the time. The wraps would then be cut and sent to the Advance Paper Box factory where they would be folded and pasted to heavy cardboard boxes. This process of printing box art on glossy paper and then wrapping it around a hard cardboard box made for supremely attractive packaging. It should have, because the box actually cost more than the plastic that went into the box.

Meanwhile, another artist would be working on the instruction sheet. At first Gretz and Bulone did some of the instruction sheets themselves, but in 1955 Anthony Furtivo took over responsibility for the instructions. He was a talented artist in his own right and a graduate of the Los Angeles Art Center. He became Revell's specialist in the humble, but critical area of instruction sheets. By the 1960s he had left the Venice plant to become a freelance artist in his home garage studio, but he continued to do Revell instruction sheets down through the 1980s.

The F-101 Voodoo embodied speed and power. *H-231*

The A-4 Skyhawk box art allowed any boy
to imagine himself in the cockpit. *H-232*

Richard Kishady's brother Charles joined the Revell staff as a model sculptor. He had trained as a wood sculptor back in Europe, and his talents suited Revell's needs perfectly. He was the primary sculptor for the tug boat *Long Beach* and did turrets and smoke stacks for other ship models. He also created the patterns for the North American B-25 and Consolidated B-24 bombers—kits for which his brother did the fantastic box art. It proved to be a winning combination, for these two World War II bombers became top sellers among Revell's aircraft throughout the 'fifties and down into the 'sixties.

project into. It may be an act of piloting an airplane in war or piloting an airplane as a transport pilot." (*Toys & Novelties*, January 1, 1967, 45) Glaser wanted models that would spark a builder's imagination when he first saw the box resting on a store shelf and, when completed and displayed in his home, would leave the builder with a sense of accomplishment and pride of craftsmanship. And that would make him want to go back to the store and buy another Revell model kit. The ideal customer was the boy who wanted to "build them all"—to have a whole set of Revell's ship or car or aircraft models.

Kishady's original Bell P-39 shows three swastika "kill" marks that were later changed to red Japanese circles to avoid anti-swastika laws in European markets. *H-222*

Box art for the smaller of Revell's two F-102 models. *H-233*

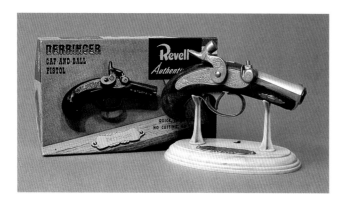

The Derringer was one of a half-dozen Antique Pistols issued in the mid-50s. *H-602*

By 1954 Revell hit its stride in model making and was filling its kit boxes with an extensive assemblage of soon-to-become classic models. Decisions about which new subjects to turn into models were made by an informal committee consisting of Glaser, Kramer, Gretz, and perhaps a couple of other men in manufacturing and sales who would be involved in producing and selling the kit. As Gretz recalled, they would sit and "kick around ideas." Glaser explained the process: "What makes us select products in kits is what is historically important and what is exciting. It's got to be both. You have to have something that a boy can vicariously

All model kit artists know that orange skies sell model kits. The F-100 Super Saber. *H-236*

Kramer, whose thinking had a strong influence on Glaser, believed that a model should duplicate as accurately as possible its real life subject. Beyond that, the model had to present enough challenge to the builder to involve his sense of workmanship; yet be so easy to assemble that an eight-year-old boy could enjoy success in completing the project. Kramer steered Revell in the direction of modern-day United States aircraft and warships because he felt that was where the public's interests centered. Every week feature stories ran prominently in *LIFE* and other national magazines and newspapers about the latest aircraft, ships, and military hardware added to America's Cold War arsenal. This amounted to free advertising for Revell's models. Beyond this, the Glasers and staff at Revell simply shared the patriotic feelings and love of modern innovations typical of Americans in the 1950s.

Gathering information for new models became easier once Revell established its reputation for producing quality products—and once Revell started building good relations with the armed services by doing things like donating built-up models to recruiting offices. Part of the credit for Revell's success in building its good public image belonged to Henry Blankfort, vice president for public relations.

Before coming to Revell, Blankfort had been a successful Hollywood movie screenwriter. He listed among his credits the 1940s leftist classic *Tales of Manhattan*, which starred black activist-singer Paul Robeson. After the war the McCarthy era hunt for "subversives" in the entertainment industry landed him on the blacklist along with the "Hollywood Ten." His new employer, Lew Glaser also had some traces of left-wing activities in his past. As a young man Glaser had frequented some Marxist clubs—a good place to meet girls, he later quipped—but he must also have been intrigued by the interplay of unconventional ideas in leftist ideology. During the Cold War years of the 1950s, Glaser occasionally worried that some hostile party might try to exploit his and Blankfort's past to poison Revell's good relations with the Armed Services and military contractors.

The Coast Guard Cutter *Campbell* lent itself to an illustration that "told a story." H-338

The Sky Squadron gift set aimed for the Christmas market. G-226

The icebreaker *Eastwind* sails on a sea of Styrofoam ice in this store display. Nice dioramas like this cost $200 and more. H-337

With new box art, a change in plastic color, and the switch of a few parts, the Air Force Sikorsky S-55 became a Navy rescue copter. H-227

Blankfort's first project for Revell was a proposed television series that featured hobbies as part of family life. The show would star Royle Glaser as a young housewife who would visit "Uncle Henry's" workshop to see what hobby craft he was working on that day. The TV show idea didn't get very far, but Blankfort stayed on in public relations. Sol Kramer later declared that Blankfort "had the most creative imagination of any human being I have ever run across." He had a way of getting stories about Revell planted in newspapers and major national magazines, and his sharp wits and smooth interpersonal style opened doors with both private companies and the armed services. "He had them eating right out of his hand," said Kramer. For example, when the movie *Strategic Air Command* premiered in Omaha in the fall of 1954, Revell appeared to deliver models of the SAC bombers to General Curtis LeMay and the governor of Nebraska. The star of the movie, Jimmy Stewart, posed with a Revell bomber model in his hands, and at Christmas Revell offered a "Strategic Air Command" gift set.

Private aircraft manufacturers like Lockheed, Boeing, and Douglas calculated that having models of their latest designs in the homes of millions of Americans made for good public relations at a time when each company was intensely involved in competition for military contracts. They would pass information on to Revell—minus classified details—and inspected Revell's prototypes for accuracy. Thus sometimes Revell's models actually were "scaled from official prints," but just as often the R and D staff had to piece together information in the form of photographs they took themselves or found in publications. Sometimes Revell's researchers put two and two together and came to an accurate conclusion about something that the military thought was classified information.

The Colt ".45" looked just like a real gun. *H-603*

All four of the Strategic Air Command modern bombers lacked landing gear—thus the box highlighted the Revell swivel stand that held them. *G-209*

The 1950s proved to be the last gasp for amphibian aircraft like the Convair R3Y Tradewind. *H-238*

The Martin P6M Seamaster is hard to find in blue plastic today. *H-244*

The first three World War II bombers, the B-24, B-29, and B-25, came in different scales so that they would turn out about the same size and fit in the same size box. *H-218, H-208, H-216*

Jack Campbell, a professional photographer, was responsible for assembling all the research data. He presided over Revell's growing reference library of books, trade journals, and popular magazines that contained stories and photographs of everything that flew, floated, or rolled. Campbell became a major player in suggesting new subjects for models. The red-haired Scotsman drove a sporty MG and led Revell to make models of a Porsche Carrera, Mercedes-Benz 190-SL, Austin-Healey 100-Six, and even the novel VW Micro Bus.

R & D head Jack Campbell steered Revell toward classic European sports cars rather than Detroit's annual new cars. *H-1238, H-1239*

The Austin Healey epitomized the 1950s muscular sports car. *H-1217*

Once documentation on a new model had been gathered, the engineering department—which had grown to several dozen men—would draw up highly specific blueprints of every part in the proposed model. The sculptors in the model shop would complete a new model's pattern, making the parts just as they would be in the final kit, except for the hollow interiors of the larger parts. Then the model and a preliminary instruction sheet would be air mailed to Kramer in Baltimore. A self-confessed clumsy builder, Kramer felt that he was an excellent guinea pig to evaluate a kit's buildability. He wanted the parts to fit precisely and to be designed in such a way that they would almost hold together without glue. Thus a nose cone and exhaust ring might hold a fuselage together, while deep recesses in the fuselage and overlapping tabs on the two wing roots would secure the wings in place with the proper dihedral. Tabs and slots would be made in "foolproof" shapes and sizes so that it would impossible to assemble parts incorrectly—such as putting the left-wing landing gear tab in the right-wing hole.

Black on orange makes for a dramatic Martin B-57 composition. *H-230*

By mid-decade the model shop had expanded to a staff of a half-dozen skilled craftsmen. Bulone made their work a bit easier by talking Gretz and Glaser into purchasing an expensive but time saving milling machine that could carve reverse images into molds. Thus only one side of a ship or plane model had to be sculpted precisely because the "True Trace" machine would duplicate the other side in reverse. Some parts of a model didn't have to be carved at all by the model pattern sculptors if the mold makers in the engineering department could work right from the engineering blueprints. As project engineer Ernest Brown described it: "The process was not always one, two, three, four. Sometimes it was one, two, four. It all depended on the model or part in question. Sometimes it was easier to work from a three-dimensional model; sometimes the mold maker could use just drawings if he could visualize the way the part would look." Brown added that mold makers had to become accustomed to visualizing everything in the negative because every dimension in the plans and mold would be reversed in the actual model that came out of the molding machines.

Chief mold maker Frank Sesto expressed pride in the jeweler-precision handiwork of his craftsmen. "We put shoelaces on human figures only one inch high and rivets on fuselages of 12-inch airplanes. ... it takes from 2,700 to 7,000 hours to make a suitable mold." (*Coronet*, April 1957, 166) But that was what made Revell's models special. Not many boys would notice, but the tiny captain figure on the HMS *Bounty* looked like movie actor Charles Laughton and his first mate resembled Clark Gable.

Philip Shelton painted only one box cover for Revell, but his HMS *Victory* was a masterpiece. *H-363*

The rivets that Sesto mentioned encrusted Revell's aircraft models in the 1950s and were an item of debate among the staff. Some complained that rivets and panel lines were inaccurately oversized, but Bulone felt that they were necessary to embellish otherwise flat, plain surfaces on wings and fuselages. Also, they helped create the illusion of super detail and suggested that the model was made of metal, not plastic. Raised decal locater lines went on the aircraft models as well because the staff felt that youngsters needed them for reference. At least Revell, unlike Aurora and some of the other model companies, usually kept their decal locaters subtle so that serious modelers would have minimal trouble sanding them off.

Eidson's art for the *Bounty* showed the same attention to detail found in the model. *H-327*

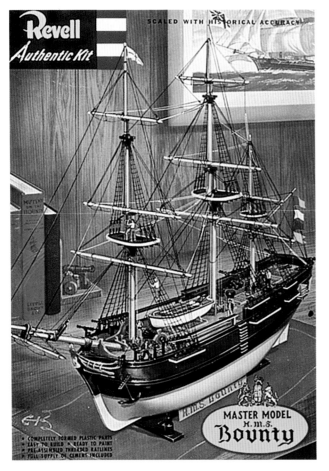

Model airplane box artists like Kishady love sunrise and sunset for their dramatic color potential. The P2V Neptune. *H-239*

The "Flying Dragon" B-25 remained a
top-selling kit for a decade. *H-216*

The issue of maintaining a constant scale in its aircraft and ship models bedeviled Revell. The Highway Pioneers and Miniature Masterpieces presented no problem because cars and wagons didn't vary too much in size. However, aircraft and ships ranged in size from PT boats to aircraft carriers; from small fighter planes to giant bombers. The production and marketing departments wanted to keep the number of box sizes to a minimum, and they had certain price points at which they wanted to sell kits. Thus Revell's models were scaled to fit specific size boxes and sell at certain prices. Gretz and Kramer later confessed that in the early days of Revell they had just not been sensitive enough to the desirability of maintaining constant scale in a model company's inventory of kits. Yet Revell's "box-scale" models of the 1950s were so good in so many other respects that many of them would remain in the catalog down through the 1970s.

The Douglas Skyrocket made headlines in
the 1950s for its supersonic flights. *H-213*

The Merchant Fleet gift set brought together
three classic kits: the freighter *Hawaiian Pilot*,
tanker *J. L. Hanna*, and the tug *Long Beach. G-322*

In 1954 Tony Bulone made another contribution to the aircraft models. He recalled that back in his days as a ceramics sculptor, he had made flower vases and candle holders to hang on the wall. So he designed a new stand for Revell's aircraft models that could either be hung horizontally on a wall or rested upright on a shelf. The key ingredient to the new stand was a ball-in-socket mount that allowed the model builder to pose the plane in any dramatic position he wished. The stand was molded in clear plastic, with a place for a colorful decal of the manufacturer's logo and the name of plane. This innovative and attractive display stand added to the desirability of the models at the time, and today it is one of the things that makes 1950s vintage kits collectible. In the 1960s and 1970s Revell reverted to a simple base-and-arm stand for some of its models—but most were issued with no stand at all.

Every one of the models developed by Revell hit a home run with America's kids—and many grown-ups, too. However, this tremendous success only marked the beginning of bigger things to come.

Models like the Martin Mariner could be posed at
any angle on Revell's unique swivel stand. *H-258*

Chapter 3 –
America's Number One Hobby

In mid-decade, 1950s America entered a model maker's utopia. Back in the olden days of the 1930s and 1940s, model building had been a hobby reserved for mature skilled craftsmen with the specialized tools and patience to create a model from the blocks of wood and handful of metal or plastic accessories that came in the relatively expensive kits sold in side street hobby shops. The switch from wood to plastic brought the cost of a model kit down to the range of a boy's weekly allowance, and the pre-shaped plastic parts made it possible for the average youngster to make a really nice looking model. A survey conducted by *Boy's Life* magazine found that model making had become the number one hobby of America's boys. In a parallel survey done by *Boys Life* in 1947, model building had not even appeared on the list of favorite hobbies.

The typical eight to fifteen-year-old American boy could hop on his bike, ride to the neighborhood Woolworth, and check out the newest assortment of kits sitting on the hobby shelves beside the toy department. If he was lucky, he could speed on to the hobby shop just around the corner with a larger kit selection, where he could check out the array of built models in the display case. A few minutes later, back home in his room, he enjoyed the supreme pleasures of popping open the box, smelling the aroma of fresh plastic, sorting through the shiny plastic parts, and imagining what the model would look like when it was assembled. A few years later, when he reached the mature age of sixteen and discovered the dual attractions of girls and cars, plastic model building would suddenly became very un-cool. But until then, making and collecting models absorbed the after school creative energies of legions of adolescent boys.

In the mid-1950s a new age was dawning in plastic modeling—
just as it was over Kishady's F8U Crusader. *H-250*

Scott Eidson's blazing USS *Arizona* box art put a sensational finishing touch on one of Revell's best ship models. *H-348*

Lew Glaser and a collection of the best selling model kits of all time.

The plastic model kit business had grown to include a half-dozen major companies and several dozen smaller companies spread across the country. Still, the industry was a relatively small world in which executives from all the companies knew each other on a first name basis, and workers frequently changed jobs from one company to another. The forth week in January each year, they would all gather in Chicago for the Hobby Industry Association convention. A cordial atmosphere prevailed because business was good and growing, and most companies that really wanted to succeed in plastic kits were making money. Lew Glaser became a member of the HIA board of directors, and would be president in the early 1960s.

Kishady's original F11F Tiger has Marine Corps markings for the Supersonic Marines gift set, but these are changed to Navy on the individual F11F kit boxes. *H-249*

Aurora Plastics of West Hempstead, New York, came closest to Revell in variety of models and volume of sales, but Aurora made simple, inexpensive models that lacked the accuracy and detail of Revell's products. Also, Aurora specialized in figure kits like knights in armor and monsters from the old 1930s horror movies. Monogram Models of Morton Grove, Illinois, closely resembled Revell in its commitment to manufacturing top quality, accurate models, but Monogram lagged far behind Revell and Aurora in sales. Monogram's president, Jack Besser, declared: "We don't want to be the biggest; we want to be the best." (*Craft, Model, Hobby,* February 1958, 100) Because it product offerings almost paralleled Revell's, Monogram became the focus of Revell's competitive spirit.

As the dominant company in the industry, Revell adopted the corporate policy of simply making the best quality models and selling the most of them. Lew Glaser discounted the idea that the market was glutted with too many models, saying, "Unquestionably, despite the enormous expansion that has taken place, the market for authentic models has hardly been scratched." (*Craft, Model, Hobby,* February 1955, 39) He declared (with some exaggeration) that Revell would be bringing out a new kit every week.

A factory-built display model of the Lockheed Electra. *H-255*

The Electra appeared in Brooklyn Dodgers colors as a premium kids could send away for in the mail. *H-255D*

When the Air Force rolled out a new plane, Aurora might rush a simple (and inaccurate) model of it onto the market first, but the Revell model that came along later would be superior and could be reissued again and again over the years. Revell's market studies showed the typical model builder to be a boy in the eight to fourteen years-old range, and Revell aimed to hit that target. But Revell also believed the adult market to be extremely important; so its kits maintained the authenticity and detail that mature builders demanded. By the end of the decade Revell estimated that about forty percent of its customers were adults—although some parents were reluctant to admit that the models they bought "for the kids" were really for themselves. Revell was not averse to admitting that adults built their models; in fact, Revell—in typical 1950s fashion—proclaimed that model building brought families together. Many a Revell advertisement showed Dad looking over Junior's shoulder at a model, and some ads suggested that Junior buy Dad a Revell model for Father's Day.

Revell's Lincoln Futura and Pontiac Club de Mer models captured the look of the real concept cars. The real Futura became TV's "Batmobile." *H-1210, H-1213*

By 1956 Revell had come a long way. It's total sales topped $10.5 million, compared to $737,000 back in 1949 when it sold Gowland toys. The Revell complex in Venice had grown to encompass eight acres and filled a half-dozen buildings, where twenty-five injection molding machines ran round the clock and more than three-hundred people worked.

Lew Glaser was lord of this domain, but—as long-time purchasing agent Betty Tomeo recalled—visitors encountering Glaser in a hallway likely wouldn't have any idea that the modest looking fellow everyone called "Lew" owned the place. Lunch time might find him sitting in the cafeteria eating with the women who ran the molding machines. Revell's wages were among the highest in the industry. Employees received lapel pins for every five years they stayed with the company, and the company newspaper *Revellations* praised anyone who accomplished something good. At the annual Christmas party, end of the year bonuses went to everyone. Perhaps Glaser was generous to a fault—to the detriment of Revell's bottom line profits—but his liberality resulted in a strong feeling of *esprit de corps* within the Revell family.

Glaser wished to be on the cutting edge of business developments. He went to conferences, hired consultants, and even employed that icon of 1950s corporate innovation, the industrial psychologist, to test applicants for executive positions and work with staff on conflict resolution. Glaser studied management techniques and business organization. Revell itself was not one corporation, but a collection of dozens of independent (at least on paper) corporations that owned molds or manufactured products or handled other segments of the company's operations. That led to a lot of internal paperwork as one part of Revell bought services from another part of Revell. It also led to a law suit by the Internal Revenue Service accusing Revell of using its complex organization to avoid taxes—but Revell won the suit in court.

Royle Glaser found living with her workaholic husband both stimulating and maddening. She later mused: "It was as if he had a prophetic vision that he would die young—and he was only fifty-three when he died. He raced the clock as if he knew that he didn't have that much time. He slept only four hours a night. He would go to bed early—maybe seven o'clock. Sometimes he would fall asleep during dinner, and I would get so angry. Then he would wake up at one or two in the morning and work through the night. He'd write and calculate with his slide rule—his most treasured tool."

At mid-decade Revell updated its original product, the Highway Pioneers, in an attempt to keep pace with the rapid evolution of the hobby field. Gone were the old-fashioned generic boxes used to package all five cars in a series. Each new model introduced came in its own individualized box with a picture of just one car on top. The first of these latest models, the 1932 Ford Hot Rod set new, higher standards for the line. It had forty-four parts, a detailed engine, a very realistic teenage boy driver, and even hub caps with "Ford" embossed on them. The improved driver figures were now sculpted by Revell's very talented team of artists, not the Gowland staff.

However, the Highway Pioneers line finally came to the end of the road in 1956-1957 with the release of three reworked earlier kits. The '32 Hot Rod *(H-60)* gained a roof, a new driver, and a few other parts to become the '32 Ford Jalopy *(H-80)*. The Franklin Phaeton *(H-81)* was a remake of the Nash Rambler *(H-47)* with a new round radiator, folded-down roof, and a lady passenger holding an umbrella. The Hudson Touring *(H-82)* was the old Pierce Arrow *(H-48)* with the top down and a little boy passenger waving a flag.

Although the Highway Pioneers had proven to be true pioneers in the model kit field and in making Revell's reputation, by the mid-1950s the hobby world had changed. The quaint, hobby craft spirit of the tiny, antique car models belonged back in the 1940s.

Revell opened the door to the future of automobile modeling in 1955 with the introduction of a set modern cars fresh off the Detroit assembly lines. As American adults reveled in an orgy of conspicuous consumption on the roads, Revell supplied America's kids with models of the latest chrome-and-tailfin products from the Big Three auto makers. Revell, a West Coast company, gained access to the Midwest world of the Detroit auto companies by forming a partnership with AMT, the model car specialists located in Troy, Michigan. AMT (Aluminum Model Toys) had started making metal toy cars back in 1948, but had since become the country's primary maker of the plastic model car "annuals" handed out as promotional items by car dealers across the country. The auto manufacturers knew and trusted AMT, and thus willingly shared advance information on new cars with AMT—and, now, through AMT, with Revell.

Kishady stretched the '55 Cadillac
Eldorado to look a block long. *H-1200*

Store banner for the Revell-AMT '55 Ford Fairlane. *H-1202*

Glaser, as was his customary practice, set up an independent corporation in partnership with AMT's president West Gallogly. Under this agreement AMT would provide Revell with the information needed to create models of the latest cars, and AMT would pay the tooling costs for some of the molds needed to produce the kits. In return, Revell's development and engineering team would create the models, tool the molds, and manufacture the kits. Revell also would package and market the kits through its large network of distributors and retailers.

The 1/32 scale Revell-AMT cars began to appear in stores in the spring of 1955. The Cadillac Eldorado convertible came first. A Ford Fairlane convertible, Chrysler New Yorker, Mercury Montclair, and Buick Riviera followed through the summer and fall. These nicely done models came complete with two figures to liven-up the car. Like all car offerings of the period, they lacked clear plastic parts for the windows, but did have "chrome" plated bumpers and grills. And, like most car models of the time, the bodies were manufactured in several pieces. This made tooling development and molding less expensive, but assembling the car body was a frustrating experience for most youngsters. One-piece bodies were still a few years away for Revell.

Art Director Richard Kishady (top), production artist Larry McAllister, and instruction sheet artist Tony Furtivo (bottom) check out the '55 Ford kit.

Revell's '55 Chrysler is driven by a black chauffeur—a rarity in the nearly all-white world of plastic modeling. *H-1201*

In the fall of 1955 Revell's tool makers got busy and modified the molds to transform the cars into 1956 models. The changes in the cars themselves were modest (as they were on the real cars), so Revell accentuated the innovations in the new releases by changing the box art, plastic colors, and the two figures that came with each kit. All five of the cars were released in their new form by the summer of 1956—but that proved to be the end of the road for Revell-AMT, Inc. Glaser purchased Gallogly's interest in the corporation and the three molds paid for by AMT. (One of Revell's model builders, Budd Anderson—who had not worked on the Revell-AMT cars—moved to Michigan and became AMT's model car spokesman in the 1960s.)

The '55 Autorama gift set contains all the Revell-AMT cars except the Mercury. *H-1206*

The Mercury Montclair received new figures and plastic color to update it to the '56 model. *H-1204-6*

The cars themselves continued in the Revell catalog with the AMT trademark removed from the boxes. In 1959, to stretch the life of the molds yet a few years longer, the models became "customizing" kits. These models reflected the latest appearance-oriented trends in car modifications, with lots of extra add-on parts—like moon disk hubcaps and bubble fender skirts—for personalized styling. There was also a decal sheet with pinstripes, scallops, and flames to add finishing touches to a real jukebox-on-wheels.

Revell cements. On the right front is a rare early tube of "A" cement for acetate plastic. Courtesy of Rusty Cowart.

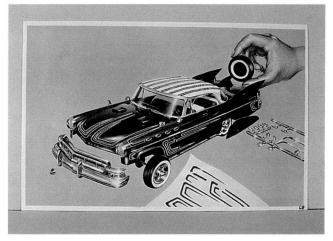

Jack Leynnwood did the box art for the Buick customizing kit. *H-1230*

By then Revell was bringing out some new Detroit models on its own. It had to sign an agreement of secrecy with the auto companies and swear its model makers to keep their lips sealed. The model shop and engineering department became a restricted, top secret area of the Venice plant. The doors remained always locked and workers from other divisions had to buzz for admission. New models under development were assigned code names to conceal their true identity. (The F-4 Phantom II's working name was "Spook.") However, the person who proved to be the greatest security risk was Lew Glaser himself. He was so enthusiastic about whatever new project his company had coming up that he couldn't resist talking about it. Royle hoped that the code names would keep both Lew and the competition confused.

The Continental Mark II continued the features of the earlier 1/32 scale cars. H-1209

Revell considered using this illustration for the Cadillac Eldorado Brougham, but ultimately decided to delete the jeweled Cadillac crest. H-1214

Leynnwood's Mobile Gas Truck. H-1402

Store display for the Ford Country Squire station wagon. H-1220

The store display for the Ford '56 Pick-Up. H-1400

The '59 Ford Fairlane Skyliner model had a roof that actually retracted. H-1227

In January 1956, Revell launched a new series of historical sailing ships with a model of the USS *Constitution*. Sol Kramer had long wanted Revell to make all-plastic models of classic sailing ships because he knew that such ship models had been favorite subjects for old-time wooden model ship builders. Plastic would allow for much more detail than wood—but that was just the problem: how to get all the small parts into a plastic kit? The biggest headache proved to be the rope ladders—the ratlines—that ran from the deck to the tops of the masts. The easy way to make the ratlines would be simply to injection-mold them in plastic, but then the ropes would be far too thick for the scale of the ship. Requiring a ten-year-old builder to tie together true-to-scale rigging was too much to ask for. After months of experimentation, Gretz and his engineers solved the problem by devising a machine that would feed plastic-coated string into a jig with all a ship's ratlines laid-out in order. The machine would then clamp down on the lines and heat seal them together. All the kit builder had to do was to lay the ratline assembly over a paper pattern included with the instructions and trim off the excess string. It wasn't a perfect solution because most builders ended up with little nubs of string sticking out from the edges of their rope ladders, but it was the best solution any hobby company had come up with up to that time—or since.

Revell's Old Ironsides plastic model kit gave the average man or boy—for the first time—a realistic chance of building a mantelpiece-quality sailing ship model. H-319

Revell's model of the U. S. Navy's oldest commissioned ship, "Old Ironsides," was destined to become a one of Revell's all-time best sellers and is still a staple in hobby shops today. The principal sculptor for the prototype model was Tom Hogg, an Englishman known around the model shop as "Captain Tom." He was a sailing ship enthusiast who filled his home with large wooden ship models. Kramer instructed Revell's model makers to avoid perfect symmetry in the parts of the ship since absolute regularity would ring false in the mind of anyone looking at a model of an old-time wooden

vessel. The molds for the Constitution cost almost $100,000; so the kit sold in stores for a hefty $2.98. But for this price the hobbyist got a very detailed model, molded in two colors of plastic, with everything a lover of old ships could want, right down to a sheet of paper signal flags.

The Santa Maria store display shows off Revell's innovative vacuum-formed sails. H-322

Revell expanded its line of heroic ships from the age of sail with models representative of major classes of vessels. There was the HMS Victory, Lord Horatio Nelson's flagship from the Napoleonic Wars, Columbus's flagship Santa Maria, the Coast Guard training ship Eagle, and the ship made famous by mutiny and movies—the HMS Bounty. There was also a rakish clipper ship, the Flying Cloud. All of these kits built-up to neat models about a foot-and-half long. Then in 1959 Revell took a gamble with a mantle piece ship model three feet long—the clipper Cutty Sark. This model had everything: parts molded in four different colors, a pre-painted hull, real chains for the anchors. The steering wheel even turned the rudder. It was an immediate success and became the best seller in the ship line. To capitalize on this success, Revell made some slight changes in the model's details and issued it as a second kit, the Thermopylae.

Marketing and distribution of its products had always been a strong suit for Revell, going all the way back to its days as a toy company. Within the United States distribution was handled by independent hobby industry distributors, like Sol Kramer and Nat Polk, and by large toy distribution companies who handled chain stores such as Woolworth and Kresge. From his first association with Revell, Kramer had pushed Glaser to get involved in overseas sales. Glaser first approached sales of Revell's kits abroad by making an agreement in 1954 with Ramos Trading Company of Los Angeles to handle foreign distribution. Bernard Ramos and his chief lieutenant Al Trendle ran this company.

They located distributors in countries overseas who were given exclusive licenses to distribute Revell models in their homelands, and Revell's kits soon became popular items around the world.

This tattered printer's proof shows how Eidson's painting could be united with a photograph to create an interesting composition. *H-358*

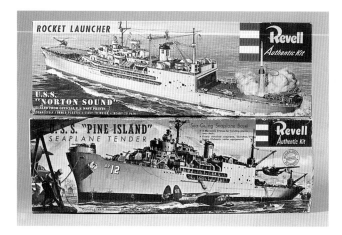

The Navy converted a seaplane tender into a seagoing missile test center. Revell reversed the order—first issuing its model as the rocket launcher *Norton Sound* and then modifying it into the tender *Pine Island*. *H-331, H-362*

The *Pine Island* seaplane tender store display. *H-362*

However, Glaser wanted an even stronger position abroad. In 1958 he brought Ramos and Trendle to Venice to become leaders of a new international operations department. Then Ramos traveled to Europe to establish Revell

subsidiaries in England and West Germany. In order to avoid import taxes and other trade restrictions, Revell had to have a presence in both countries because England belonged to the European Free Trade Association, while West Germany was part of the Common Market.

The *Forrest Sherman* was the Navy's newest destroyer. *H-352*

The Naval Academy gift set combined the aircraft carrier *Ranger*, the guided missile cruiser *Canberra*, and the destroyer *Forrest Sherman*. *G-359*

Revell Great Britain, Ltd. opened for business with an office in West London on Berners Street, and a warehouse near Heathrow airport served as a distribution center for kits imported from the United States. To consolidate operations and escape the high costs of doing business in London, Revell moved all its activities to Potters Bar in Hertsfordshire. In its new plant Revell, GB began molding kits using tooling imported from the United States. This made good economic sense because shipping costs were much lower for a mold than the transportation costs for the kits that could be produced from that tooling. The molds that went overseas were for those models that no longer remained best sellers in the United States.

Revell's British unit created its own instructions sheets and packaging, hiring noted English illustrator Brian Knight to paint its box art. By the early '60s the British also started to develop and make tooling for some small scale cars and aircraft that had special appeal for the English market. With this degree of autonomy, Revell, GB could hope to compete on its home turf with local companies Airfix and Frog, which until then had held a hammerlock on the English market.

The Navy Log gift set came with both ABC and CBS markings. It contained three missile ships: the *Nautilus*, *Boston*, and *Norton Sound*. G-330

The cruise liner SS *Brasil*. H-346

to be serious about their modeling, and Revell, Germany, enjoyed strong growth in sales. Indeed, Revell's subsidiaries in Europe generated better profits than the home plant in Venice because they strictly focused on producing and selling model kits.

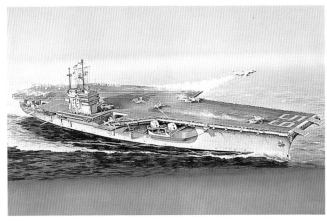

The super carrier USS *Forrestal* remained a top-selling kit for years. H-339

Eidson's illustration for the USS *Buckley* catches the moment when the destroyer escort rammed a U-boat. H-355

Revell Plastics, GmbH, West Germany, first set up shop in a tobacco warehouse in the rustic little town of Bünde near the Dutch border. This was the home of managing director, Heinz-Georg Schöneberg. Thanks to a subsidy from the German government, Revell soon built a state-of-the-art manufacturing plant at Bünde. In the beginning, it imported kits manufactured in England and California, but quickly the Germans began manufacturing their own kits using molds brought over from the United States. Unlike Revell, GB, however, it did not have the resources to develop new models or molds. German customers tended to purchase basic ship and aircraft models, especially those with a strong relevance to historical events. They proved

Revell took a different approach to sales in Japan. It first made a licensing agreement with the Japanese company Marusan in 1959 to market Revell kits in Japanese stores. When this did not lead to the volume of sales hoped for, Revell switched to Gunze Sangyo, a silk clothing manufacturer that wished to enter the toy and hobby field. This partnership lasted until the mid-1970s, when Revell again changed vendors to Takara. The Japanese embraced Revell models enthusiastically. Al Trendle, Revell's agent in Japan noted, "To my utter amazement, the biggest seller of all was the B-29. The battleship *Missouri* was also a very big seller." He chalked this up to Japan's understandable national preoccupation with World War II.

Revell of England reissued the B-25 with
new British version box art and decals.

The Swedish Saab Draken was a natural for Revell, Great Britain.

By the early 1960s Revell earned about twenty percent of its profits from overseas, and that figure would continue to grow into the 1970s.

Back home in the U. S., Revell began to issue models of military armor, artillery, and army vehicles in 1956. The decision to enter the "Army hardware" field came after some debate within the new products committee about whether Revell should get into such earthbound engines of death and destruction. Somehow mud-covered, olive drab war machines seemed more sinister than silver aircraft or great ships on the high seas. So Revell started with a small step into this new field, just one kit: the M4 Sherman Tank, America's easily-recognized stalwart from the Second World War. The model was a hit, and Revell quickly joined the rest of the hobby industry in issuing more army models.

The Sherman tank was just a great subject
to kick off Revell's armor series. *H-522*

Whenever possible Revell attempted to tie-in its models
with movies or television shows to stimulate interest.

To expand its line, Revell again linked-up with Steve Adams, the mold-maker who had done the Miniature Masterpieces collections. Adams financed production of the next models to come on line, although the work was done by the Revell staff. Sculptor Tony Bulone created the figures that went with these models. He modeled the general in the GI Battle Action figures on George Patton, right down to his two pearl-handled six shooters. (By this time Bulone had left Revell to work as a freelance artist. One of his commissions was a slender, leggy doll inspired by a figure Mattel's Ruth Handler had seen in Europe. Bulone used his wife Lylis as his personal inspiration. Mattel thanked Bulone, paid him $800 for his sculpture work, and produced the doll under the name "Barbie.")

The Long Tom with Tractor store display. *H-523*

The M-40 Combat Car proved to be one of the
most popular of the Revell armor collection. *H-524*

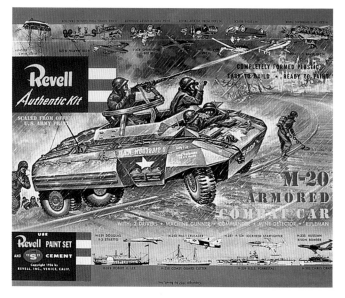

The Revell-Adams partnership turned out to be very short-lived. In 1957 Adams decided to launch his own company, Adams Action Models. (Adams's sales representative was ex-Revell sales chief Milt Grey.) Adams took the five molds he owned with him: the 155 mm Long Tom cannon and High Speed Tractor (H-523), the M-20 Armored Car (H-524), the Jeep and Trailer (H-525), and the GI Battle Action Figures (H-526). However, the Adams model company soon folded after producing a collection of very interesting models on its own. Adams's molds for the five Army armor and artillery models that Revell used in 1957 would later be employed by several other companies to reissue the kits, but they would never again reappear under the Revell trademark.

This paint set from 1956 gave model builders a choice of flat or glossy paints, thinner, and liquid cement.

The High Speed Tractor without the Long Tom turned out to be a poor-selling kit. H-536

In 1957 the Russians launched Sputnik, and America found itself in a space age arms race to develop missiles and rockets to close an alleged "missile gap" opened up by its Cold War adversary. The result was rapid proliferation of a variety of new rockets—and a parallel missile race among the nation's model companies to bring out kits of the new space-age marvels. With the aircraft, ship, and car model fields already saturated with competing models from hobby companies, rockets offered a whole new field for potential kits. No one was more enthusiastic than Revell's forward-looking president Lew Glaser, and no model company brought out more missile kits than Revell. Between 1957 and 1959 Revell introduced an even two dozen new kits based on United States rockets.

The 105mm Howitzer. H-539

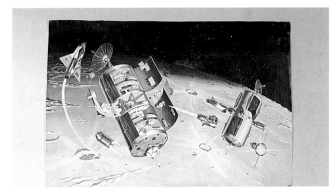

Revell's complex Space Station shows company president Lew Glaser's interest in the future and in science. H-1805

Store display of the Snark air-breathing missile. H-1801

Revell developed well-conceived models, with excellent detail, lots of accessories like support vehicles and launch towers, and teams of ground crew figures. Most of the models depicted actual military and scientific rockets, but some were imaginative creations by Revell's staff of what future spacecraft might look like. Engineer Gretz was pleased when Revell hired Convair astronautics scientist — Krafft Ehricke to develop the Space Shuttlecraft. (Ehricke had earlier designed models of Convair rockets for Strombecker.) Ehricke was Convair's lead public relations spokesman for a strong United States space program, and he considered helping Revell one way of building support for future undertakings like the man-in-space project. Gretz later observed that Revell's model "was quite visionary for the time," and embodied some of the features later used in NASA's real Space Shuttle.

But Gretz also observed that Revell had gotten too far in advance of the market with its array of guided missile products. Sol Kramer agreed. "The missiles were Lew's idea. He was ahead of his time. We thought at first they would sell, but they didn't." This first generation of rocket models just did not capture the imaginations of model builders. Part of the problem was that they were just machines, without human pilots. The men in Revell's own model shop derided the Space Station as the "Coffee Can," and one Revell salesman complained that the rockets had about as much sales appeal as ballpoint pens. By 1962 almost all of the rocket kits had disappeared from the Revell catalog. Later in the 1960s when the space program started putting men on top of rockets, missile kits would make a comeback; but, there would never again be an explosion of rocket models in the hobby industry like that of the late 1950s.

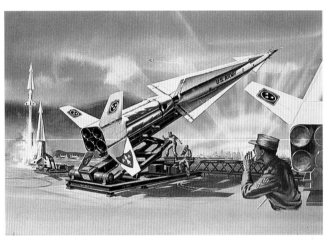

Leynnwood put the viewer right in the middle of the action with the Nike Hercules box art. *H-1804*

The Terrier anti-aircraft missile included its ship-board launcher. *H-1813*

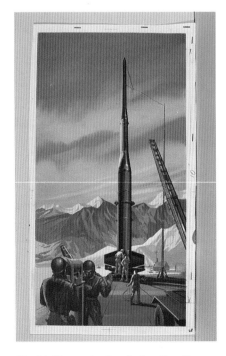

The X-17 was obsolete before Revell got its kit into the stores. *H-1810*

Leynnwood used a photo of a Regulus parked on the ground as reference to paint this airborne illustration—but he forgot to leave out the locking wires that held the landing gear in place! *H-1815*

The Hawk mobile missile battery. *H-1817*

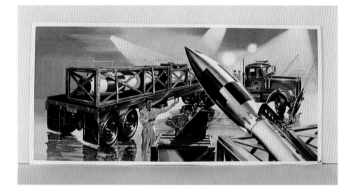

Revell converted its Bekins moving van into a flatbed truck for hauling the Honest John rocket. *H-1821*

The store display for the Atlas shows its elaborate launch complex. *H-1822*

The Moonship made a dramatic model, continuing the 1930s Buck Rogers concept of streamlined space rockets. *H-1825*

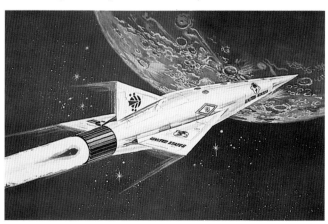

The Jupiter IRBM. *H-1824*

Another repercussion of Russia's surprising Sputnik triumph was a national outpouring of concern over the state of science education in America. Congress appropriated money to support the purchase of educational materials for the country's classrooms. Lew Glaser saw this as an opportunity to extend Revell's model line in a direction close to his heart. He went to Westinghouse Corporation and managed to persuade them to help finance the cost of tooling for a model atomic power plant that Revell would market to schools, as well as to the general public. Westinghouse was, of course, interested in selling the public on the peaceful use of atomic energy. The resulting model and its accompanying booklet on generating electricity through nuclear power were quite interesting to serious science students, but to the typical shopper in a hobby store or toy department, it looked like nothing but a jumble of pipes and wires. It never became a successful product.

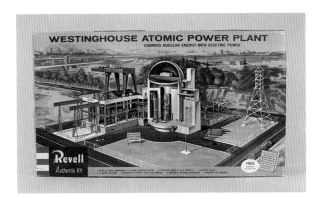

The Atomic Power Plant just didn't make an exciting model. *H-1550*

Teddy the Koala. *H-1901*

While all this military and hi-tech activity pleased America's boys, very little in the Revell catalog had any appeal to girls. The nation's model kit company executives were only too well aware that half the nation's potential customers—the females—were not being reached by their model offerings. Thus, they tried to find subjects that would appeal to girls. Aurora had its Guys and Gals of All Nations figure kits; Bachman offered birds and dogs. Revell seemed to have an advantage in dealing with this problem since it's new director of product development, Royle Glaser, came from the model-neglected female portion of the nation.

Her promotion to R & D department head had taken some years. "It began," she explained, "with my serving as hostess when Lew would hold new product meetings at home with his associates. I'd sit back and listen until the others left, then express my views. After a while it occurred to Lew that, as long as I was offering worthwhile ideas, I ought to be a full-fledged member of the team." She first became a member of the new products committee in 1955, and in 1958 a new research and development department was created with Royle at its head. "I had no idea what to do at first," she later declared, "but I wasn't shy about asking questions and I learned on the job. Also, I hired some very talented people who did know what to do."

She thought that animals might appeal to girls, and Gretz, an animal fancier, agreed it was worth a try. Revell signed a contract with Walt Disney Productions to make a model of Disney's True-Life short feature movie star, Perri the Squirrel™. To go with Perri, Revell added some animals of its own in a Nature Series: Teddy the Koala Bear, Friskie the Beagle, and Sassy the Kitten.

Gretz went to a pawn shop and purchased a stuffed squirrel that became part of the research materials for Perri. Companion models of Friskie and Sassy were modeled on a real beagle puppy and a kitten who had the run of the shop while the model patterns were being made—and then the pets were adopted by Revell staffers. The model for the Koala was done by freelancers Roma Coe and Tony Bulone. Coe later recalled that she cut a eucalyptus branch and stuck it in the wet clay she was modeling. To her surprise, the branch started putting out new leaves. Bulone finished off details on the model, which was sculpted in the same scale as the finished model. He then cut the clay model into its component parts, taking care to make the parting lines in places that would be inconspicuous and that formed parts that would pull easily from the production molds. These clay parts were then used to make pattern molds in dense epoxy, and these epoxy molds were utilized by the tool makers to cut the steel production mold.

The wildlife kits were nicely done, with transparent plastic eyes and natural postures. Each came with plastic packets of flocking and paint-on glue. Model builders were supposed to coat the completed model with glue and then puff on the flocking while the glue was still wet to make a coat of fur. But it was hard to get it to stick and look right.

The animal models did reach female customers—Revell estimated that half the kits were sold to girls—but overall sales were too low to keep them in the Revell catalog for long. These models confirmed that even if the subject had appeal for girls, model building was just not something girls liked to do. A fifth wildlife figure model, a young raccoon, never made it into production. A real raccoon cub lived in the model shop for a while until pattern maker Ron Campbell adopted it and took him home as a pet.

This preliminary proof of Perri does not include the children's faces later added on the left side. *H-1900*

Store display for Friskie the Puppy. *H-1902*

Royle Glaser's first major project as head of the new product division put Revell into a partnership with another producer of childhood fantasies: Theodore Geisel—Dr. Seuss. An old school-mate of Geisel's approached Royle and offered Revell exclusive rights to produce Dr. Seuss toys and games. Mrs. Glaser had raised two daughters on Dr. Seuss and thought the idea was great, but she ran up against opposition from other key Revell leaders. Gretz believed that the Dr. Seuss characters worked as illustrations in a book, but would not translate into models. Kramer labeled the project "kooky" and felt doing such figures would be a waste of time and money.

However, Royle wanted to get Revell out of the plane-ship-car rut and plunged ahead with the program. She flew to San Diego to visit Geisel and took Revell's new staff sculptor, Harry Plummer, along with her. Plummer was a handsome, genial, bow-tie wearing Native American. The visits eventually lasted almost six months as Geisel objected to nearly every preliminary sculpture Plummer showed him—resulting in many revisions of each piece.

Problems continued in the production phase. Revell normally purchased its polystyrene from Monsanto and Dow, but Grace Chemical offered to promote the Seuss line if Revell would use Grace's newly developed plastic in the kits. The guiding concept of these toys was that they could be played with by younger children. The snap-together parts from one model interchanged with parts from another; so kids could create their own fanciful animal characters. When the first test shots came out of the molding machines, Royle tried to assemble one of the figures and found that the plastic had no give at all: "It was like trying to assemble steel."

The Cat in the Hat and the Birthday Bird were regular glue-together kits. *Z-2000, Z-2051*

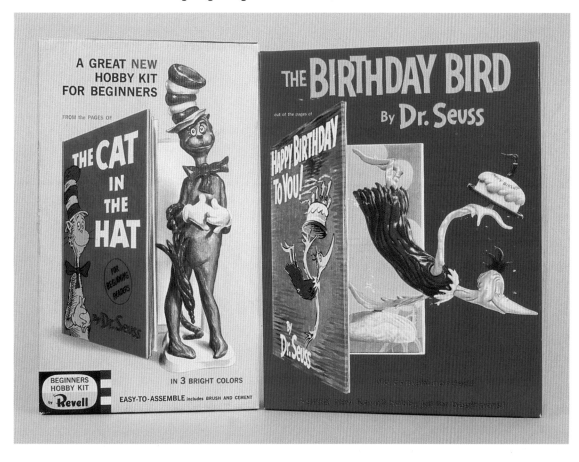

The Dr. Seuss Zoo sets included all six of the snap-together animals. G-2080, *G-2081*

Troubles continued when Revell showed The Seuss Zoo at the hobby show and toy fair. "We got laughed out of the place," recalled Mrs. Glaser. "The buyers were unsophisticated. They hadn't heard of Seuss, didn't know what to make of them, and didn't think they would sell." But Revell had committed to go ahead, and in 1959 the Cat in the Hat model came out, followed by the rest of the series the following year.

They turned out to be a sales disappointment. A second issue of the kits appeared, switching them from regular model boxes to cellophane window boxes to give customers a look at the parts inside. However, sales remained low and the whole line quickly was abandoned. In post-mortem verdict on the Dr. Seuss series, hobby distributor Nat Polk asserted that the product had no market: kids young enough to be interested in Dr. Seuss lacked the dexterity to build even these simple models, and older youngsters who had the building skills simply weren't excited by Dr. Seuss.

As the decade of the 1950s drew to a close, Revell had firmly established itself as the world leader in plastic modeling. However, despite its excellent reputation, quality products, and superior work force, Revell, Inc. lost money in 1958 and 1959. Part of the problem resulted from the slump in the whole country's economy during the last years of the Eisenhower administration, but some of the causes

Richard Kishady's colorful
F-105 Thunderchief. *H-285*

Lorenzo Ghiglieri painted several of Revell's classic 1950s aircraft illustrations, including the PBM Mariner. *H-258*

were internal at Revell. The company had brought out several model lines that didn't sell, and thus it had to eat the tooling costs for those molds. Also, for several years Revell tried to enter the model train market and produced some very high-quality products, but ultimately that venture had to be abandoned due to production problems and low sales. The five million dollars invested in this big project became a near total loss.

Revell created a nice collection of buildings to go with its HO train sets—including the "Revelltown" station. *T-9001*

One possible solution to Revell's money woes already existed in South Plainfield, New Jersey. In the mid-'50s Revell had opened a warehouse and molding plant there to service its customers east of the Mississippi. John Deegan, head of the South Plainfield factory, approached Lew Glaser and suggested that all manufacturing operations be shifted to New Jersey where labor, material, and shipping costs were lower than on the West Coast. Deegan had twelve molding machines running twenty-four hours a day pumping out kits, and he declared that it would not take much more effort to handle all Revell's production needs. But Glaser was a California person, and he could not envision leaving home. Thus the New Jersey plant closed and Revell consolidated operations in Venice. Deegan became head of Revell's European (and later world) enterprises.

Some of Revell's problems came from company management, a subject that had long fascinated Lew Glaser. Marketing executive Dave Fisher once observed that Glaser was always searching for just the right mix of management structure and inter-personal relationships that would make Revell a well-oiled, friction-free machine. Fisher believed that Glaser enjoyed the challenge of the problem. "His weekend hobby was changing the management structure. He was thoroughly obsessed with the business." Glaser experimented with management by a committee of department heads. He also put in eighteen hours a day on the job. It wasn't working; so he and export manager Barney Ramos sat down together and decided to reorganize the company's chain of command. Ramos became executive vice president in charge of budget, finances, and day-to-day operations, while Glaser continued with long range planning and new product development. In Ramos's words: "It was a duumvirate. We made a good team." However, Ramos also became the company's hatchet man, cutting costs and personnel. It wasn't pleasant for him or some of the company's staff; but it worked, and a leaner, transformed Revell, Inc. entered the 1960s on an even financial keel.

Chapter 4 –
Hot Rods and Monsters

When youthful John Kennedy entered the White House in January 1961, many Americans sensed that a new era of history had begun. The plastic model hobby also turned a corner about 1961 and moved forward to the brink of maturing into its modern form by learning what subjects worked in the marketplace and what standards of accuracy were appropriate for mass produced model kits. However, a couple more years of experimentation would be required before the transformation reached completion.

The F-106 was one of the last box illustrations Richard Kishady did for Revell. *H-298*

In the early 1960s Revell—and the whole plastic model kit industry—badly needed some fresh ideas for new products. Most of Revell's recent releases had been recycled kits from the 1950s. The Highway Pioneers, for example, came back in bright spiffy turn-of-the-century box art in 1960. Some of the ships, cars, and tanks received battery-powered electric motors—a fad in the hobby business at the time. A selection of aircraft were dubbed the Air Cadet series, packaged in plastic bags to hang from wall pegs and priced to sell at the low cost of forty-nine cents. Other old aircraft kits received changes to become Whip-Fly-It models that boys could build, attach to a length of chord, and twirl around their heads. There was nothing here for a serious modeler or any innovation with staying power.

The Martin B-57 became a British Canberra in the Whip-Fly It series. *H-157*

Lew Glaser always valued educational projects and thought Revell might try selling some products touted as learning tools. Behind his desk stood a large table piled a foot deep in manila folders with ideas for new products. He supported new endeavors like electronics kits that he had enjoyed as a boy back in the 1930s. Thus Revell brought out a short wave radio, a stereo record player, a weather laboratory, and an amplified speaker system. However, in the stores they retailed for too much and sold too little.

Lew and Royle Glaser still hoped that Revell's models could be used in an educational setting and hoped that the schools would become a market for the right kind of model. After *LIFE* magazine ran a series of articles on the miracle of birth, Royle was inspired to suggest a model of Chicken Little (H-1554) illustrating the gestation and hatching of a chick. An aquarium model with fish from the seven seas and another showing the life cycle of frogs were in development and in line for release next, but dismal sales of the chicken cancelled that idea.

Revell's 1950s military Atlas missile model became launch vehicle for John Glenn's Mercury capsule in the 1960s. *H-1833*

The V-2 Rocket came apart to show its interior. Revell suggested modelers frame John Steel's box illustration. *H-1830*

Revell briefly re-entered the toy business with Montini building sets.

Most of Revell's rocket models went out of the catalog in the 1960s, but the Redstone survived by adding a Mercury space capsule. *H-1803, H-1832*

In another attempt to diversify, Royle Glaser experimented with a plastic house divided into modular sections that would allow girls to play modern architect—but it never went into production because buyers at the hobby and toy shows didn't think it would sell. They believed girls and their moms wanted only traditional doll houses.

One of the product planners, Don Ernst, discovered a new toy in Europe—a knock-off of the popular Lego construction blocks called Montini. The toy came from Holland and improved on Lego by offering flexible plastic parts. Ernst showed it to Lew Glaser, who liked it, and Revell began importing sets for sale in the United States. Shortly thereafter Revell received a letter from Lego's attorney threatening a law suit, and Revell dropped the project. Ernst thought Revell should have stood its ground, but Glaser wanted to avoid the controversy of a court case.

English-born model shop supervisor Ron Campbell came up with the bright idea of a one-quarter scale model of a V-8 engine—something educational and exciting. Glaser endorsed the concept. The R & D boys brought a Chevy motor into the model shop, disassembled it, and recreated almost every part—right down to the raised lettering on the cylinder covers. Campbell then made an aluminum mold, placed it in the "die try" machine used for testing new molds, and shot enough parts for six engines. One complete working model was built and another set of parts was placed on a display board. Campbell, who had made real engines in his first career back in England, pronounced the finished product a "thing of beauty." Glaser took the model to Detroit to try to interest General Motors in backing production of the model, but GM said no. Campbell later declared the death of the Chevy V-8 the biggest disappointment of his twenty-five year career at Revell.

The Allison Prop-Jet was the aviation equivalent to Revell's Chrysler Slant Six engine. *H-1552*

Having been rejected by GM, Glaser turned to Chrysler Corporation and made a deal: Revell would produce a line of models if Chrysler would partly underwrite the mold tooling costs. The Revell kits would depict the whole range of Chrysler's 1962 car lineup, as well as their most innovative new engine, the Slant Six. Campbell made an excellent, working model of the Slant Six, but grumbled that the V-8 would have made a more mechanically efficient model. Revell also received advanced material on the Chrysler '62 lineup so that the plastic model cars would be in hobby shops in the fall just as the real new cars were being unveiled at Chrysler showrooms. During the summer, after the Plymouth Fury had already been tooled, Chrysler contacted Revell to announce that the raised rib running the length of the Fury—on line-of-sight with the driver—had been removed, so would Revell please remove it from the model! However, everything else went fine, and Revell produced a nice-enough line of six Chrysler car models.

Unfortunately, America's boys didn't buy many of the Chryslers. Family sedans just did not excite them. A new employee in the R & D department, Jim Keeler, came up with a bright idea to spice-up the Chryslers. He had recently received several packets of metallic flakes from a company that thought Revell might find some way to use them in creating metal flake paint for its custom cars. Keeler saw that the flakes were far too large to be true to 1/25 scale models, and he put the packets aside for several weeks. Then one day an idea suddenly struck him. He went down to the molding room where a run of Plymouth Fury's was just being completed on one of the machines. Keeler asked the shop foreman to load the machine with clear plastic and to dump the metal flakes into the mix. The shots that came out looked pretty awful (Keeler was just relieved that the flakes hadn't damaged the machine). He put the Plymouth body aside and forgot it for a few more weeks. Then he got the idea of painting the insides of the transparent body. He thought that the result was not half bad and showed it to Mrs. Glaser. She said, "That's cool." Thus the "Metalflake" Chrysler cars were born. They lasted only one year in the catalog. Royle Glaser later explained that many of the shots coming off the assembly line had to be rejected because the metal chips clogged up the runners in the mold and this led to most of the flakes clustering in just one area of the model.

The Plymouth Valiant had the most sports car appeal of the Chrysler car set. H-1250

The Valiant appeared in a Metalflake plastic version, as well as standard solid colored plastic. H-1260

In its second issue, the Austin-Healey became a rally racer. H-1244

The low-cost Cadet cars, like the Rover 3-Litre, came from Revell, Great Britain. H-956

Jack Leynnwood used mostly shades of gray to create what he called his "European wet look" for the VW Deluxe Sedan. *H-952*

In spite of the failure of the Chrysler model cars, Revell had to try again to establish a presence in the automotive field because model cars had emerged as the fastest-growing segment of the plastic kit industry. That was why Jim Keeler had been brought in.

The first model car Jim Keeler ever built was a Highway Pioneers 1910 Cadillac sedan purchased in a hobby shop near his home in Salt Lake City in the early 1950s. He detailed the model by painting the roof with black model airplane dope and then smoothed a Kleenex tissue over the wet paint to simulate cloth texture. As he got older his family moved to San Diego, and he started entering model car contests like those sponsored by the Fisher Body Craftsman Guild. Keeler would take model kits bought right off store shelves and modify them by adding detail parts to the interiors and engines. He cut away the doors from the side panels and added hand-made parts so that the doors would open and close. To gather information and ideas for his next model, he prowled the auto shows with his camera, taking photos of the cars from all angles. At these car shows he met people like speed merchant Mickey Thompson and a big, uncouth fellow named Ed Roth who sold hot rodder T-shirts with gross, hairy, bug-eyed caricatures spray-painted on them.

By the late 1950s Keeler was running model car contests, and he asked Revell to donate model kits as prizes. He struck up an acquaintance with public relations man Henry Blankfort. Soon Keeler began peppering Revell with suggestions for new models they ought to bring out and new features they should put in their models. Blankfort thought the brash, lanky kid deserved a tryout. He gave Keeler some HO scale cars from a model train set and asked him to customize a few. Keeler took them home and cut open some doors, chopped tops, lowered bodies, and generally turned them into contemporary show cars. "When he saw what I had done, Blankfort flipped," recalled Keeler. Blankfort brought Keeler and his models in for a talk with new

products manager Royle Glaser. She liked what she saw and hired the nineteen-year-old in April 1961, giving him the task of revitalizing the car model line. Keeler moved to Los Angeles and lived with Ed Roth and his wife until he found an apartment.

To make the old 1950s Chris Craft Cruiser model more interesting, Revell converted it into a deep sea fishing boat. *H-387*

Revell entered the HO scale model railroading field in 1956 and issued this set of 1961 Chrysler cars not long before it gave up on model trains. *T-6019*

The Sherman Tank received an electric motor and new box art in the early 1960s. *H-544*

Jack Leynnwood thought red was an appropriate
color for the Russian Stalin tank. *H-546*

Now Keeler got his chance to present some fresh ideas to his new employers. He was told to take three weeks and pull together a presentation for the New Products Committee to consider. Although Keeler was already writing articles for *Rod & Custom* magazine, he considered himself a student in the "bonehead" school of English prose. But he sweated-out production of a neatly typed, multi-page exposition of his proposals. He began by explaining that in recent years AMT had revolutionized the model car field with its 3-in-1 car kits, containing extra parts that allowed builders the options to create their own custom car models. Keeler wanted to do something like that. His recommendations came down to three different kinds of models: a speed car (Mickey Thompson's Challenger I), a stock/custom car (the 1956 Ford F-100 pickup), and a show rod (Ed Roth's *Outlaw*).

When Keeler stood up before the New Products Committee to present his proposals before all the company's executives, he began by outlining the merits of Thompson's Challenger. At that point one of the committee men interrupted to declare: "Yes, yes. That car's fine. I want to hear about the Roth guy!" He had a hunch that "the Roth guy" might turn out to be something special. In the end the whole committee liked what Keeler had to say and gave R & D the go-ahead to proceed with all three car models.

Keeler and Ron Campbell drove down to Long Beach to gather research material on Thompson's land-speed-record car, Challenger I—what Keeler called "the ultimate hot rod."

(*Hot Rod Model Kits* 2000, 32) They took measurements of the car and photographed it from all angles—then Thompson's mechanics took the car apart so they could photograph each part separately. After this, all the paperwork and photos went back to engineering and the model shop where Revell's small team of craftsmen used wood, brass tubing, and sheet metal to produce a model of the car. This pattern was then copied by the mold makers. The tooling cost $80,000—twice that of a standard car model. Keeler kept careful watch over the first of his babies, spending his lunch hour observing the tooling department cut the molds and then haunting the molding room past midnight to see shots come out of the machines.

The Challenger I launched Revell's line of
super-detailed 1/25 scale car models. *H-1281*

To research the '56 Ford Pickup, the R & D boys drove a truck right to the Revell parking lot and gave it a thorough going over. The kit that came out of the development process was an instant winner. The Ford itself had a classic shape, and Revell's model gave kids lots of things to play with. There were two V-8 engines: a '57 T-bird and a '60 Pontiac (from the Challenger I). The hood, doors, and tailgate opened and closed—something no other model company offered. There were chrome customizing extras, racing slick tires, and a surfboard. Something it did not have were little human figures to sit in the models. Keeler felt that boys wanted to build "hardware"—the cars, not the people who drove the cars. The Ford Pickup would become a regular in the Revell catalog for decades and appeared in a myriad of kit variants.

Meanwhile, Ed Roth received a phone call from Royle Glaser asking if he would like Revell to produce models of his custom show cars. Roth's answer was a hearty affirmative: "It freaked me out to see a mainline company even tryin' to dig this stuff." Roth signed a ten year contract with Lew Glaser—who he described as "this happy little square fella"—that gave Roth two cents for every licensed kit Revell sold and provided him a steady income. (*Confessions* 1992, 18) (It worked out well for Revell, too, because by 1964 Roth cars were generating almost sixteen percent of Revell's annual revenues.)

Roth trucked his *Outlaw* to the Venice plant parking lot and worked with the R & D team to make sure they did the model right. The car deserved first-class treatment for it truly was an innovative blending of the classic hot rod and way-out contemporary styling. Roth liked the boys at Revell because they grooved on the same things, spoke the same language, and enjoyed kicking around ideas. The only difference was that Roth made his cars out of steel and fiberglass in 1/1 scale; while Revell made its cars out of polystyrene in 1/25 scale.

Revell made a classic model of the classic '56 Ford Pickup truck. *H-1283*

Jack Leynnwood's awesome painting of Ed Roth's Outlaw. *H-1282*

The '31 Ford could be built either as a "woody" wagon or a Tudor sedan. *H-1275*

Revell's art department took Roth to a prop rental agency and fitted him out with an array of outlandish clothes and accessories. Then he spent a week at the Glasers' home around the swimming pool posing for photographs to be used on kit boxes and in advertisements. "He was a great, great guy. I adored him," said Royle Glaser. "He was off-the-wall creative." The only nagging problem was coming up with a nickname for Roth—who thought his high school moniker "Big Ed" worked just fine. But PR man Henry Blankfort didn't. So Blankfort and Roth dickered over the nickname for months; then Blankfort suggested "Big Daddy" for a handle. "Cool!" Roth agreed.

In February 1962, Revell took Roth and his *Outlaw* car to the Hobby Industry Association annual show in Chicago. Roth found that his customary sports shirt and blue jeans wardrobe did not suit Chicago in mid-winter, so one of the Revell boys took him shopping for some warmer duds. Roth made a big hit with the hobby industry men who crowded into Revell's parlor, and the *Outlaw* won the show's prize for best display. The model kit continued the "show car" theme by providing boys with a pedestal sign to go with the built car and tiny stanchions to rope-off a display area.

Over the next four years Revell would bring out five more of Roth's hot rod creations. As Keeler put it: "We realized we didn't need regular car kits. We had specialty cars, dragsters, and the Roth rods. We chose this niche and chased it." It didn't matter that Revell lacked inside contacts with Detroit's auto makers—the center of custom rodding was Southern California, and Revell operated right in the middle of the action at just the time when show rodding was the hottest thing going with teenage boys.

The Mysterion was Roth's most popular car model. *H-1277*

Ed Roth's Beatnik Bandit. *H-1279*

The R & D staff sculpted this solid model prototype of Ed Roth's Rotar car, but that was as far as the development process went.

In December of that year the company newsletter *Revell Reporter* cast a sentimental look back more than a decade to the first sales of Highway Pioneers. "Here we are at Christmas time 1962. In an ironical way, we are almost back where we started from—with authentic model cars. Only this time it is custom, speed, and show cars, rather than the antique variety."

To hype the model customizing aspect of its new car models, Revell launched a nation-wide Model Car Customizing contest in 1963, inviting every hobby shop in the country to participate. The contest was developed by Rich Palmer and Dick Schwarzchild, two East Coast hobby shop owners who had been responsible for Aurora's wildly successful Grand National slot car racing competition the year before (and who would design the Aurora monster model customizing contest in 1964). Lew Glaser wanted something similar for Revell. Palmer and Schwarzchild arranged a tie-in with Pactra, the hobby paint company, which would offer its own prize for the model with the best paint job. Hobby shops received promotional banners, contest rules, suggestions for holding in-store competitions, and prizes for local winners in three age categories.

Revell's R & D staffers handled the judging end of the contest. They sent out instructions to local hobby shops to mail in their store winners packed in popcorn—but they should have been a little more specific because one model arrived packed in unpopped kernels, another used buttered popcorn, and one used Cracker Jacks! Thousands of winning cars from 2,600 participating dealers arrived at the Venice plant, and a mound of popcorn grew in the warehouse where the entries were opened and sorted. When the contest models had been narrowed down to a few top-notch entries, Ed Roth and speed parts manufacturer Dean Moon came in to decide the national champions. The senior division winner, Richard Johnson of Ohio, had submitted a stylishly modified '62 T-bird. When it was all over, Revell bought another thousand pounds of popcorn to repackage the entries for shipment home.

The Second (and, as it turned out, the last) National Open Custom Contest featured some rules changes based on lessons learned from the first try. This time local hobby shop winners went to twelve regional competitions—so Revell received only forty-eight entries at the Venice headquarters, not the nearly 10,000 of the year before. The senior title was divided between Augie Hiscano of Miami for his *Beatnik Bandit*/Jaguar XK-E hybrid and Nebraskan Bob Norberg for a scratch-built semi truck. All the winners went to Disneyland and got to meet Ed Roth and other well-known car personalities holding contracts with Revell.

In 1964 Revell began an annual Sweepstakes contest that youngsters could enter just by sending in a box end panel or a coupon enclosed in a kit box. This sweepstakes program became a central promotional vehicle for the rest of the 1960s and 1970s. Store owners even had a chance to win prizes. The sweepstakes encouraged kids to buy kits with the hope of winning a nifty prize, and Revell hoped dealers would stock Revell kits on their shelves with the prospect that they too might win a prize. To further encourage shop owners to carry its kits, Revell put together package deals of kits at reduced wholesale prices. Window streamers, posters, and other promotional items went into the package.

The prizes were aimed at the aspirations of young boys. Over the years they included a sailboat, a Cessna airplane, a trip around the world, a Datsun pickup, All Terrain Vehicles, a Toyota pickup, a trip to Boston, Philadelphia, and Washington for the Bicentennial celebrations, a custom van, a Ford pickup, a Chevy pickup, a Turbo Mustang, and each year a galaxy of second and third place prizes. In 1965 Revell gave away two surplus Air Force F-86 fighter jets to be placed in playgrounds near the homes of the winners.

During brainstorming sessions for the 1967 Sweepstakes, advertising manager Howard Rieder came up with the bright idea of giving away a Gemini space capsule. His inspiration brought roars of dismissal from the others at the table. Marketing specialist Dave Fisher asked why a boy would be interested in a prize that he couldn't keep, but had to donate to a museum. Besides, everyone agreed, you can't even get a space capsule from the government! They all belong to NASA or something. But Rieder remembered an incident from early in his career when he worked as an ad man for a musical instrument company, and the boss asked him to get free editorial mention in a magazine. When Rieder replied that it couldn't be done, his boss leaned over the desk and bellowed: "How do you know if you haven't asked!" So he asked, and the magazine published just the sort of piece his employer wanted.

Now a more experienced but frustrated Rieder decided to telephone McDonnell Douglas to ask if they just might have a space capsule to spare. He called their head of advertising. As Rieder later recalled, "There was about a ten second pause. ... Then he replied, 'We have one'." Revell was able to purchase it for $5,000, and Rieder enjoyed "the biggest promotion we ever had." The capsule ended up in the Portland, Oregon, Museum of Science and Industry.

A couple of years later Rieder suffered through "the worst promotion ever." In response to suggestions made by previous Sweepstakes winners, Revell offered a college scholarship as grand prize. Entries plummeted that year. Kids just couldn't get excited about a grand prize so intangible and so practical.

Another promotion began in 1961, but it turned out to be a false start. That year Revell announced the Master Modelers Club. To join you had to buy a newly released Revell kit containing a membership application inside and send it back along with a quarter. In return youngsters received a membership card, an engraved membership certificate, a subscription to *Modelers World* magazine, and a stamp album for collecting the stamps that came with each new Revell kit. Kids who accumulated enough points by purchasing Revell kits became members of the Consumer Advisory Panel and could suggest new models for Revell to bring out. Hobby shops became Master Modeler Headquarters, with store banners and shelf streamers. Unfortunately, the response was so overwhelming that Revell's staff could not keep up with all the club paperwork, and the Modelers Club was allowed to die.

In 1963 it was Hawk Model Company's turn to create a sensation at the Hobby Industry Association annual meeting with its outlandish "Weird-Ohs." A year earlier Aurora Plastics Company had paved the way for offbeat plastic horrors with its models of Frankenstein, Dracula, and the other old Universal movie monsters. Now Hawk mated the monster idea with cars, planes, and boats by putting its caricature figures in high-power vehicles. Revell's representatives at the convention took notes on Hawk's models and hurried home to Venice to plan Revell's response. The obvious answer: take some of the freaky cartoon characters Roth had been spray-painting on T-shirts and turn them into three-dimensional models. But first Lew Glaser appointed a committee to study whether monsters were a wholesome product to sell to America's children. After all, Revell had been portraying its models as "family" fun, while Roth's outrageous creatures were calculated to delight kids and offend parents. After consulting with psychologists, the committee decided that "monsters help youngsters cope with their problems."

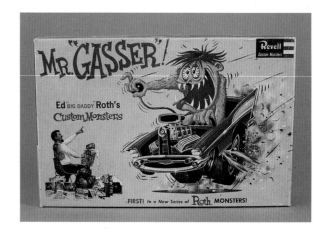

Mr. Gasser went from the back of a T-shirt to a Revell model kit. *H-1301*

Drag Nut came with his little friend Rat Fink. *H-1303*

The first Master Modelers Club of the early 1960s didn't last long.

C'MON ALONG...
be a MASTER MODELER, too!

Creation of the Roth Monsters went to Revell's former staff figure sculptor Harry Plummer. Roth went to Plummer's home to conjure up the monsters. "It was a real cool place to work because there were no interruptions, no phones, or nosy kids. ... Harry and I created monsters beyond my worst nightmares. My beloved monsters." (*Confessions* 1992, 20) Plummer sculpted his figures several times larger than the size intended for the model, layering plaster over a bent clothes-hanger armature. Roth contributed his artistic inspiration, while Plummer made sure that the figures were shaped so that the parts would easily pull from production molds.

Once the plaster model reached completion, Revell's technicians made a cast of the model in wax and then cut the cast into the kit parts. These parts would be copied and reduced in size by the tool makers as they engraved the steel production molds. The major drawback in this approach to making a figure kit was that Revell's figures had only a few parts—for example, the whole torso only had a front and back half. Aurora Plastics, the industry leader in figure kits, took a different approach. Aurora asked its sculptors to carve each model part separately in acetate plastic, and then these parts would then be cast, not cut, into beryllium copper alloy molds. The result was that Aurora's figure kits had many more separate pieces than their Revell counterparts.

The first fruit of the Roth/Plummer collaboration was Mr. Gasser (H-1301), a big-eyed, wild-haired, gape-mouthed hot-rodder happily shiftin' and steerin' his '57 Chevy.

Revell added more Roth Monsters like crazy—twelve in all over a three year period. At first they sold well. Revell had caught the peak of "monster" fever in 1964, when the "Addams Family" and "Munsters" were popular shows on TV. The name of Roth's signature character, "Rat Fink," became a household word in the vocabularies of America's teens. But the fever subsided as quickly as it rose, and by 1966 all the monsters had departed the Revell catalog.

Superfink. H-1308

Brother Rat Fink, like Ed Roth himself, could really dig a cycle. H-1304

Ed Roth's alter-ego: The Rat Fink. H-1305

Harry Plummer designed and carved most of Revell's figures, from the Roth monsters to the tiny 1/28 scale pilot for the Fokker Dr-1. H-270

The Roth rod cars stayed a while longer, but by the mid-1960s Roth had gone off riding with outlaw motorcycle gangs, and Revell did not want to tarnish its public image by being associated with roughnecks. Four of the Roth monsters would return in 1971 as "Freaky Riders"—without Roth's name on them.

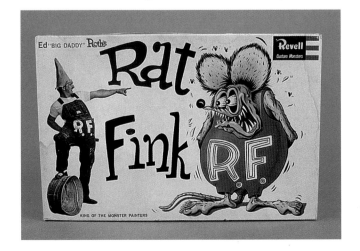

In 1963, while visiting the Revell plant in England, Lew and Royle discovered that every adolescent girl on that island had gone insane over a pop music group calling themselves "The Beatles." The Glasers checked out the guys with the rag mop haircuts and found the music not half bad. Royle had a hunch that the Beatles phenomenon would soon jump the Atlantic; so on their return to New York the Glasers located the Beatles' agent in New York City, who was just unpacking to set up an office. Revell negotiated exclusive right to market Beatles hobby products in the United States, but had to agree to pay a whopping fifteen percent royalty on sales, not the customary five percent.

Magda Kopek, a newly-hired figure sculptor, hurried to create models of John, George, and Ringo, while Tony Bulone helped out freelance by doing Paul. Revell quickly got the kits produced and out into the stores—and even movie theater lobbies—just as Beatlemania struck the country. Royle patted herself on the back for achieving such a timely coup for Revell, but, as she later declared: "Surprise, surprise! They didn't sell." The target audience, teenage girls, still would not build models, even of their beloved rocker heart throbs.

Revell tried several other kits in an attempt to cash in on the figure model craze of the 1960s: Flash Gordon™, The Phantom™, Flipper the Dolphin™, and the Cartwright family from Bonanza™. Three other figure kits got part way through development: Prince Valiant™, Disney's Winnie-the-Pooh™, and Alvin and the Chipmunks™. The three chipmunks were snap-together models, molded in textured plastic so kids could color them with crayons. But when Revell showed them at the hobby convention, buyers declined to place orders and all three proposed kits never went on the market.

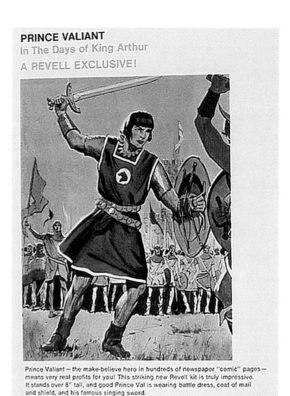

Prince Valiant™—as well as Winnie the Pooh™ and Alvin the Chipmunk™—never went on sale after they received a cold reception at the annual hobby industry show.

The one figure kit line that did enjoy modest success and found a regular place in the Revell catalog was the horse line. Several Revell staffers owned horses and wished the project well. Engineer Ernest Brown later recalled that R & D brought in some strands of horse tail to match up with fibers that might be used for manes and tails on the model horses. There was a big debate over whether an anatomically correct model of a stallion should be made, but ultimately Revell went with the usual toy-horse modest suggestion of reproductive organs. Only two horse molds were cut, but by molding kits in four different colors, four distinct breeds of horses could be depicted. The idea was to make a very simple seven-piece model that would not discourage girl customers and to add accessories like saddles, blankets, brushes, and other horse tack that kids—especially girls—could play with. It worked pretty well and the horses went in and out of the Revell line several times.

About this time a television production company approached Revell with an offer of licensing rights to model kits based on a new TV series about the bold voyages of a rocket ship and its crew through the final frontier of space. Royle Glaser watched one episode of the show and thought it was terrible. To her, the crewmen's space craft, called the Starship Enterprise™, looked devoid of detail and pretty boring, so Revell declined the offer. At the time it seemed like a sound decision since the space serial lasted only three seasons on NBC before being cancelled. But, of course, "Star Trek" took on a whole new life in syndicated re-runs, and models of its space hardware have ever since become standard hobby shop fare.

Box artist Jack Leynnwood had no problem depicting human figures; in fact, he enjoyed a career in fine art separate from his commercial work. Flash Gordon and The Phantom. H-1450, *H-1451*

Of all Revell's figure models, only the horses proved to be decent sellers. The Palomino had peel-and-stick silver decorations for its saddle. *H-1921*

Flipper and his pal Sandy were based on the popular TV series and movie.

Blaze King™ starred in NBC-TV's "National Velvet" series. *H-1920*

If figure kits turned out to be a bust for Revell, its new lineup of car models roared off from success to success. Keeler knew that boys liked to put their own individual stamp on the model cars they built; so he and the R & D team came up with a proposal to make small kits containing nothing but extra parts for use as add-ons to a boy's latest automotive model creation. Revell could reap profits selling customizing parts for AMT, Johan, MPC, and Monogram kits, as well as for its own. A builder could even create a unique custom model car by combining the parts from several customizing kits. It was late in the year when the idea caught on, so everyone had to scramble to produce exhibit items for the February 1962, trade show. They printed dummy boxes and filled them with one-off parts produced from test molds. Some of the parts came from existing Revell cars and some parts came from the kits of other companies. They even stuck fake mold runners on the parts and gave everything chrome plating. These hand-made display packages worked at the trade show, and the industry embraced the "Custom Car Parts."

The Double Car Kit contained enough Custom Car Parts to assemble two complete cars. *H-1223*

Modelers loved them, too. Roth explained, "It was like havin' your very own 1/25th scale junkyard." (*Confessions* 1992, 60) Once in regular production, many of the Custom Car Parts consisted of pieces from other Revell model kits. It made good sense to get double use out of a mold if possible. Later Keeler recalled, "We ran the molding machines twenty-four hours a day cranking those puppies out." Unfortunately, the Custom Car Parts soon ran out of steam and were dropped from the Revell catalog. It seemed that there were not enough custom builders out there in the marketplace to justify their continued production. Some of the components from the Custom Car Parts enjoyed a second life as parts for new kits coming on line.

In 1963 Keeler continued developing kits in his three categories of cars. There were more Roth cars, of course. The racing category included TV personality Tommy Ivo's four-engine dragster *The Showboat*, Mickey Thompson's *Attempt I*, and Bob Tindle's *Orange Crate*. All of these cars were identified with well-known personalities, and Revell proudly announced its ties to the "Show and Go Team." Publicity the real cars received at drag strips and auto shows and in car magazines represented free advertising for Revell.

Bob Tindle's Orange Crate show car is a perennial favorite among car modelers. *H-1289*

Tony Nancy's two dragster models represented early '60s vintage slingshot layouts. *H-1224*

The third category, stock/custom autos, gained a magnificent (and expensive-to-tool) model of a '57 Chevy. This car had all the usual custom extras, plus opening doors, hood, and truck—and front wheels that turned and rear quarter windows that went up and down. It was followed by '55 and '56 Chevrolets that utilized the same chassis and much of the same underbody components as the '57 model (just as GM's real cars did). Revell tried to scale individual parts to authentic size, and if two parts were separate items in a real car, Revell made them separate parts in the model.

Thus many pieces were extremely small and delicate. The high part count and intricacy of these kits discouraged many younger modelers with short attention spans, who often gave up in the face of what these kits demanded from builders. Nevertheless, these cars became tremendous best sellers and staples of the Revell line over the ensuing years. "The Chevies were like striking gold," recalled Dave Fisher.

The '55 Chevy included the names of Revell's R & D staff on the door: Keeler, Paeth, and Jones. *H-1276*

However, by the mid-'60s Jim Keeler had burned out and decided to call it quits with Revell. He had grown tired of the Los Angeles rat race and thought it high time that he went to college. In addition, the electric slot car boom was roaring full-throttle in mid-decade, adsorbing development money Keeler would rather have seen go into model kits. He returned to Utah to attend college, then a few years later became product manager for Aurora Plastics of New York in both slot cars and model kits.

Back at the beginning of the decade when Keeler shook up the company's thinking in the automotive department, Revell's line of aircraft models also underwent a revolution. Revell's booth at the 1962 Hobby Industry Association may have featured Roth's *Outlaw* custom rod as its focal point, but hobbyists interested in aircraft were drawn straight to Revell's exhibit of the *Memphis Belle* B-17F Flying Fortress. This large model featured exquisite detail and loads of moving parts: turrets that rotated, opening bomb-bay doors, flight control surfaces that moved, and landing gear that could be built down or retracted. Of course, the riveting and panel lines were exaggerated, continuing the custom of the times among model manufacturers. But, most importantly for Revell's future in aircraft models, the B-17 was made in standard 1/72 scale—a change that marked a revolution in Revell's aircraft modeling philosophy.

By 1962 pioneer decision makers from Revell's early days like Sol Kramer, engineer Charles Gretz, and researcher Jack Campbell had departed Revell, and new men such as shop supervisor Ron Campbell were coming to the fore. The new Revell model development team responded to demands from Revell's customers in Europe and serious adult builders that Revell adopt a standard scale for its models.

The B-17 "Memphis Belle" kicked off Revell's second generation of authentic, standard scale aircraft. Jack Leynnwood at his best. *H-201*

Most American companies such as Aurora, Monogram, and Lindberg generally adhered to 1/48 scale for their fighter planes because that made a model sized about right for a ten-year-old to build and play with. But 1/48 scale would have been too big a departure for Revell in 1962, especially in a bomber like the *Memphis Belle*. The plane in 1/72 scale built-out to a wing span of seventeen inches, and that was plenty big enough. The 1/72 scale had an additional advantage of being the most popular size in Europe, where Frog and Airfix had long issued kits in that standard. Thus, 1/72 became Revell's official scale for the 1960s, and the company quickly brought a whole new generation of aircraft models on line.

Jack Leynnwood's FW-190 solved the swastika problem by substituting another cross on the tail fin. *H-615*

In the 1960s Revell issued an excellent series of 1/72 scale World War I aircraft. This is Leynnwood's art for Herman Göring's Fokker D- VII. *H-632*

Brian Knight's Revell, Britain Me-109, like all European kit box art, omits the swastika from the tail fin. *H-612*

In a way, Revell had a chance to start all over again in the model airplane business, with a decade of experience behind it to strengthen its new effort. These second generation models would still maintain high standards of quality, but additional research would make the kits more accurate and authentic than before. This time around Revell focused on World War I and World War II aircraft, not the latest jets coming on line with the American armed services. Partly this was because the Cold War arms race no longer elicited quite so many new aircraft prototypes as in the hot house atmosphere of the 1950s. During the 1960s Revell issued a never-equaled collection of World War I pursuit planes and an even larger assortment of bombers and fighters from the Second World War.

Revell needed a new manager to shepherd this line, and Henry Blankfort again found the man for the job. He had noted the excellent aircraft models built by Lloyd Jones on display in a local aviation museum and discovered that Jones had also written the book *US Bombers: B-1 to B-70*. Jones ran a hobby shop in Van Nuys that, as Jones said, "barely fed his family," so he quickly accepted Blankfort's offer to come to work for Revell. He brought an extensive library of resources about aircraft to Revell—and he brought himself.

As one staffer put it: "Jones knew everything about airplanes, down to the pilot's underwear."

His first project at Revell was the "Dam Buster" Avro Lancaster that had bombed the Ruhr River hydro-electric dams during World War II. Great Britain had just declassified material on the plane, and Revell obtained a set of plans from Avro still marked "Most Secret." Revell picked the Lancaster as the subject for a model because it was England's illustrious equivalent of America's B-17 and because of the great story that went with the plane. Also, the model might be released in two versions—giving Revell more bang for its mold tooling bucks. One "change block" in the tooling held the cavities for the "Dam Buster" skip bomb and extended landing gear, while another substitute block contained the normal bomb bay parts and landing gear.

With the move to standard scale and increased accuracy, Revell entered deeper into the realm of the "serious modeler"—adult model fanatics armed with micrometers and hyper-critical attitudes. When the Lancaster came out, some critics in the International Plastic Modelers Society sniped at details of the model, but Jones showed the editor of the IPMS newsletter his reference material and silenced the critics.

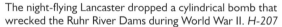

The night-flying Lancaster dropped a cylindrical bomb that wrecked the Ruhr River Dams during World War II. *H-207*

Not all the criticisms of Revell's 1/72 aircraft kits were off the mark. Part of the problem arose because Revell tooled many of these kits in England where costs were lower. In the normal course of operations at the Venice plant there were several opportunities to catch errors as a model was developed—in engineering or the model shop or in the tool shop—but once an error was cut into steel, it became difficult or impossible to correct. When Revell sent its materials overseas it was hard to look over the shoulders of the mold makers to prevent slip-ups. Thus Jones, a hyper-critical modeler himself, found some of the models coming out of Europe woefully below his exacting standards: The P-51 Mustang was "so bad." The Fokker Triplane, "everything was wrong with it." The B-26 Marauder was "a complete disaster."

In 1964 the Yak-25 was reissued in the Jet Command series with new box art. *H-274*

Of course, most of the 1/72 aircraft line met with Jones's warm approval, and most model builders considered them gems of detail and accuracy. Jones encouraged Revell to expand the range of the line beyond the normal Mustang-Spitfire-Messerschmitt offerings. Thus hobbyists got a chance for the first time to build a Morane-Saulnier N monoplane, a stubby Polikarpov I-16, a Brewster F2A Buffalo, a Kawasaki Hien Ki-61, and other delightfully obscure craft from the world wars.

In order to improve the accuracy and detail of its models, Revell changed the way it developed a new kit. Up to this time the engineers and model craftsmen had done the preliminaries in exactly the same size intended for the final model. Now model shop supervisor Ron Campbell introduced a new procedure in which the model patterns were created in a larger scale than that intended for the production model. Thus the engineers and model makers started working in sizes from one and a half to three times the size planned for the kit. A 1/25 scale car, for example, would usually be developed in 1/10 scale.

The process began in the usual way with R & D gathering blueprints and photographs of the subject and handing them over to engineering to draft working drawings of the parts of the model. The model shop would then sculpt a model from the plans and photos in clay or wood or a combination of materials. An epoxy cast would then be made of this model, and this cast would be used as a mold to create a duplicate model in epoxy. Working with this epoxy model (which had a hollow interior core), all the parts could be assembled together to test accuracy and fit. Openings such as windows and wheel wells would be cut into the pattern model at this time. Finally, all the epoxy model parts would go to the tool room and the steel production mold would be cut directly from the pattern model. During the tooling process, a pantograph would reduce the model to its intended production scale size.

The model shop boys liked this approach because it allowed them to work with larger, easier to handle parts, and the mold engravers loved it because they just copied exactly what they were given without having to refer to both blueprints and a demonstration model. The result was a steel mold that usually produced excellent quality parts right from the very first test shots.

The boxes that held Revell's kits gained a new look in the 1960s. Groundwork for the changes began back in the late 1950s when Richard Kishady and Scott Eidson started having trouble keeping up with box illustrations for all the new kits Revell was bringing out. As art director, Kishady began to assign more of the illustrations to outside artists like Lorenzo Gigliera and Nixon Galloway. However, the most important new artists Kishady drew into the Revell orbit were Jack Leynnwood and John Steel.

Then in 1960 Kishady decided to part company with Revell to work on his own. George Saito briefly took his place as art director, followed by Howard Goldstein. About the same time, Steel replaced Eidson as Revell's ship kit illustrator. (Eidson had no trouble finding other commissions—including Life Like and UPC model companies—and continued his busy illustration career for another two decades.)

The Bell X-5 model has variable sweep wings, retracting landing gear, moving flight control surfaces, and opening air brakes. The kit came out in 1960 when models with moving parts were popular. *H-187*

The Famous Artist Series became the Famous Aircraft Series after only a few months. A new talent George Akimoto did the F8U Crusader, while old hand Leynnwood did the P2V Neptune. *H-167, H-170*

Jack Leynnwood did the P6M Seamaster for the Famous Artist Series. *H-176*

Jack Leynnwood painted the Sikorsky helicopter for the Famous Aircraft Series. *H-172*

Thus the 1960s began with a new pair of artists presenting Revell's face to the world: Kishady and Eidson gave way to Leynnwood and Steel. This was a fairly normal development in the hobby industry because model companies like to change the art work on their kit boxes from time to time to refresh the image of the line. A company could revise the

art work on its packaging at much less expense than changing the models inside the boxes. Thus an old model could be made to look new with just a fresh box illustration and a switch in package design and layout.

Saito and Goldstein revised the design and layout of Revell's packaging, which Goldstein thought had previously been "totally undisciplined" (but which today's kit collectors love). The new 1960s look abandoned the old practice of wrapping the box top art around to the side panels and filling the panels with rows of small pictures of other kits in the Revell line. The box top layout of many kits now included a square panel at the left containing the kit name and description, while the art work occupied the rest of the top without being cluttered with text. In fact, for a time Revell printed its box wraps on textured paper and told youngsters to cut out and frame the box art. A final change—marking the end of an era—the familiar "use type 'S' cement" message disappeared from the box end panels.

The illustrator who did the lion's share of the new box art, Jack Leynnwood, was a true renaissance man. He flew a war surplus T-6 Texan and drove a new Jaguar XKE. His home near the ocean held a huge pipe organ in the basement rescued from an old movie theater. Music had always been a vital part of Leynnwood's life. As a youngster during the Great Depression he had helped support his family by touring as a child prodigy saxophone player. He even did some bit parts acting in the *Our Gang* movie comedies. As a young man he played in a swing band, and when World War II came around he played in an Army Air Corps band. During the war he flew P-40s and P-38s in stateside service.

While still in the army Leynnwood painted some safety posters for the Air Corps, and after the war he used the GI Bill to pay for lessons at the Los Angeles Art Center (where he would later teach for twenty-five years). His first job was illustrator for Northrop Corporation, but as soon as he established a reputation, he went off to freelance with several companies, movie studios, and magazines as clients. Kishady saw his work, judged him "a fabulously gifted artist," and hired Leynnwood to paint for Revell.

Leynnwood's style suited Revell's needs perfectly. He would begin a painting by roughing-in a background, often in the hot orange end of the color spectrum to create an aura of excitement. Then he selected a photograph of a plane, ship, or car and projected that photo image on art board with his trusty opaque projector or *camera lucida*—affectionately known as "Lucy." This insured that all the complex angles and proportions of the subject were correct, but then Leynnwood would begin distorting the image—stretching a fuselage section, twisting engine nacelles—to create a more dynamic composition. He knew how to capture the essence of an airplane, ship, or car—and how to produce an illustration that seemed about to explode from the box top. His paintings are filled with action and movement, and his airplanes usually crowd the box top since Leynnwood found things like wing tips uninteresting.

A typical Leynnwood airport scene featuring the Air Cadet series X-3. *H-113*

Leynnwood used thick layers of paint to portray the Piasecki H-16. *H-138*

Leynnwood did his second rendition of the C-130
Hercules for the Picture Plane Series. *H-183*

The Bison bomber as Red Menace. *H-182*

in a well-equipped studio. Instead he discovered that Steel produced his magnificent seascapes seated at an artist's table pushed into a corner of his wife's kitchen. As a painter, Steel was not a colorist—most of his paintings tended to stay at the blue-gray-black end of the palate. His favorite medium was casein, a milk based poster paint that lacked luminosity, but his compositions captured the hulking beauty of the navy's big aircraft carriers and battleships as they plowed through dark seas under ominous skies.

When John Steel began painting for Revell the Picture Fleet was created to show off his work. Many a boy cut out and displayed Steel's box art.

Skies were seldom blue in Leynnwood's paintings—as seen with this pair of F-105s. *H-166*

John Steel, Kishady's other find from the art world, had a well-established reputation as a commercial illustrator in Southern California in the 1950s. When Kishady first visited Steel's Palos Verdes home he expected to find him working

Everyone in John Steel's painting—and the viewer of the art—is watching to see what will happen to the AD-6 Skyraider. *H-260*

When subjects like the tug *Long Beach* required it, Steel could do an illustration rich in color. *H-314*

Steel's life story surpassed even Leynnwood's in drama and excitement. Born in New York City in 1921 to a family of actors and musicians, Steel grew up in Europe with his mother and then appeared as a singer on stage and radio in New York City in the years just before World War II. When the war broke out, he joined the Marines and saw action in the dirty, bloody battles on Guadalcanal and Peleliu. While in the South Pacific he started doing sketches of what he witnessed. After the war he—like Leynnwood—used the G. I. Bill to pay for training at the Art Center. Then he went off to his second war in Korea and again fought in the most desperate engagement of the conflict at the Chosen Reservoir. He emerged from these wars with the Navy Cross, a Bronze Star, and two Purple Hearts.

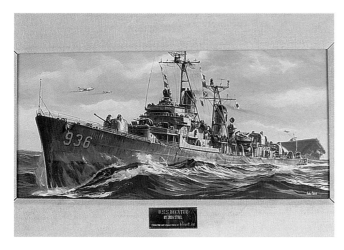

Steel's USS *Decatur* illustrates his ability to capture salt water and steel in a painting. *H-430*

Steel's career as a commercial artist took off in the mid-fifties as he painted for aircraft manufacturers, the Air Force, movie companies, *Skin Diver* magazine, and even Disneyland. Soon Revell joined his list of clients; but, unfortunately, his years at Revell turned out to be few. His personal life fell into turmoil in the mid-sixties. Art director Goldstein recalled that one day Steel submitted a new painting for the Old Ironsides kit that had to be rejected. The outline of the

ship was distorted and the colors were washed out with no luminosity at all. Shortly afterwards Steel spent the night as guest at Leynnwood's home; then he departed at dawn the next morning without saying goodbye. Steel went into self-imposed exile in Mexico, and the staff at Revell soon lost track of him. Leynnwood later heard a rumor that Steel had drowned at sea.

The Science Program, a company in Garden City, New York, advertised with several model companies by inserting fliers inside kit boxes. It offered the Revell X-15 as a premium for subscribing to its monthly series of science bulletins. Courtesy of Rusty Cowart.

The PT-212 box wrap shows how John Steel could pack a lot of action into a small space. *H-421*

Steel put the viewer's eye at sea level to emphasize the massive hulk of the USS *Lexington*. H-426

Since civilian ships didn't sell, Revell turned the *Hawaiian Pilot* and *J. L. Hanna* into the war time variants *Burleigh* and *Mission Capistrano*. H-341, H-342

Revell's World War I German commerce raider *Seeadler* model was just the old Coast Guard training ship *Eagle* with deck guns added. H-382

The USS *Olympia* was one of the most complicated models Revell ever produced. H-367

Actually, Steel had accepted an offer from the Marine Corps to go to Vietnam as a combat artist and photographer. He spent the next five years in Southeast Asia, where he picked up another battle wound. Then Steel returned to settle in Northern California and resumed his life as a commercial artist specializing in wildlife subjects.

When Steel left, Goldstein informed Leynnwood that from now on he would have to paint Revell's ship art, as well as the aircraft and cars. Leynnwood protested, but he had the talents a commercial artist needed to handle the increased load: he was very good and he worked very fast. Almost single-handedly, Leynnwood would go on to do hundreds of Revell box illustrations down through the 1970s. Although photos had become the standard box art medium by the '70s, Revell still liked to use Leynnwood occasionally for "romantic" subjects like ships and spacecraft.

By then Leynnwood's work had already inspired a new generation of artists. Years later, one of his students at the Art Center, Mike Machat, introduced himself to Leynnwood by opening a tattered file of all the Revell box tops he had carefully cut out and saved from his childhood twenty years earlier. When Machat later became president of the American Society of Aviation Artists, he discovered that many of his colleagues had also begun their art studies by revering Leynnwood's Revell box wraps. "Those box tops were simply intoxicating, with their dramatic depictions of aircraft screaming off the

covers right at you! That moody lighting, coupled with such razor-sharp detail and an almost overwhelming sensation of speed, motion, and flight, made for some very compelling art work that just begged to be taken home."

The Supersonic Gift Set of 1961 marked the end of Revell's gift sets for a number of years. G-161

The 1962 issue of the Boeing 707 came with unique "air mail envelope" box art. *H-243*

The Convair 990 took commercial airliners to the edge of the sound barrier. *H-254*

The canvas on which Revell's artists painted—the kit boxes—changed in the mid-1960s. Since 1954, Revell's models had been packaged in heavy cardboard boxes with a slick paper wrap pasted on. Warehousing these bulky made-up boxes took up a lot of space, so Revell ordered them from its box company as they were needed. That required pain-in-the-neck planning and coordination between the molding room and the box company. Many of the boxes were damaged in shipment. Thus Revell decided to switch to fold-down boxes made of thin cardboard that could be printed-up in advance and stored at Revell's Venice complex. Although the cardboard was coated to achieve a smooth, shiny surface, it was not quite as good as the old paper wraps. As today's kit collectors know only too well, the new boxes sagged and creased more, too.

The old Boeing B-29 model flew on in the 1960s with new Leynnwood art. *H-141*

Leynnwood employed his "wet look" on the Fairey Rotodyne. *H-185*

During the 1960s, while Revell put added emphasis on car models and focused on extending its line of 1/72 scale aircraft, many of Revell's vintage "box scale" models from the 1950s continued to be strong sellers. The three 1/28 scale World War I pursuit planes always found willing buyers. To make these kits seem new they assumed different identities.

The Eddie Rickenbacker Spad became the Frank Luke Spad; the Manfred Richthofen Triplane became Werner Voss's mount; and the Roy Brown Camel assumed the marking of William Barker's plane. The original six bombers—the B-24, B-25, B-29, B-36, B-47, B-52—actually outsold most of the newer models. The B-52 also became the launch vehicle for a tiny X-15 research plane. (Alas, only this B-52 kept its nice 1950s clear plastic stand.) The P-39 fighter became a Thompson Trophy pylon racer, with a new four-bladed propeller and bright yellow civilian plastic.

Leynnwood's SAS Caravelle is about the only box art that offered purchasers a pink sky. *H-184*

New box art and decals turned the old Buffalo
Bill B-24 into a "Pacific Raider." H-237

The B-36 intercontinental bomber in the Air Power series. H-139

The old P-39 fighter became the Cobra II pylon racer
with new box art and bright yellow plastic. H-144

The A3J Vigilante model had
many moving parts. H-165

The Lockheed Electra airliner from 1957 survived, but
in an altered form. The tool shop cut its mold apart, threw
sections away, and milled new mold parts to turn the model
into a Navy P-3 Orion anti-submarine plane. Thus the original
Electra can never be reissued—making it a favorite among
kit collectors today.

As new airplanes came on the scene, Revell continued
to bring out models of them. The aircraft that epitomized
space-age innovation was Lockheed's top-secret "Blackbird." The YF-12A had been flying for a while and had
been subject of a lot of speculation in aviation and technical
magazines. Finally, Lockheed announced a public unveiling
for the news media at Edwards Air Force Base. Revell's
airplane expert Lloyd Jones knew a newspaper reporter
friend who provided him with press credentials to get into

The YF-12A Blackbird showed that Revell could be both fast and accurate in bringing out models of the latest aircraft. *H-206*

The mold for the Lockheed Electra was retooled to create the P3 Orion sub hunter. *H-255, H-163*

the briefing, and he had another friend working at Edwards who shepherded him around the place. Since the Air Force allowed photos, but frowned on note taking, Jones wondered how he was going to get the plane's dimensions. He knew that the insignia and numbers on the plane were a standard size, and that would help. Then he noted the aircraft's silver Firestone tires.

Back at the Revell plant, Jones put in a phone call to the friendly people at Firestone, who were happy to tell him all

about the fine qualities of their tires, including the dimensions. Jones was thinking he might have to scale the plane just from this data, when the *Los Angeles Times* ran a photo of the plane taken from above showing the Blackbird resting on a concrete pad—with a nice grid of lines between the sections of concrete. Another phone call to his friend at Edwards netted the length and width of the concrete sections—and thus the size of the plane sitting on them.

A few months later the Air Force had a big celebration in Dallas, Texas, during which the YF-12A's record breaking performances were recognized. When Revell presented pilot Col. Robert L. Stevens with a built model of his plane, he was amazed and asked how Revell could produce such an accurate model of a still-classified plane. Revell turned its answer into an advertising slogan: "You've got your secrets, we've got ours."

Leynnwood gave the F-100 new box art for the Academy Series. *H-127*

Chapter 5 –
New Products, New Challenges

One day after returning from vacation in Hawaii, Lew Glaser bounded up to Al Trendle, R & D's second in command, and announced: "We're going to make big airplane kits with lots of detail!" Glaser then rushed to his aircraft expert, Lloyd Jones and declared that Revell would revolutionize the model airplane field with a new series of big, super-detailed models. Glaser had already decided that the first three planes would be the Spitfire, Messerschmitt Bf-109, and Curtiss P-40, and, he instructed Jones, all the models had to fit in the same size box and sell for the same price. Jones, of course, loved the idea of models in a larger scale that would allow for much more detail and give builders something to work with if they wanted to modify their creations. He thought the choice narrowed down to the recognized 1/24 or 1/32 scales. Jones sculpted rough models of the planes in foam plastic to get an idea of what he had to work with, and it became clear that 1/24 was just going to be too big—so 1/32 it was.

Artist Jack Leynnwood enthusiastically embraced the new series because it gave him an opportunity to paint planes that he had piloted during the World War and because the large new kit boxes gave him an expansive canvas to lavish with detail. Leynnwood later told his student Mike Machat that these illustrations ranked as his all-time favorites "because they were big enough where you could get real juicy with 'em."

Jack Leynnwood painted new box art for the Academy reissue of the Douglas Skyrocket. H-121

However, marketing executive Dave Fisher considered the big aircraft project a risky venture. The larger a model became, the more important detail and accuracy became. These would have to be very precise models if they were to look good, and, of course, that meant very high tooling costs. As it turned out, the risk paid off. Years later Trendle recalled, "We did the large scale aircraft line, and off it went, and it was extremely successful. We owned that category of kits in those days."

The 1/32 Aircraft kits gave Jack Leynnwood a big canvas to work with.
He responded with wonderful art like that for the P-47. H-296

away." The models featured sliding canopies, retractable landing gear, and cowl panels that removed to show intricately crafted engines. Cockpit interiors reproduce the real thing down to minute particulars. Rivets were raised when they were supposed to be raised and, thanks to beryllium copper alloy inserts in the molds, flush when they were supposed to be flush.

The P-51 Mustang fighter, with new yellow plastic and a couple of mold modifications took on an air show personality. *H-272*

Cardboard diorama kits that could be used with any of Revell's 1/72 scale plane models seemed like a good concept, but didn't sell.

Gift sets made a modest return to the Revell catalog in the late 1960s—as in this set of two 1/32 scale models. *H-288*

Two 1/72 scale planes, the FW-190 and P-47, came in the Battle of Berlin diorama kit. *H-663*

Model airplane enthusiasts immediately fell in love with the kits when they hit store shelves in the spring of 1967. *Scale Modeler* magazine (August 1967) declared: "One of the most farsighted and ambitious projects ever undertaken by a modeling firm, Revell's new 1/32 scale series is already on its way to pioneering a landmark in scale modeling. ... These models are so realistic, you'll feel like climbing in and flying

Packaging 1/72 scale aircraft in sets of three played on the hobbyist's desire to build complete collections of related models. *H-682, H-685*

Of the first three models, the P-40 received the best reviews: "It is almost devoid of errors, and those are of the nit-picking variety," said *Scale Modeler*. (October 1967, 45) Of course, presenting models that claimed absolute accuracy invited nit-picking from some experts and pseudo-experts. In the case of the P-51 Mustang, Jones was forced to admit the nit-pickers were right. The model had been tooled in England, and when the first shots came back Jones compared the fuselage part to the engineering drawings sent to the tool shop—the nose of the part was too tapered! When called to account for this, the mold maker protested: "But we were only 1/16 of an inch off!"

For Revell's ship model line, the decade of the 1960s began with a rousing national controversy over one of Revell's new models. On June 19, 1961, the front page of the *New York Times* carried a photo of Revell's Polaris guided missile submarine USS *George Washington* along with a story revealing secret testimony given by Admiral Hyman Rickover, father of the nuclear submarine. Rickover claimed that a plastic model of the Polaris sub revealed classified information. "If I were a Russian," declared the admiral, "I would be most grateful to the United States for its generosity in supplying such information for $2.98." (Actually it was cheaper: $1.98.) Rickover claimed top secret data had been leaked to a hobby company. He did not mention the name of the company, and both Revell and Renwal had Polaris subs in their catalogs—but the media spotlight focused on Revell because it was the nation's best known model company.

When Henry Blankfort read the story he immediately recognized this as a marvelous opportunity for some free publicity. He contacted the press and told them Lew Glaser, President of Revell, would be available to answer questions at his home the following day. Then he phoned Lew. "I'm going to tell you what to do," he said, "and then I'm going to disappear." Blankfort did not want the old allegations about

his supposed Communist past to muddy-up the story. When the media men arrived at the Glaser household, Lew dived into the backyard pool with a model of the Polaris sub and surfaced blowing bubbles. "Lew was a ham," observed his wife. A photo of the episode appeared in the next day's *Los Angeles Times* and later as the picture of the week in *LIFE*. The Glasers were invited to appear on radio and TV for interviews.

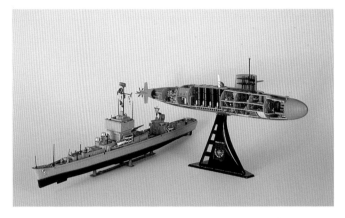

The guided missile cruiser *Long Beach* and the Polaris sub *George Washington*, with its incorrect complement of just eight missile tubes. *H-365, H-368*

Lew Glaser surfaces with the notorious Polaris sub model.

Lew found himself forced into the awkward position of arguing for the inaccuracy of a Revell model. He pointed out that Revell got one big item wrong, giving the Polaris sub only eight missile launch tubes, rather than the actual sixteen. (An error corrected in later issues of the kit.) Glaser avowed that Revell had received no secret information, but had simply gleaned facts from trade and technical journals "available to anyone who wants to take the time and trouble to look them up." (*Los Angeles Times,* June 19, 1961, 1)

The box art shows a missile being launched from a rear tube of the Polaris Sub, but the model had two forward missiles that fired via spring power. H-425

The Navy launched only a few new classes of ships in the 1960s; so there was not much fresh material for Revell to turn into models. Thus attention reverted to World War II era vessels like the carrier *Enterprise*, the battleship *North Carolina*, and the destroyer *Aaron Ward*. With John Kennedy in the White House and the movie *P.T. 109* on theater screens, a new rendition of the mosquito boat entered the Revell line to join the old PT-212 from 1953. In fact, a third PT boat, the PT-73, joined Revell's fleet to attract fans of the "McHale's Navy" television show.

Nationally syndicated columnist Walter Winchell picked up the trail of the controversy and someone fed him material for one of his columns in which he called Lew Glaser a Trotskyite and denounced Blankfort for taking the Fifth Amendment during the Congressional Un-American Activities hearings of the early 'fifties.

The boys in the model shop at Revell found this all very amusing. They had, of course, researched the model just as Glaser said, piecing together data on the submarine from whatever sources they could find. One of the model's creators, Englishman Ron Campbell, recalled that the craftsmen in the model shop had no idea what kind of motor the sub had, so he just gave it a three-stage turbine like those he had once manufactured in his previous job back in Britain.

In the end Royle Glaser pronounced it "the best piece of PR we ever had, thanks to Admiral Rickover and Henry Blankfort. We sold a jillion of the sub models because they were already in the stores."

With Jack Kennedy in the White House, a model of PT-109 was a natural choice. H-310

To mark the Centennial of the Civil War, Revell issued models of the Confederate commerce raider *Alabama* and its nemesis the USS *Kearsarge*. (Actually both ships were made

Revell introduction of the battleship Bismarck showed its increasing interest in World War II subjects. H-350

from the same basic mold, with just a few alterations in details.) These models continued the features of the *Cutty Sark*—that is, they were big and highly detailed. Ship enthusiasts and Civil War buffs loved them. To extend this success, Revell decided to make a larger size model of one of its classic models: Old Ironsides. At the time the USS *Constitution* was basically just an empty hulk, quietly rotting at its moorings in Boston Naval Yard. But major plans were underway to refurbish the ship in time for the nation's bicentennial in 1976. Revell went to the Smithsonian and obtained copies of the plans for restoring the vessel. Then it started work on making the model. Lloyd Jones recalled that it became such a big project that everyone in the model shop received one aspect or another of the kit to work on. Once again, Revell made one mold do double duty by also reissuing the *Constitution*, with a few modifications, as its sister ship the *United States*.

Ben Lench, whose company built display models for Revell in the early 1950s, designed an acetate display case to protect models from dust.

Peter Pan's Pirate Ship continued a long-standing, if intermittent, relationship between Revell and Walt Disney. *H-377*

The PT-167 used the same mold as the PT-109, but Leynnwood's painting of the craft in zebra stripe camouflage made it look different. *H-342*

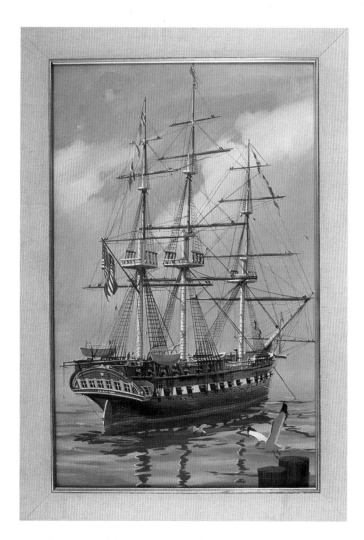

As its other major ship building project for the 1960s, Revell introduced a new line of small scale modern warships that sold for just one dollar. During the previous few years the various Japanese model companies had collaborated to bring out a collection of Pacific theater warships from World War II in constant 1/700 scale. These waterline models could be displayed on a flat surface as if they were sailing on the high seas. Revell wanted to do the same for America's ships and for vessels that fought in Atlantic waters. Lloyd Jones decided to size Revell's fleet to 1/720 scale because it made a multiple of the established 1/72 scale, but still came close to 1/700. The first ship to be developed was the battleship *Arizona* because Revell still had materials in its storage vault used to make its larger size *Arizona* kit. The new kits were very nice models, with hulls split at the waterline so that hobbyists could build either a full-hull model or a waterline version. The original plan had been to issue an extensive armada of models, but when the series hit ten kits, Revell decided to call it quits since it had more than enough ship models in its inventory to keep track of.

Leynnwood's Old Ironsides captures her in calm repose. Perhaps for this reason Revell never used it on any of its many USS *Constitution* packages.

The USS *Wisconsin* used the same tooling as the original *Missouri*. H-352

The *Massachusetts* and *Ark Royal* helped usher in a whole new series of 1/720 scale Revell ships. *H-485, H-483*

Revell's third model of the USS *Constitution* was an easy-to-build two-foot long model. *H-362*

Royle Glaser had a big problem with Revell's ship models—and she thought that it might also be a problem for many of Revell's customers: She could not understand the instruction sheets. When any new model came off the assembly line—ship, plane or car—she sometimes attempted to build it herself to get an idea of how the customer might experience the product. She found it frustrating. The instructions appeared to be drawn-up by engineers for other engineers, not real people. Once she attempted to assemble the popular B-25 kit, but it didn't seem to be coming out right. She called in Lloyd Jones and showed her handiwork to him, and he laughed. Somehow she had managed to jam the wings in upside down!

Royle brought in a remedial reading teacher from a local school and asked him to draw up his own version of an easy to follow instruction sheet. Then she called a staff meeting to tackle the instruction sheet question. After the teacher presented his critique of the instruction sheets, Tom Hogg, Revell's ancient mariner, spoke up: "What does he know about ships? Why, you're trying to design them so just anyone could build a ship model." "Precisely," Royle replied.

She didn't get very far with her protest. After all, Revell had built its reputation on sales of complex, authentic models—something Royle called "the flush rivet syndrome." However, at least Revell began to offer some "simplified construction" ship models with reduced part counts and streamlined rigging suggestions. New products manager Don Ernst came up with a novel idea for two of the new models: Instead of trying to find a different new subject for a model, why not make another model of a top selling kit in a different size? Thus the public's favorite Revell ship models, Old Ironsides and the *Cutty Sark*, appeared in two-foot long versions, midway between the original sixteen-inch models and the large three-foot models. Since they sold at different price levels, they did not compete against each other directly.

By the 1960s car models dominated sales in the model kit field. At mid-decade, with the departure of Jim Keeler, stewardship of the model car line passed to Bob Paeth, a man Keeler had hand-picked to join him in the research and development department. Paeth, a tall, exuberant fireman and car enthusiast, ran the model car contest at each year's Oakland Roadster Show. Through this connection Keeler met Paeth and invited him to join the staff at Revell.

Revell's model car line continued along the paths established earlier in the 1960s. A very nice '41 Willys coupe dragster debuted as Revell's first true funny car model. The model depicted the blue Stone-Woods-Cook "Swindler II" made famous by its series of match races with John Mazmanian's red Willys. Management asked Paeth to add more funny cars to the catalog, but also directed him to avoid expensive tooling costs. So he rummaged through the tool warehouse to see what existing molds might be recycled into drag racers. The first thing he located was the body mold for the old 1962 Chrysler Dodge Dart. He mated this with the vintage "22 Jr." dragster frame and cut out a section of the Dart's trunk lid to create a cockpit for the driver. With racing wheels and a "Revellion" race decal, he had a new kit for almost no new tooling costs.

The second new funny car had an even more interesting genesis. Years earlier Revell had begun development of a 1953 Studebaker and got as far as cutting the body mold. But in the midst of this work Revell's "spy network" learned that AMT also planed on bringing out a '53 Studebaker. Since companies generally tried to avoid duplicating each other's kits—and even had a rough gentlemen's agreement to that effect—Revell put its Studebaker project on the shelf. Paeth remembered this abandoned Studebaker body mold, which had not yet received engraved door or trunk lines, and thought it would work just fine as a funny car body, since real dragster bodies were just fiberglass shells. He used an existing chassis and the Chrysler V-8 engine from the Custom Car Parts. The only problem was that the chassis had a shorter wheel base than the Studebaker, but enlarging the body's wheel wells resolved that satisfactorily. With its "Miss Deal" decal added, the cobbled-together model ended up as a quite respectable kit—despite its questionable past!

The "Miss Deal" Studebaker funny car helped build Revell's reputation for exciting drag racing models. H-1266

On one occasion, Revell's industry spies did it a disservice. Revell was developing a 1949 Oldsmobile model when a photographer who did work for both Revell and Monogram mentioned to the Revell R & D staff that Monogram also planed to bring out a '49 Olds. Revell's management decided to cancel its Oldsmobile program. However, time went by and no Monogram '49 Olds model appeared. At an industry trade show Bob Paeth ran into his equivalent in product development at Monogram and asked him why their '49 Olds kit had not been issued. The reply was: "Well, we were working on one, but then we heard that Revell was doing the same model; so we cancelled ours!"

Revell's next proposed funny car dragster received some opposition from within the company's management. Paeth wanted to do a model of an English Anglia, but Revell's resident Englishman Ron Campbell considered the Anglia "a bucket of bolts ... a dull auto." Nevertheless, Paeth received permission to do his Anglia, signing a contract with Skip Hess to make a model of his "Skip's Critter." Once the model came out, Campbell had to admit his skepticism had been misplaced—the Anglia stayed in its molding machine month after month churning out parts to meet popular demand.

Paeth's follow-on project faced a different obstacle. He wanted to do a model of the Anglia's cousin, the Thames panel truck. But where could you find an example of this exotic vehicle in Southern California? As it turned out, while driving in North Hollywood Paeth happened to spot one parked alongside the street. He immediately pulled over and walked up to the house were the Thames was parked. The older couple that answered the door said that the truck belonged to their son and invited Paeth back for breakfast on Saturday to meet him. Naturally, Paeth arrived on their doorstep bright and early that day. He sat down with the family over coffee and learned that the owner of the truck was Ken Berry, star of television's "F Troop" and "Mayberry RFD." He turned out to be a regular down-home guy who was happy to loan his Thames to Revell for a couple of weeks to be copied and, in payment, he asked only for a case of models.

The Austin was the last in Revell's line of cute little gasser dragsters. H-1208

The Thames panel truck proved relatively easy to develop because it shared front-end parts with the Anglia. Likewise, the model shop also found it easy to make a model of the '41 Willys delivery truck by simply taking the wooden pattern (or "buck") of the Willys coupe, sawing it in half, and adding the truck rear end. Paeth's collection of these "neat little cars" concluded with a gasser-class '51 Henry J Coupe and a '50 Austin Sedan. Paeth wanted to do more kits of these popular drag strip cars, but management said no. They probably were right. The Austin turned out to be a poor seller; so perhaps this breed of dragster had reached a saturation point with the buying public.

By this time Revell had become deeply involved with a whole new family of kits: motorcycles. In the 1960s America's teenage boys fell in love with the light-weight, sporty bikes recently introduced by Japanese manufacturers, and Revell offered them kits of their favorite mounts. In 1965 it rolled out a model of the stylish Triumph Tiger 100, setting the standard for what would grow into a large and varied collection of cycle kits. Revell designed the Tiger to a large 1/8 scale that built-out to a nine-inch long model and put in lots of chrome parts, spoke wheels, real rubber tires, flexible vinyl tubes for cables and wiring lines, and intricate details down to the spark plug level. To exploit the mold further, Paeth took the engine and wheel parts from the Tiger kit and designed Custom Show Bike and Drag Bike versions around them.

Takara of Japan developed Revell's line of 1/12 scale motorcycles, like the Kawasaki KZ900. H-1520

Next came a trio of Hondas, also popular cycles among America's teenage riders. The first was the off-road Honda Scrambler trail bike. A Super Hawk and a racing bike with a streamline cowling followed in its path. Paeth wanted to stretch the Honda line just a bit farther and pieced-together a demonstration model of a customized Honda, with an aerodynamic cowl fashioned from the bow of the Polaris

Revell's Triumph 100 model set the industry standard for high-quality motorcycle models. H-1231

sub model. The new products committee bought the idea because it could be pulled-off without spending too much in new development money.

The obvious next step in the motorcycle world was a model of a Harley-Davidson. Development of the Harley model faced a simple obstacle: the freight elevator leading to the R & D department on the second floor of the Revell plant. With the Triumphs and Hondas, engineering and the model shop boys had simply brought them up to their work area to copy them—but would a Harley-Davidson fit in the elevator? Yes, as it turned out, but just barely. Paeth first designed a custom "Chopped Hog" model because he could cut corners on some of the details, like inventing a easy to make, but never-seen-in-the real-world Chevy II single-leaf suspension for the rear end. The model of a Harley-Davidson Police Bike took a little longer to develop because it had more accurate real-world details.

Revell's Japanese distribution partner Takara sent over a set of 1/12 scale motorcycles developed by its mold making company, Otha Tooling, for Revell to inspect. Glaser liked the nice details in these smaller-sized models; so Revell started adding Yamaha, Husqvarna, and Kawasaki kits to its line.

Accuracy was never a question when it came to the outlandish set of Corvair engine-powered custom trikes Paeth designed for Revell just at the time hippie fashions blossomed into vogue. To sell management on the idea, Paeth made up a display model of a trike with extravagantly long front spokes

and extra-wide rear slicks (made in the prototype model by taping two paint jar lids together). The molds for these tric-trikes were cheap and easy to make, but engineering had a headache designing tooling for those fat vinyl tires that would hold their shape after being ejected from the molding machine.

The demand for new car and cycle designs became so great that management allowed Paeth to hire another man to help with the load. The new guy, Darrell Zipp had come to Los Angeles from Minnesota to study automotive design at the Art Center, but it eventually dawned on him that his chosen career path would take him right back to the Midwest, and he liked sunny California. So he started looking for a job in the

Jack Leynnwood's illustration for the Triumphant Trike shows that mod, hippie styles were in bloom around 1970. *H-1223*

The Six-Pack Trike was just a pure fun three-wheel cycle. *H-1221*

local area, and his mentor in hot rod design, Ed Roth, pointed him to Revell. Zip was thrown into the cycle frenzy at the Venice plant. "For six months we did nothing but trikes," he later recalled. "We all got sick of them."

Meanwhile, Paeth continued playing around with ideas for additional quick and easy models, and he started carving big 1/12 scale models shaped from poly-foam plastic. Once he had a pretty good idea of what he wanted, Paeth built a 1/25 scale display model in styrene to show the new products committee. It was a street rod with an antique car body, sporty mag wheels, and a Corvair engine. The committee liked the idea, but, as usual, required that several different model variants emerge from the design process. The result was the Meter Cheater Taxi, the Der Guber Wagen truck, and a basic flatbed truck. One day engineer Lonnie Flanders showed Paeth something interesting: put the 1/96 scale Apollo space capsule model on the bed of the truck and it looked like a cement mixer. Thus the flatbed was transformed into The Amazing Moon Mixer.

Dave Deal did the box art for the whimsical Amazing Moon Mixer hot rod. *H-1210*

In the late '60s the old VW minibus came back as the Bed Bug with new Dave Deal box art. *H-1203*

Revell's final line of new car kits to emerge during the 1960s reflected an evolutionary change in the model industry and in national retailing. Plastic models were no longer the fad novelty they had been in the heady days of the late 1950s and early 1960s. The number of hobby shops operating across the country had declined from its high of about 5,000 at the start of the decade. Increasingly kit sales were dependent upon finding shelf space in the toy sections of big chain stores like K Mart. By 1970 Revell sold seventy-six percent of its kits in mass merchandising outlets and only fourteen percent in hobby shops.

Among Revell's new series of 1/32 scale car models were a set of timeless classic 1957 models, led off by the T-Bird. *H-1290*

Cars remained the most popular subjects for plastic models, so Revell began a new category of 1/32 scale, snap-assembly car kits designed for younger boys and intended for sale in the toy sections of big retail stores. Revell became the first company in the industry to began the practice of marking the boxes with age-appropriate numbers to indicate the degree of building difficulty. The hope was that a youngster would enjoy success with a simple model kit and then move up to more complicated models as that youngster grew older. Marketing manager Don Ernst also thought some grown men might pick one up just to have a model of their own car to put on their desk at work.

The first four kits were popular new "pony cars"—the Mustang, Camaro, Firebird, and Cougar. Unlike the cars Revell had been doing, they had few parts and no opening hoods or doors. To develop these simple kits, Revell would borrow new cars from area dealerships and drive them to the Venice plant's parking lot to be photographed. The R & D team would shoot them with a telephoto lens from across the lot to get a flat image, then make photo prints in exact

The original Corvette gave America a
sports car it could be proud of. *H-1291*

1/32 scale so that the engineers could just trace the outline to
create precise blueprints. Close-up photos would be taken
after strips of masking tape had been stuck vertically on the
side of the car every foot or so to accentuate the contours
of the body. Altogether about two-hundred close-ups would
then be taken for use by engineering and the model shop to
get proper shapes and all the details.

Mold modifications and new box art kept the
old F-102 model flying into the 1970s. *H-130*

Nobody at Revell—outside some in the marketing
department—liked the 1/32 scale cars very much. The R & D
and model shop car aficionados couldn't take the simple kits
very seriously. Royle Glaser declared: "They went against all
Revell stood for. It was like we had gone back to where we
started, selling disassembled toys." These models did help
Revell secure a place in the model car market, but Revell
had not found a product that challenged the supremacy of
AMT and MPC in model cars.

The '57 Chevy sold very well in 1/25 scale,
but not so well in 1/32 scale. *H-1293*

This is the third of three box wraps
Jack Leynnwood painted of the X-3
over a period of a dozen years. *H-135*

The Apollo Spacecraft allowed kids to assemble
and disassemble the final stages of the rocket
that took men to the moon. *H-1838*

The field of guided missile and rocket models had been an area pioneered by Revell in the late 1950s, and a decade later Revell again launched a major new initiative in this area. The first time around the missile model category had been heavily military, but the new issues were totally civilian and linked to America's man-in-space program. The Glasers and other top Revell's executives liked the scientific, educational aspects of models tied to America's efforts to land a man on the moon. This time men sat atop the missiles, and that added a compelling human element to the models. America's boys could actively involve themselves in the adventure of space travel by building Revell's models.

Revell's models of the Apollo command module and lunar lander
appeared in 1967 at the start of the Apollo flights. *H-1836*

Revell returned to gift sets with the American Space Program collection. *H-1839*

When American families watched their TVs in 1968 to see the first orbital test flights of the Apollo-Saturn program lift-off, Revell already had models on store shelves of the moon mission vehicles. The first of the new kits was a diorama of the Apollo command and service modules orbiting over a lunar terrain base with the Lunar Excursion Module resting amid a field of craters. The second, a twenty-inch tall model of the final three payload stages of the Apollo Mission rocket, included lots of opening panels and moving parts to interest youngsters curious about the vehicles that would carry men to the moon and back.

Astronaut in Space depicts a Gemini space walk; while the Apollo Lunar Module packaged the lunar lander model separately from the command module. *H-1841, H-1842*

Marketing director Dave Fisher wanted a really big product to sell during the Christmas season of 1969 to mark man's final conquest of the moon. His proposed building a model of the whole, huge Saturn V booster rocket. To make his point, he had the model shop build an eight-foot tall demonstration model that he unveiled to the new products committee. Fisher thought the sheer size of a Saturn model would give it great "sex appeal;" but, of course, he had something smaller in mind for the market place: a four-foot tall model! The committee liked the proposal, but no model of such proportions had ever been manufactured before, and producing it meant overcoming some engineering and molding problems. The engineers decided to make the fuselage of the rocket by asking the builder to roll thin sheets of plastic into cylinders and then slip rings around these tubes to secure them in place. Lloyd Jones recalled that R & D's method of testing the sturdiness of this construction technique was to have him step off a chair on to a rocket section to see if it would hold his weight. It did. This $12 kit proved to be a very popular item.

Revell's second generation of rocket models sold much better than the first collection from the late 1950s, yet they never became really big sellers, and their popularity dropped rapidly after men walked on the moon. It is one of the great mysteries of America's psychology that the missions to the moon never captivated the public's spirits as did Charles Lindbergh's modest hop across the Atlantic a half-century earlier. As the Apollo program wound down in the early 1970s, Revell retired—at least temporarily—all its aerospace model kits.

Super Jack Leynnwood art: The Gemini space walk. *H-1835*

Revell's huge Saturn V model paid tribute to a monumental event. *H-1834*

The Russian half of the space race equation received attention in the Vostok model. *H-1844*

The Apollo Astronaut on the Moon represented the end of Revell's line of space program models for the 1960s. *H-1860*

With the decade of the 1960s drawing to a close, Revell remained the world leader in model kits, but it was hard work to maintain this position in a highly competitive industry. Revell had grown to become a fairly large company. It owned or leased a whole complex of buildings around the old Venice plant and employed about six-hundred people. Unfortunately, its bottom line profits suffered in the final years of the decade. In 1968 the slot car frenzy collapsed—almost overnight. The rage for large scale slot racers simply crashed and burned. Many hobby companies were hurt, and Revell had to absorb about a half-million dollar loss on its slot car product line. When N scale model railroading emerged as a hot field in the late '60s, Revell jumped into

Two of Revell's old spacecraft concept models from the 1950s came back a decade later as pop-art space vehicles. *H-1850, 1851*

that as a way of diversifying, but it also turned out to be a money-losing proposition.

Finally Royle Glaser, newly promoted to Executive Vice-President, took the lead in a major corporate restructuring designed to cut operating costs. In the fall of 1969, on what became known as "Black Friday," several company executives and some staff lower down on the organizational chart received word that their jobs had been eliminated. This radical corporate surgery resulted in a leaner, more streamlined company with a better shot at recording black ink on its bottom line.

These years proved painful for the whole hobby industry. The venerable Frog model company of England, originator of the all-plastic model kit, went bankrupt. Aurora Plastics of New York chose to sell out to food industry leader Nabisco in order to raise working capital. Toy giant Mattel absorbed Monogram Models, and Monogram's president Jack Besser retired, saying the hobby industry just wasn't the same old close fraternity anymore. Plastic models had now established themselves as staple products in the marketplace, but just exactly how they would fare with the next generation of kids and hobbyists in the 1970s remained to be seen.

Chapter 6 –
The Troubled Seventies

As America entered the 1970s, the patriotic feelings and close bonds of memory that tied the public to World War II faded, only to be replaced by the national agony of the Vietnamese conflict. Tensions over the issues of war, poverty, and race threatened to rend the nation's social fabric. Oil shortages and growing awareness of threats to the environment added elements of doubt to the country's spirits. America seemed transformed from the country it had been back in the 1950s, and as new episodes in history played out, Revell continued to construct a record of the times in plastic.

Leynnwood's original comp for the Bell Huey showed the copters firing rockets at a sampan, but that suggested firing on civilians; so the target became a bridge. *H-259*

From time to time the Glasers would be called upon to make talks before civic organizations, and one of the questions repeatedly came up—especially as the Vietnam War escalated: Why did Revell make so many "war toys." Royle Glaser's stock answer was: "If you won't buy them, we won't

make them." However, this question struck Royle close to the heart because both she and Lew hated war and would have preferred to manufacture non-violent, educational products. However, to their great frustration, models of civilian ships and aircraft—not to mention human and animal figures—just didn't sell.

The box art for the A-7 Corsair shows that the Vietnam War had an impact on model subjects in the 1960s and '70s. *H-133*

Jack Leynnwood gave Revell's big 1/32 scale Stuka a colorful paint scheme. *H-298*

In 1969 Lew Glaser's personal life took on ominous overtones. His doctors discovered cancer spreading through his body, and informed him that he might have as few as six months left to live. However, Glaser had never been a person to allow distractions to divert him from his work, and he simply told himself, "I'll lick this." By force of will, he conjured-up a mighty internal army to do battle with the cancer. He underwent chemotherapy and allowed the doctors to try some experimental treatments on him—and with that taken care of, he went back to work.

Glaser turned day-to-day company operations over to Royle, and she became president and chief operating officer in 1970. Lew continued with long range planning and also returned to one of his old interests: the educational possibilities of plastic models. He wanted to create learning modules for sale to schools that would package Revell models along with a film-strip, phonograph record, and booklets. A "world exploration" unit featured the *Santa Maria*; one on space travel used the NASA space capsule and rocket models. Beyond that, however, it proved difficult to conceive enough learning modules to create a saleable catalog of products to offer school systems, and finding a way to reach the diverse market of schools across the country presented another problem. Product planning director Dave Fisher felt that Lew was trying to push models beyond their reasonable sphere. The educational kits never went into production.

By 1972 Glaser's cancer had progressed to the point that it became difficult for him to come in to his office on a regular basis: so he set up a work place at the dining room table in his home. He continued working in his robe and pajamas, studying materials prepared by psychological consultants on the value of educational toys for preschool children. Then, on September 12, 1972, his work finally concluded.

Lew and the company's board of directors had prepared the way for Royle to assume control of Revell. For twenty years under Lew Glaser's leadership Revell's goal had been to become and remain the world's largest and best model company—no matter what the cost. The transition to Mrs. Glaser ushered in a decade of more practical, tough-minded management at Revell. As Royle explained it: "My husband had an insatiable desire for perfection. He willingly sacrificed everything for being the best. When I became president, we amended the company goal to 'leadership consistent with profitability'." She and chief operating officer, Marshal Metlen, initiated a new cost/profit approach designed to insure that Revell made money on every new piece of tooling and on every unit sold. "Lew was the dreamer, the founder, the entrepreneur—I was the consolidator," explained Royle. Money that Lew once spent on expensive business consultants and speculative product development projects now went to shore up Revell's cash-poor finances.

In 1975 Revell President Royle Glaser made the cover of *Playthings*, the toy industry's trade journal.

In the model industry it was commonly believed that red cars sold best. A red Mustang was a natural anyway. Jack Leynnwood created this excellent art for a small 1/32 scale kit. *H-1250*

One of the new generation, hard-headed managers was Don Ernst, who had joined the marketing department back in 1963. He left a position as paint company salesman for a job that promised to have much greater appeal to a rabid car and motorcycle enthusiast. Ernst worked with Revell's slot car line until the crash of slot car fever, then moved up into the management department.

In 1967 he spotted a notice in *Car Craft* magazine for the "Mexican 1000," a thousand-mile dirt-road race from Tijuana to La Paz, on the Baja California peninsula. This inaugural race premiered what later become known as the "Baja 1000." Ernst approached speed equipment manufacturer EMPI and suggested that EMPI and Volkswagen co-sponsor a car in the race. As part of the deal, he would drive the car, and Revell would make a model of the car. Revell put up the $350 dollar entry fee for the car and painted its "Revell" name on its side.

The Freaky Rider Shift Kicker reincarnated Ed Roth's Mother's Worry. Revell, Japan brought back Drag Nut as Gaga. H-901

Revell's Dave Deal and Don Ernst drove the Spark Bug in the Baja 1000. The art department enjoyed creating dioramas to show off the built model in the box art. H-1318

Ed Roth's Tweedy-Pie returned with an updated new look in 1973 as The Rodfather. H-1444

That first year Ernst and his co-driver did very well, winning their class, but the following year's race did not turn out so fortunately. Dave Fisher later recalled that Revell staffers were waiting in Venice to hear how Don had fared when a telegram came in reporting a disaster. It turned out that Don had just broken down, but the message took on ominous overtones in translation from rustic Spanish to English. During this race Ernst crossed paths a hearty, bearded racer named Dave, but at the time he was just another face in the crowd of competitors.

Since Ernst was so deeply involved in the automotive scene, management handed him the daunting assignment of coming up with a proposal for a completely new line of car model kits. Searching for inspiration, Ernst flipped through a copy of *Road & Track* one day and happened across a cartoon by Dave Deal. Ernst had long enjoyed Deal's over-the-top, distorted caricatures of well-known autos with big, fat tires. Why not turn these cartoons into 3-D models? He walked over to Dave Fisher's office, showed him the cartoon, and asked, "Do you think this might make an interesting model?" Fisher immediately replied: "It would make an interesting series of models!"

Ernst phoned Dave Deal and asked him to drop by the Revell plant to discuss his idea. When Deal stepped through the door, Ernst immediately recognized him as "Dave" the Baja race driver. It turned out that Deal had already been connected with Revell in the past. Back in the mid-1960s he had done a few illustrations for instruction sheets and had even served as interim art director briefly. They hit it off right away. Ernst explained that Revell's management had not agreed to anything yet, and asked him for some sketches of a set of four cars that could be made into models. It would be done totally on spec, with no promise of payment for his work. Deal quickly complied and gave Ernst a stack of drawings.

Ernst's idea of preliminary market research was to carry Deal's sketches to a local hobby shop and hang out with the ten-year olds. He didn't want the reactions of older, more auto-wise boys who might have already seen Deal's drawings in car magazines. When Ernst showed Deal's drawings to the younger kids and asked them if they would like a model of these cars, their response was enthusiastic: "That'd be bitchin'."

With the ten-year old crowd on board, the next problem for Ernst was selling the concept to Revell's management because cartoon cars were way beyond the realm on which Revell had made its reputation. The engineering and model shop personnel also expressed skepticism. Revell manufactured authentic, accurate models, not wildly inaccurate models. Ernst swore to the new products committee that tooling for the kits would be inexpensive and that the line would sell tens of thousands of units. He got the OK to go ahead.

At this point, Ernst introduced Deal to Darrell Zipp in the R & D department where the model prototypes would be produced. Zipp and Deal got along well right from the start because both were enthusiastic about the project and both enjoyed designing autos. The problem was how to turn Deal's two-dimensional cartoons into three-dimensional models. The first four models selected were a VW bug, a dune buggy, a Corvette Stingray, and—most outrageous of all—a five-wing Fokker airplane like the kind that never flew in World War I. For each model Deal submitted a three-quarter front view, a side view, and a three-quarter rear view before getting the OK to go ahead. Zipp, who had learned to sculpt car bodies at the Art Center, loaned Deal his sculpting tools so he could make the VW bug. When Deal brought his VW bug model back, it clearly didn't have the look Revell wanted. Ernst was nominated by the R & D boys to break the bad news to Deal, who later admitted that his preliminary model had indeed "gotten out of hand. ... It was horrible." But he quickly got busy and started to produce models that the shop could copy into production tooling.

"Deal's Wheels" ZZZZ-28 Chevy Camaro. *H-1353*

Deal's Red Baron Fokker sports a dragster V-8 and blower. *H-190.* Courtesy of Mark Mattei.

Dave Deal's first creation was a VW Bug. Revell designed the Deal's Wheels cars so that components from one kit could be used in a second kit. *H-1351, H-1361.*

Flt. Lft. Rif Raf and his chubby, hilarious Spitsfire. *H-192*

With all the preliminary difficulties behind them, Revell's team went to the Hobby Industry Association trade show in February 1970, confident that they had an innovative new product that would appeal to anyone with a sense of humor. To their horror, they discovered that the Monogram parlor featured "Snap-Draggin's," cartoon cars designed by Tom Daniel that looked astonishingly like the first conceptual drawings for Deal's Wheels. How had this happened? Some at Revell suspected that one of the employees terminated the previous year had leaked preliminary sketches of Deal's Wheels to Monogram. However, other Revell staffers thought that it was simply one of those striking coincidences where two different companies come up with very similar products at the same time.

Despite the competition from Monogram, Deal's Wheels turned out to be a top selling line. They were easy to build and appealed to both younger kids and to the whimsical adult with an appreciation for the ridiculous. Deal went on to create a line of four aircraft and twelve cars. (Zipp and Dennis Rich sculpted the bodies for the Tirebird and Ferd Phony Car.) The twenty-four year old Deal received only a paltry one percent royalty on wholesale unit sales (one cent a kit), but since he also received payment for his box art and instruction sheet illustrations, he did well enough. And one cent multiplied thousands of times eventually amounted to a goodly sum, too.

The Deal's Wheels line stopped abruptly after three years, perhaps because, like all products, it had reached a saturation point in the market. As often happened, some proposed models never saw the light of day. A Porsche 911 made it as far as the pattern stage. The P-51, F4U Corsair, Japanese Zero, and P-47 died on the drawing board.

Having worked well together on creating small model cars, Ernst assisted Deal in building an honest-to-goodness VW off-road racer: the Champion Spark Bug. They co-piloted it in the Baja 1000 three times between 1969 and 1971, and then drove a solo-effort time trial that set a Tijuana to La Paz time record that will never be broken—because the roads have been paved since then! Deal and Ernst presented Revell's model of the Spark Bug to the mayor of La Paz, and later Deal's real car became a prize in Revell's Sweepstakes give-away.

Meanwhile, Darrell Zipp dreamed up a new project of his own. Monogram and *Model Car Science* magazine were co-sponsoring the "Build a Dream Dragster" custom-design contest with Darryl Starbird's *Predicta* show car as the top prize. Everyone at Revell considered Monogram their chief competitor, and a friendly rivalry existed between the two companies. Zipp walked into promotion manager Howard Rieder's office and said something like, "You know how Monogram is getting a lot of mileage out of its *Predicta* contest?" Rieder admitted that it was true. "How would you like it if I won?" Rieder explained that certainly there must be disclaimers that would disqualify professional model builders from the contest, but a close reading of the contest entry turned up no roadblocks. "OK," said Rieder, "but I don't want to know about it." So Zipp left Revell's management in the dark and went about building his entry.

He employed bits and pieces from seven Monogram kits in designing his dream dragster. "It was the most far out, wild thing my mind could imagine." Then he sent it in and waited to see what would happen. One day a phone call came in

Dave Deal's wacky creations had tremendous appeal to adolescent boys. Swine Hunt and VAN. H-1356, H-1362. Courtesy of Tim Nolan.

There is action on all levels in Leynnwood's U-99. *H-408*

to his home, and his wife referred the caller to the R & D department at Revell. It was the director of Monogram's advertising agency, and he was calling to tell Zipp that he had won the grand prize. "Cool!" responded Zipp. Then the ad man wanted to know about Zipp's wife and child, and when he learned that Zipp was a product designer, he thought that was great. "What company do you work for and what do you design?" Zipp replied, "Revell, and I design model cars." There was dead silence for a few seconds as the ad man finally caught on. "Are you still there," asked Zipp. "Yeah," said the ad man. "Did I win?" "Yeah, you won."

Monogram's planned promotional events for the *Predicta* winner were cancelled, but Revell workers held a small celebration for Zipp that Revell management discreetly stayed away from. After a few weeks wait, a Buick hauling the Starbird car on a flat-bed trailer pulled up in front of Zipp's home. Friends and family excitedly gathered around as Zipp opened the bubble canopy of the *Predicta* and started the engine. The car immediately leaped off the rear of the trailer—just missing Zipp's wife—since what Zipp thought was neutral turned out to be reverse. The brakes failed because the chains that had secured the car during the trip had cut the brake line. But no harm was done, and Zipp enjoyed driving his new car around the neighborhood and taking it to car shows. "It was an early 1960s show car, and it drove like a toad," observed Zipp. He soon traded it to a fellow for a custom Harley cycle, and eventually the *Predicta* found its way back into Starbird's hands.

During the 1970s Revell renewed its reputation as a preeminent model car company with a superb lineup of spectacular funny car and rail dragster kits. Drag racing achieved a pinnacle of popularity in the United States in the 1970s with a national circuit of top-name competitors matching thunderous, nitro-burning, fire-breathing machines over a measured quarter-mile. At a time when NASCAR track racing was regarded as a regional idiosyncrasy of the old Confederate states, the drag racer ruled as king in the minds of America's speed-thirsty men and boys. Several model companies jumped into the drag car arena, but Revell achieved a near monopoly of the top racers and their cars.

Revell's affair with drag racers went all the way back to the Tony Nancy models of the early 1960s and had continued with cute little fuelers like the Anglia and Miss Deal. But in the 1970s a more muscular breed of funny cars evolved,

The Maverick Funny Car hit low marks for accuracy, but it opened the door to a series of amazing dragster models. *H-1302*

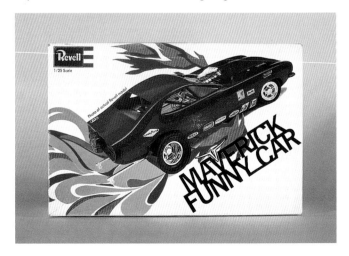

sporting fiberglass bodies that imitated late-model Detroit iron like Mustangs, Camaros, Chargers, and Grand-Ams. R & D model-maker Darrell Zipp started Revell off in this new domain with a generic funny car chassis that could mount either a Mustang, Maverick, or Camaro body. Zipp admitted that the model was based on scanty research and represented "just the idea of a funny car ... something that had the look."

Marketing's Dave Fisher and Don Ernst teamed up with R & D's Zipp to take it from there. Not only did they want to do more dragster car models, they proposed doing them in big 1/16 scale. The debate in the New Products Committee centered on the same risks involved in the decision to make the large 1/32 scale aircraft. Tooling for the larger-scale car models would be expensive, and it would have to embody excruciating details like fuel lines, spark plug wires, and textured rubber tires. The kits would also break the industry-wide $2.00 price ceiling on car models.

Ernst argued that drag racing fans were older teens and adults who could spring for the extra bucks the kits would cost. Also, the more expensive kits would have appeal as Christmas gifts. Finally, the tooling costs could be spread over several models since one chassis could be used on different models and the costs of producing various body shell molds would be modest. After all, the real cars looked pretty much alike on the inside. All of them ran versions of the Dodge Hemi engine. With an assortment of distinctive decals, different plastic colors, and minor part changes Revell could market a wide array of colorful, exciting kits.

Ernst and Fisher received the go-ahead to launch the Big Car program. They first sat down with the very successful team of owner Art Whipple and driver Ed McCulloch to discuss making a model of their car. Revell planned to tie the new kits in with big-name race personalities since human interest helps sell models of impersonal machines. To further enhance the individual character of the car models, Ernst and Fisher proposed that Revell design an artistic, distinctive paint scheme for the cars and give them unique names. In exchange, Whipple and McCulloch would get a $5,000 cash advance on the five percent royalty they would receive on kit sales. The cost to Revell was a bargain, but Whipple and

McCulloch liked it too. They needed the up-front money to plow into preparing their car for the race season, and they (and their other corporate sponsors) just liked the idea that hundreds of thousands of race fans would have a model of their car sitting on a shelf at home.

Cars like Ed McCulloch's Revellution displayed the Revell name at drag strips across the country. *H-1447*

In that initial 1972 season Gene Snow's "Snow Man" joined the Whipple & McCulloch "Revellution" as the first of the large scale funny cars. Revell renewed its old ties with Tony Nancy by issuing a 1/16 scale model of his "Wynn's Sizzler" front-engine rail dragster, and paired it with the "California Charger" rail of Keeling & Clayton. Jim Liberman, the biggest racer on the East Coast, wanted in on the action too; so Revell molded a copy of Zipp's 1/25 scale Camaro funny car in blue plastic and put a "Jungle Jim" decal on the side to turn it into a model of Liberman's car. Thus began a series of 1/25 scale funny cars and rail dragsters that paralleled the larger scale models.

From there, Ernst and Fisher went out looking for other drivers to sign-up for the Revell Race Team. Mickey Thompson, another old-timer with modeling ties to Revell, signed up to have a model made of his Pontiac Grand Am "Revelleader." Fisher went to lunch with Liberman and dis-

The big 1/16 scale model of Gene Snow's Snowman funny car showed off the paint scheme designed by Revell's art department for the real car. *H-1481*

It is no wonder why Jungle Jim Liberman's 1/25 scale Camaro led all Revell cars in sales. *H-1449*

cussed plans for a new large scale Camaro with new body art created by Dave Deal depicting wild "Jungle Jim" swinging from a vine. By then the drag racing community caught on to what was happening, and owners started telephoning Revell asking to get in on the action. Eventually twenty-two racers joined the Revell team. Revell's marketing department developed press kits for Team members that promoted both the real cars and their small plastic counterparts.

Don "Super Shoe" Schumacher's 1/25 scale '74 Vega funny car. *H-1453*

Ultimately "Big Daddy" Don Garlits also came on board. Dave Fisher stayed late one night after a drag race and signed the contract with Garlits while they sat in his pickup in a deserted parking lot. Garlits changed the real drag racing world—and Revell's miniature mirror image of it—with his revolutionary rear-engine rail. After nearly losing a foot when the clutch of his conventional front-engine machine exploded, Garlits put his time in the hospital to good use designing a rear-engine dragster. Revell immediately issued a model of a rail with this new configuration and retired its front-engine dragster when the whole competitive world followed Garlits to rear-mounted power plants.

Don Garlits and his Swamp Rat rail. *H-1460*

At the peak of drag race hysteria in 1974-1975, Revell sold a million dollars worth of these specialty car kits a year. Promotions director Howard Rieder feared Revell had oversold the market in dragster models. "We pushed it too far." Either because of that or just because nothing lasts forever, by 1979 the funny car/dragster craze had passed. Not a single

quarter-miler remained in the catalog. While it lasted (and drag races don't last much longer than a thunderclap) Revell sold almost one million 1/16 scale models and more than three million units in 1/25 scale. It was quite a ride.

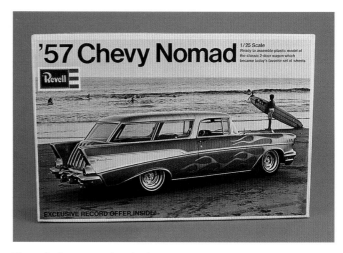

Through the magic of trick photography, the chrome reverse wheels on Bob Paeth's Nash Rambler appear on the '57 Nomad. *H-1260*

All of the dragster kits featured photographs of the real cars on their packaging, and during the 1970s Revell began using photographs of built models on its other kit boxes, rather than the traditional box art paintings. The whole industry followed this trend. Marketing departments thought that photographs projected a cleaner, more up-to-date product image. Don Ernst believed photos of well-built models showed kids what they could do with the kit. Also, since the practice of sending factory-built display models to hobby shops had declined, the kit box itself could now serve as a point-of-purchase display of the finished model. Art department personnel enjoyed photographing the built models in diorama settings to create a sense of movement and life. Royle Glaser and other old-timers regretted the switch a little bit since a dramatic box art painting lent an air of romance to a model kit.

Ernst still had another trick left in the race car market. He knew that one of the biggest expenses of producing a funny car kit was the decal sheet—it actually cost more than the plastic that went into the model. Much of the decal sheet consisted of assorted automotive product company trademarks. The sides of Revell's car models amounted to free advertising billboards for speed equipment companies. Why not ask them to pay for the privilege of appearing on Revell's models and model kit boxes? So Ernst went to the auto equipment companies—like Goodyear—and asked them for the small sum of $1,200 per million decal sheets for the exclusive right to appear on Revell's models. In the case of Goodyear, for example, Revell promised not to use the name of any other tire company. Ernst found that twenty-six companies were quite happy to make this deal. Thus Ernst developed a generic decal sheet that could be dropped into any Revell car kit at virtually no cost to Revell.

Promotion Director Howard Rieder had his own idea for sparking interest in Revell's models: Why not give the Master Modelers Club another try? After all, the club provided Revell a link to its best customers and was a way to "pre-sell" each new Revell kit before it even reached stores. The trick to success this time around was putting all club information on a computer. Revell's new, almost-room-size computer had a storage capacity totaling an impressive 32K! It needed all of it to keep up with the quarter-million members of the club.

In its second incarnation the club retained the usual membership card and certificate, but now kids also received an iron-on T-shirt emblem, a small assortment of plastic tools, and a new magazine, *Get It Together*. People from various departments contributed to the magazine's contents—how to built it essays, answers to questions sent in by readers, and even the serialized adventures of Revell's ace master modeler Delmo Kitsalp ("plastic" spelled backwards—sort of) in his never-ending battle with that other model company's evil champion Monty Graham. Club members could see their names printed in the magazine as they built more models and rose in the "proficiency levels." Photos of members with their model creations also appeared. Of course, there were profiles of new Revell kit releases to look for in your neighborhood hobby shop.

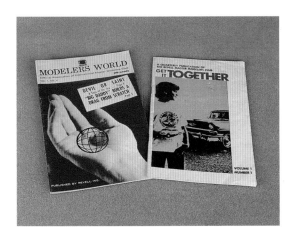

The Master Modelers Club appeared first in the 1960s and then again in the 1970s. Each time it had a magazine for members.

The second Master Modelers Club came to an end in the late 1970s as the cost of keeping it going continued to rise. Promotions director Rieder considered it worth the cost—marking it down as an advertising expense, but upper management decided otherwise. It took a while for the club to wind down because old membership blanks remained in kit boxes on store shelves for several more years.

By the 1970s Americans were becoming aware of environmental problems, and in 1973 these concerns forced themselves on the national consciousness when an oil shortage threatened to drag the country to a halt. As drivers lined up at their neighborhood service stations to wait for a chance to buy gas, shock waves rippled through the hobby industry since plastic, a petrochemical product,

seemed to be next in line for shortages. The price of plastic tripled and availability became a worry as industrial plastic users hoarded supplies. Royle Glaser devoted a good deal of time to worrying about the problem: "I was terrified we'd go out of business." As she mulled-over the predicament, a solution came to her dramatically one night in a dream. It was a great relief. The next morning, in the cold light of day, she reconsidered her revelation of the night before: replacing plastic in the molding machines with molten chocolate did not seem like such an inspired idea after all! As it developed, the price of plastic stabilized after a few months and the scare blew over.

Revell attempted to take advantage of the growing interest in environmental issues by teaming-up with the World Wildlife Fund to originate a set of snap-together construction kits of threatened animals like the California Condor, Mountain Gorilla, and Komodo Dragon. Part of the profits from sales of the models would go to the World Wildlife Fund. Royle's sister, Gale Ebert, became the champion of Revell's Endangered Species series. Ebert, Dave Fisher, and sculptor Chris Mattson went on safari to the San Diego Wild Animal Park and Los Angeles Museum of Natural History to take photographs and make sketches. Each animal figure employed moving parts, snap-together construction, and a landscaped base with a name plate giving some basic details

The Endangered White Rhino had snap-together parts that moved. *H-700*

about the rare beast. It seemed likely that young kids would go for these nifty wild things, but the kits suffered a quick exit from the catalog due to modest sales. Like all figure kits, they required delicate detail painting to make them look realistic, and most kids couldn't handle that.

One of the world's pioneer environmentalists was Jacques Cousteau, whose TV show "The Undersea World" was a fixture on America's television screens. Popular folk singer John Denver had just recorded a hit song about Cousteau's oceanic research ship the *Calypso*. Dave Fisher originated the idea of making a model of the *Calypso*.

Four preliminary "comps" were done for the Me-262 before Leynnwood eventually did the "final" for the 1971 issue. *H-218*

Cousteau's son Philippe lived nearby at Marina del Ray, and Fisher approached him about the possibility of a model that might be a fund-raiser for Cousteau's conservation society. Philippe replied that the Cousteau Society did need financial support, but that a "toy" would not be dignified enough for association with the Cousteau name.

Undeterred, Fisher arranged for a breakfast meeting, with Royle Glaser and Jacques Cousteau joining the negotiations. Fisher explained to the elder Cousteau that Revell's model would be educational and would include a booklet explaining the mission of the Cousteau Society. This meeting broke the log jam, and Cousteau signed a contract agreeing to furnish the information necessary to make models of his

Jacques Cousteau's *Calypso* was just the sort of non-military, educational kit Revell aspired to make. *H-575*

To cash in on the movie *The Great Waldo Pepper*, Revell issued its 1/28 scale Sopwith Camel with new packaging. *H-910*

ship and amphibian airplane. Mrs. Glaser came away from the meeting impressed with both the handsome Philippe and charismatic Jacques. "I've fallen in love with Jacques Cousteau," she announced to the staff back in Venice. "He's brilliant and charming."

Fisher flew off to Monaco and Toulon, where he visited Cousteau's museums, and then to Greece to measure and photograph the *Calypso*. The resulting model incorporated lots of nifty details like Cousteau's two-man diving saucer, a helicopter, a Zodiac boat, and a shark cage with two tiger sharks. The *Calypso* flying boat was a modification of the PBY model, molded in white plastic with Cousteau Society

Revell turned its PBY model into
Philippe Cousteau's amphibian. *H-576*

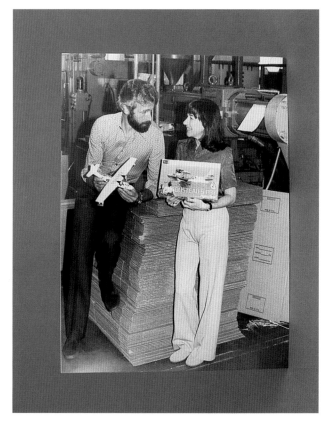

Philippe Cousteau and Royle Glaser pose with the
model of the aircraft in which Philippe would die.

Fisher ran the idea past Royle Glaser, and she thought the concept totally lacked excitement. Civilian aircraft were poor sellers; besides, there was nothing to a blimp model. It was just a big cigar-shaped object. "It's nothing," she told Fisher. But Fisher would not be deterred. He thought about the proposition some more; then came up with an inspiration: When the blimp cruised the evening skies of Southern California, it spelled out messages in twinkling lights on its broad silhouette. Fisher went back to Glaser with the idea of an electrified model that allowed people to create their own messages on its side. Now she was intrigued. A simple, toy-like gadget went against Revell's whole philosophy of realistic, accurate models, but Revell had always looked for products to extend its range beyond model kits. "That's terrific," she told Fisher and sent him back to see if the concept could become a practical product.

The store display for the Goodyear Blimp featured
a revolving, lighted message about the kit. *H-999*

decals. Royle Glaser thought the pair of models made a great product idea, but, like most civilian planes and ships, it turned out that they didn't sell well. Then Philippe Cousteau died in a crash landing of the *Calypso* aircraft, and Revell decided to pull the plane model from the market.

Over the years Revell and Goodyear Tires had developed a good working relationship. Most of Revell's car models rolled on vinyl tires with the Goodyear name imprinted on them. Revell's head of product planning, Dave Fisher, frequently crossed paths with Goodyear's public relations director and somehow the notion of a Goodyear blimp model popped up. It was a natural idea since Revell made models of things that flew, and the Goodyear blimp was a familiar sight in the Los Angeles sky.

The R & D team went to work on the crucial lighting system, and Revell hired an outside research house to tackle other aspects of the problem. Finally, the idea of a lighted drum that rotated on the axis of the blimp emerged, and from there R & D man Don Willis constructed a workable system. Fellow R & D worker Lon Cooper sculpted a simple model without going through the normal model shop/engineering process. Customers assembling the model and its inner workings would need a little patience and skill, but most people would find it pretty simple. The hull of the blimp folded open to expose the rotating cylinder. Anyone with a modicum of creativity could spell out messages with colored pens on sheets of paper that wrapped around the cylinder and clamped into place. Two D batteries powered the cylinder's motor and lit the flashlight bulb inside.

Leynnwood's action-packed cover for the F4U Corsair. H-278

Revell chose to produce the Grumman Wildcat, rather than the more common Hellcat. H-299

The Hughes OH-6 Cayuse in both military and civilian colors. H-146, H-161

Jack Leynnwood created a scene of air combat over Vietnam for the MiG 21. H-267

of them had been steady sellers for years. The best known of the Renwal models were the Visible Man, Visible Woman, and the Visible V-8 Engine.

Fisher and Don Ernst carried the prototype to a formal meeting of Goodyear's board of directors, who totally embraced the idea. Goodyear agreed to pay for tooling-up the blimp in exchange for the exclusive right to market the model in Goodyear retail stores during 1976. The next year Revell showed it at the HIAA show in Dallas, Texas, with the Goodyear Blimp itself on hand to give rides to hobby industry conventioneers. It was the hit of the show and became Revell's all-time best selling item for a one-year period. However, the blimp suffered the usual toy-syndrome drop-off of sales in succeeding years, but it was profitable and fun while it lasted.

In 1975 Revell decided to purchase the mold inventory of Renwal Products when it went out of the model business. Royle Glaser justified the purchase as an inexpensive way to acquire more production tooling and an easy way to extend Revell's product line and thus strengthen its domination of the model field. Although the molds and the models that came out of them were not up to Revell's standards, some

About that same time, America's aerospace program commenced Space Shuttle flights, and Revell again brought out a model to document an historic event, and, of course, to capitalize on the public's interest in the new endeavor. The shuttle *Enterprise* model featured an opening cargo bay

The 1/72 scale Corsair II. *H-114*

The clipper ship *Stag Hound*. *H-345*

The F-111 could alter the sweep of its wings, and so could Revell's model. *H-208*

In the '70s Revell paired-up some 1/72 plane kits as "Fighting Deuces." The P-47 and Ki-61 Hein. *H-224*

As the Navy brought out new ships like the jet powered gunboat *Tacoma*, Revell continued to make models of them and Leynnwood kept on painting fabulous box art. *H-432*

The *Coral Sea* transports the imagination into a tranquil sunset. *H-374*

Leynnwood box art for the 1/720 scale *Enterprise*. *H-489*

The English Man O' War looks like it sailed
right off a Hollywood swashbuckler. *H-397*

The USS *Forrest Sherman. H-459*

The assault ship *Tarawa* was one of the
few new ship models of the 1970s. *H-406*

The Space Shuttle with its 747 mother ship is one of the
last paintings Jack Leynnwood did for Revell. *H-177*

The *Growler* fleet submarine is a big, twenty-one inch long model. *H-436*

The Apollo-Soyuz came with box graphics and instructions in both English and Russian. *H-1800*

door and movable robot arm. If a space enthusiast wanted the complete Space Shuttle story, he could buy the *Enterprise* with launch boosters kit and the *Enterprise* with the Boeing 747 that flew it from its landing base in California back to Cape Kennedy. It turned out that the Revell Space Shuttle would become a permanent fixture on store shelves for the next two decades and more.

The historic linkup of the American Apollo capsule with the Soviet Soyuz furnished another opportunity for a model that would capture a moment in history. When the Soviets put the Soyuz on display in Montreal's Expo, Royle Glaser and a staffer hurried to Canada and took all the photographs needed for an accurate rendition of the space vehicle. To play up the international cooperation aspect, Revell put the names of the spacecraft in both English and Russian on the box—and also printed the instruction sheet in both languages. It hired a UCLA language professor to do the translation. Shortly after the kit's release, Revell presented several cartons of

the Apollo-Soyuz model to a delegation of visiting Soviets. When the Russians opened a box and read the instructions, they let out a hearty laugh, explaining that the Russian idiom used in the instructions was as old as Shakespeare's English! They promised to send a carton of caviar in payment for the kits, but it never arrived.

Revell had a chance to enter the realm of space fantasy at the time as well. 20th Century Fox Films offered Revell the rights to make models based on the forthcoming movie *Star Wars*. Howard Rieder thought this a great idea since it might give Revell a product every hobby shop and store would want, and thus Revell would have leverage to obtain more favorable treatment from its marketing outlets. However, the proposal was rejected. MPC later brought out models from the movie.

One of the first Opel GTs imported into America went to the Revell plant to be copied for a model. *H-1248*

The Austin-Healey 100 in 1/32 scale. *H-1256*

In the 1970s Revell brought back its 1/32 scale snap-together cars in contemporary packaging. *H-1132*

Revell had never gotten into the popular 1/48 scale until the mid-1970s. The F-104 made a great subject in this size. *H-236*

Revell added a "Memphis Belle" B-17F in 1/48 scale to go along with its best-selling 1/72 rendition. *H-197*

Freddie Laker made big news for a while with his low cost DC-10 flights between London and New York. *H-271*

When the English company Frog went out of business, Revell purchased a few of their German subjects. Revell, Germany, packaged the kit without swastika markings, while Revell, US, had no legal obstacles to authentic markings. *H-96*

As sales of its funny cars and rail dragsters declined in the late 1970s, Revell began searching for another line of model cars to take up the slack. It hit upon pickup trucks and vans—a natural choice since America was going through a *Smokey and the Bandit* love affair with rough, rugged trucks and the CB radios that were a signature item of equipment with the good ol' boys. Trucks and vans also seemed like an item that would have good sales appeal in big Wal-Mart stores where the volume market in model kits now centered. Plus, pickups are easy to customize into a variety of kits, and vans have billboard-size sides that are ideal for distinctive decals.

John Buttera came to Revell and asked them to make models of his custom cars like the Ford T. *H-1331*

When a Chevy Scottsdale pickup truck model received the OK for development, the marketing and R & D boys started thinking of variations on the basic model and ways it might be livened-up a bit. Jimmy Carter of Plains, Georgia,

had just been elected president, and somebody saw a magazine picture of the president's brother Billy in front of his red-neck-rustic gas station. This sparked some brainstorming that led to the brilliant idea of customizing a real Scottsdale, giving it to the nation's number one bubba, and then making a model of "Billy Carter's Pick-Up."

Revell used its Chevy 20 Van mold to make a hypothetical Charlie's Angels van as well as a model of the real California Cruiser given away as grand prize in Revell's annual sweepstakes. *H-1397*

Vice President of Advertising Howard Rieder telephoned the White House—which referred him to Plains—which sent him to Billy Carter's agent in Nashville, Tennessee. They struck a deal promising the younger Mr. Carter a cash advance, a royalty on sales, and a new pickup truck. Revell worked with the R. V. I. Customizing shop in Torrance to devise a vehicle tricked-up to South Georgia standards. The truck then went to the Venice plant to be copied and made into a model: the "Redneck Power Pick-Up." It had a wooden front bumper, a CB radio, chrome 8-spoke wheels, a case of "soft drinks" in back, and the Revell logo on the side.

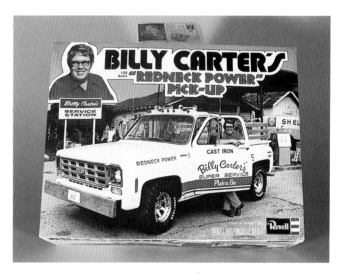

Billy Carter's Pick-Up was a gift from Revell to the President's brother. *H-1385*

Billy and his wife flew out to California to meet Revell's executives and have his picture taken with the pickup for publicity. Royle Glaser welcomed him to the plant and took him on a tour of the building. Workers on the assembly line recognized him, and the whole shop floor immediately shut

Royle Glaser and Billy Carter ink the contract for the Redneck Power Pick-up.

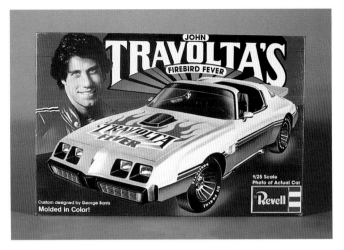

Custom car designer George Barris created John Travolta's Firebird. *H-1387*

down. Glaser, a thoroughly West Coast person, stood dumbfounded. "He was like a pop star!" Everybody wanted to shake his hand or get an autograph. A few months later at the hobby convention in Dallas the reaction was the same. Billy, nattily dressed in a leisure suit, presided over hand-shaking, autograph-signing sessions in the Revell display parlor until he would get tired and go to his room to recuperate. After the convention, Howard Rieder took the truck east by rail and delivered it to Plains. Billy gratefully accepted the pickup and gave Rieder an autographed can of Billy Beer in exchange.

an ambulance. The basic concept involved taking an existing model in the line, placing it on a large base that held batteries and electronic components, and giving the package "lights and sound action." The product had potential, but assembly of the electronics package proved to be too much of a challenge for the casual shopper. Only mechanically-minded hobbyists who enjoyed the challenge of wiring the system bought the models. The "models of the future" turned out to be a dead end.

Revell's art staff went wild with the graphics for the Midnight Cowboy Wrecker. *H-1383*

To compete with computer games Revell made "Electronic Action" kits such as the Paramedic Van. *H-800*

Revell's next ambitious line of models attempted to build on the success of the Goodyear Blimp. These were the "Electronic Action" kits, advertised as "models of the future," which would compete with the new computer games for kids' attention. Lon Cooper, who had done the Goodyear Blimp, oversaw development of these kits. There was a rescue helicopter, a police bike, a fighter plane, and

Chapter 7 –
The Tradition Continues

In 1976 Revell's total sales hit their highest level ever in dollar terms. Revenues reached thirty-four million, and the company declared: "Revell is now in the strongest financial position in its thirty-five year history." The sale of model kits in the United States outpaced sales growth in Europe for the first time in a while, and the company paid off some of its long-term debt. On the downside, increased costs of doing business ate into bottom-line profits considerably, but things still looked pretty good for the future.

In that same year a new product appeared in American stores: an electronic device that hooked up to TV sets and allowed youngsters to play games on their television screens. It was another straw in the wind signaling changes that threatened the model kit industry. Back in the 1950s model building had been one of the few diversions that youngsters could choose from to occupy their time at home. By the 1970s things had changed, and young people had more options available to absorb their interest. Over the years Revell's marketing department kept a careful running tab on what America's kids were doing, and long-term developments raised red warning flags. Indeed, as the baby boom of the 1940s and '50s subsided, the cohort of model-building

twelve-year-olds dwindled. As Royle Glaser explained: "We watched our charts, and the trends were down. We could see possible extinction coming."

The store display for the Pirate Ghost Ship shows the old *Golden Hind* model in black plastic with glow-in-the-dark paint. *H-519*

The *Great Eastern* first appeared in 1963 with John Steel box art. This is Leynnwood's rendition for the 1980 reissue. *H-393*

Revell's sales of model kits declined steadily during the late 1970s. Profit margins, which had always been thin, were squeezed by increasing costs of packaging and shipping. Even when Revell opened a mold making plant in Hong Kong, the costs of developing new tooling remained sky high. For a while the company maintained profits, and even increase them, by raising the price of kits. However, breaking the traditional $3.00 price barrier on standard kits changed the dynamics of the model kit market, making it harder for the typical kid to afford a new kit out of his weekly spending money.

At the same time, in the front office of Revell, Royle Glaser strained under the burden of leading Revell through the growing thicket of obstacles. "I was just tired of fighting all the dragons." She and the board of directors began quietly discussing the possibility of selling out to a larger, more financially robust company. The ideal partner would have a synergy with plastic models, but be outside the hobby industry. CBS Television explored the possibility of acquisition, but Revell judged its purchase offer too low.

Leynnwood's updated art for the four-stacker destroyer never reached the public because the kit was not reissued.

Jack Leynnwood's 1980s painting of the Firefighter boat was one of the last he did for Revell.

The F-16 continued Revell's tradition of bringing out models of the latest aircraft. *H-222*

Just then a suitor came calling on Revell. The Rothchild Group of Strasbourg, France, which owned the toy company handling distribution of Revell's kits in France, contacted Revell. Rothchild explained that it wanted to expand its toy and game operations into the United States and Germany, thus Revell seemed to them a desirable acquisition. Royle Glaser thought this union would work to the benefit of both companies, and a great weight lifted from her shoulders. Suddenly she felt the excitement of a challenging new enterprise. In March 1979, the merger of Revell, Inc. with Compagnie General du Jouet was announced, and in August the buyout reached its conclusion. A transition team of French executives moved into the offices in Venice, and Glaser assumed the new position of vice chair of the board with a three year contract.

At first all of Revell's existing executives and staff retained their positions; but, as is usually the case when one company acquires another, the new French managers soon decided to restructure Revell. Under the guiding concept of the new organization, employees within the Venice plant were let go and outside vendors were hired to perform the same tasks. This reduced the costs of salaries and overhead inside the company. However, Revell lost a very dedicated team of experienced specialists who knew their assignments and could flexibly work to complete the complicated tasks of bringing the various components of Revell's products together and then marketing them to the world. Many old-time Revell employees who had played important roles for years received pink slips in 1980. Most landed good positions with new companies, but they departed with a tremendous sense of loss. None found a place with quite the same atmosphere as Revell—and Revell was never the same company again.

In 1982 Royle Glaser reluctantly departed the company her husband had founded forty-one years earlier. Before going, she visited Revell's plants in England and Germany to bid farewell to some old friends. The Hobby Industry Association honored her by making her a lifetime member. Then she departed to embark on a new life with her husband of two years, Michael Freund, and to enjoy her family in retirement.

The Rothchild Group's plans for Revell never matured as envisioned, and in September 1986, they sold the company to Odyssey Partners of New York, which also acquired Monogram Models at the same time with the intent of consolidating the two companies. Odyssey announced that Revell's operations would move to Monogram's location in Illinois.

When the process of packing and moving Revell's assets began, many old-time Revell employees returned to the plant on Glencoe Boulevard for one last, sentimental walk around the familiar halls. Some took photographs of their old work stations and picked up a souvenir or two for keepsakes. Ed Roth remembered it as a very sad time. He wandered through the rapidly-emptying building, and somebody gave

Donald R. Shepherd
Managing Director
Revell (Great Britain) Ltd.

Royle G. Lasky
President and Chairwoman of the Board

H. G. Schöneberg
Managing Director
Revell Plastics G.m.b.H.
(West Germany)

Nuremberg Toy Fair - 1977

Directors of the three Revells: Donald Shepherd, Great Britain; Royle Glaser, US; Heinz-Georg Schöneberg, West Germany.

him a couple of old photographs once used to publicize his "Big Daddy" monster cars.

As one epoch in Revell's history closed, another with great potential opened. Two of the greatest names in the hobby industry—Revell and Monogram—now resided under the same roof. In fact, Aurora Plastics—the third renowned name in modeling—also rested with the same owners since Monogram had purchased Aurora's assets in 1977. As a result of separate corporate maneuvers, the three finest model companies in America—in the world—now merged into one force. Together over the previous four decades they had accumulated a collection of molds for nearly three-thousand different models. Each year Revell and Monogram combined sold far more model kits than all the other model companies in the United States put together, and they likewise led the whole world. In 1991 Revell closed its plant in Great Britain and consolidated European operations in Germany.

As world history continued to roll onward, Revell and Monogram continued to manufacture history in miniature. During the Gulf War of 1991-1992, America's youngsters flocked to Toys-R-Us and Wal-Mart to purchase Humvees and F-18s with the same enthusiasm that their fathers had purchased Jeeps and F-84s at Woolworth. When the Air Force took the wraps off the F-117 Stealth Fighter, Revell quickly put models of it into boys' bedrooms across America.

The accuracy and detail of these contemporary kits surpasses anything produced in the past.

During the Gulf War the venerable battleship USS *Missouri* sailed into battle once again, while Revell's first original model, the *Missouri*, continued to hold its place in the Revell catalog along with a scattering of other classic models from the past. In fact, in 1993 Revell-Monogram dramatically tipped its corporate hat to the past with the "Selected Subjects" series of vintage model kits packaged in facsimile reproductions of their original boxes. Ed Roth even came back with reissues of his classic 1960s cars, as well as a brand new Beatnik Bandit II. (When Roth died in the spring of 2001, Revell reissued the Rat Fink kit with a Roth/Revell cloth patch included.)

In December 1994, Revell-Monogram agreed to a merger with Hallmark Cards, Inc. Under the purchase agreement Revell-Monogram became a part of Binney-Smith, the division of Hallmark that makes Crayola crayons. This marriage worked well for the rest of the decade; then in the fall of 2001 Revell-Monogram and its sister company Revell AG of Germany were purchased by Alpha International of Cedar Rapids, Iowa. Alpha is the manufacturer of Gearbox and Empire brand toys and collectibles. When the announced purchase was made, Alpha's spokesperson declared, "It will be business as usual" for Revell-Monogram. In other words, Revell-Monogram expected to maintain its position of leadership in the world of plastic modeling.

The beginning of a new century in 2001 marked the end of Revell's first fifty years of model making—as well as the launching of a new era of recording history in plastic.

In 1998 Revell-Monogram issued Frankenstein's monster. The model had originally been developed by Aurora Plastics; then the mold was purchased by Monogram, and finally it was reissued under the Revell trademark.

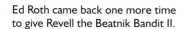

Ed Roth came back one more time to give Revell the Beatnik Bandit II.

Revell Kits You Never Saw

In the 1950s Richard Kishady painted preliminary art work and did the package design for three model kits that Revell chose not to release.

Revell considered bringing out its Bell P-39 in white plastic as a Soviet fighter; however, Lew Glaser thought the white/red color combination looked too much like a toy and killed the kit.

The Martin B-57 would have made a striking model in red plastic.

The Honest John missile could have been mounted on the back of the M-35 Truck, but instead Revell chose to mate a LaCrosse missile with the M-35 (H-1816) and brought out the Honest John on the Kenworth Truck (H-1821).

Selected Bibliography

"Age 25 and Growing," *Toys and Novelties* (January 1, 1967), pp. 42-47.

Boyle, Hal, "Tycoon of the Toy Industry," (AP press release), January 11, 1954.

Burns, John. *Collectors Value Guide for Scale Model Plastic Kits.* Edmond, Oklahoma: John Burns, 1999.

Craft, Model, Hobby Industry. This is the trade journal of the hobby and craft industry.

"From Kitchen to Boardroom," *Forbes* (January 15, 1976), p. 50.

"From Toys to Hobbies," *Business Week* (January 28, 1956), p. 56-58.

Graham, Thomas. *Greenberg's Guide to Aurora Model Kits.* Waukesha, Wisconsin: Kalmbach Books, 1998.

Graham, Thomas. *Aurora Model Kits,* Atglen, Pennsylvania: Schiffer Publishing Ltd, 2004.

Hamilton, Andrew. "The Prince of Put-It-Together," *Coronet* (April 1957), pp. 160-68.

Hansen, Brad. *W. W. I in Plastic.* Clovis, California: Brad Hansen, 1986.

Hardwick, Kay. "California in the Toy Picture," *Playthings* (September 1950), p. 152.

"Hobby Model Kit King," *Fortune* (November 1954), p. 179.

"How Many Plastic Kits?" *Craft, Model, Hobby Industry* (February 1958), p. 100-01.

International Plastic Modelers' Society Journal. This is the journal of the IPMS, an organization of model hobbyists.

Jesse, Terry. *Hot Rod Model Kits.* Osceola, Wisconsin: MBI Publishing, 2000.

Playthings. The is the trade journal of the US toy industry.

"Revell, Inc.—The Big Business of Little Models," *Craft, Model, Hobby Industry* (April 1968), p. 35.

Reder, Robert. *Brief History of Monogram Models, Inc.* Robert Reder, 2000.

Roth, Ed and Howie Kusten. *Confessions of a Rat Fink.* New York: Pharos Books, 1992.

Scale Modeler. This magazine began publishing in January 1965 and was the country's only general-interest commercial model magazine through the 1960s and 1970s.

"What to do When Profits Refuse to Grow," *Business Week* (February 13, 1978), pp. 102-03.

The Model Kits Index

Compiling an index of Revell kits is a daunting task since Revell issued so many models and usually changed the kit identification number each time it reissued a model. To make this compendium more manageable, the kits are divided into three groups according to the decade in which they were originally issued: 1950s, 1960s, and 1970s. They are then sorted into subject categories. The car and aircraft models are also subdivided into standard scale groupings.

The first issue of each kit will have a list of all subsequent reissues made from the original mold, even if the mold was modified and the model issued under a different name. The dates given for each kit are those years that the model appeared in the Revell annual sales catalogs.

Kits originated from the mid-1950s to 1960 had the marking "Use Revell Type 'S' Cement." These highly collectible kits are identified in this index with the letter "S." Subsequent issues without the "S" are not as valuable.

During 1979 Revell marketed some of its older models under the "Advent" label as low-cost kits for sale through department stores and mass retail outlets.

In the 1990s Revell-Monogram reissued many old kits in facsimile boxes in the "Selected Subjects Program." These kits can be distinguished from original issues by the added 1990s copyright dates on their side panels.

This model kit guide is limited in its scope to just those issues made by Revell of the United States between the years 1951 and 1979. The molds used to manufacture these kits have been used since 1979 to make additional issues, and they were also employed to create a myriad of issues by Revell's foreign branches and agents. This guide, however, does provide a solid foundation for the collector wishing to delve further into the arcane universe of Revell kits.

The standard resource for kit collectors covering all model companies is John Burns, *Collectors Value Guide*. Bill Coulter and Bob Shelton, *Directory of Model Car Kits* provides a price guide for automotive kits. For this book Dean Sills of Dean's Hobby Stop furnished kit values from the perspective of a major dealer in vintage model kits.

The value of an unbuilt plastic model kit is dependent on a variety of things, but chiefly price is a function of two factors: the rarity of the kit and demand for the kit from collectors. Naturally, mint kits in factory sealed boxes are most highly valued, and any departures from mint condition decreases value. The prices in this guide are for mint condition kits. Values listed in any guide, of course, can only approximate the prices any given buyer or seller may encounter in the marketplace.

H-197 Sopwith Camel, 1959-64, 1/28, $30-50.

H-245 Lockheed Super G Constellation "S", 1957-59, 1/128, $90-110. H-279 Lockhead WV-2 Warning Star "S" 1958-60, 1/128, $60-80.

H-252 Convair B-58 Hustler "S", 1958-61, 1/94, $50-70.

H-255 Lockheed Electra American, 1950s, 1/115, $100-120.

H-256 Spad XIII "S", 1957-64, 1/27, $40-50.

H-257 Douglas DC-7c Pan Am Airport Scene, 1955, 1/122, $500-700.

H-259 Douglas X-3 Stiletto "S", 1957-59, 1/65, $40-50.

H-270 Fokker Dr-1 "S", 1957-64, 1/27, $40-50.

H-296 Yak-25 Flashlight "S", 1958-61, 1/50, $50-70.

H-282 Convair F-102A Delta Dagger "S",
1958-59, 1/49, $250-270.

H-299 A4D Skyhawk with Bullpups "S",
1959-60, 1/50, $40-60.

G-195 Man Into Space, 1959, $400-450.

G-243 Dawn Patrol "S", 1956, $450-500.

G-268 Supersonic Jets "S", 1957, $450-500.

H-1808 Bendix Navy Talos "S", 1958-60, 1/40, $60-80.

H-1800 XSL-01 Manned spaceship "S",
1958-59, 1/96, $350-370.

H-1801 Northrop Air Force SM-62 Snark "S", 1958-60, 1/81, $40-50.

H-1823 Douglas Thor/Thor-Able "S",
1959-65, 1/110, $200-220.

H-303 USS Nautilus, 1953-54, 1/305, $150-170.

H-1828 Convair Space Shuttlecraft "S",
1959-65, 1/150, $200-220.

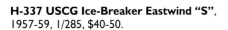

H-337 USCG Ice-Breaker Eastwind "S",
1957-59, 1/285, $40-50.

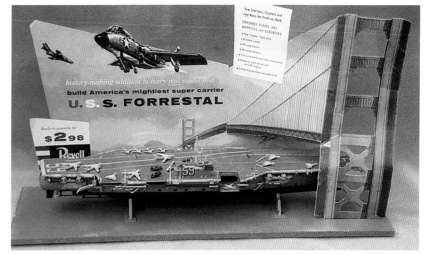

H-339 USS Forrestal "S", 1957-80, 1/542, $60-80.

H-336 Santa Maria "S", 1957-71, 1/90, $20-60.

H-364 Cutty Sark "S", 1959-63, 1/96, $60-120.

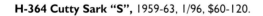

HNF-6 Admiral's Fleet, 1954, $500-600.

H-522 M4A1 Sherman Tank "S", 1956-59, 1/40, $80-100.

H-535 M2 155mm Long Range Cannon "S",
1958-59, 1/40, $80-100.

H-538 Russian T-34 "S", 1958-60, 1/40, $70-90.

Revell-AMT 1955-1956 Modern Cars: the H-1200
through H-1204 kits, $70-90 each.

H-540 M-56 Self-Propelled Gun "S", 1958-60, 1/40, $70-90.

Revell-AMT 1955-1956 Modern Cars: the H-1200-6 through H-1204-6 kits, $70-90 each.

H-1203 1955 Buick Riviera "S", 1955, 1/32, $70-90.

H-1211-6 Autorama Gift Set, 1956, 1/32, $500-600.

H-1210 Lincoln Futura, 1956-60, 1/27, $150-175.

H-1213 Pontiac Club de Mer, 1957-62, 1/25, $150-175.

H-1402 White Gas Truck "S", 1956-57, 1/48, $60-80.

H-1403 Kenworth Bekins Van "S", 1956-57, 1/48, $200-250.

H-606 Antique Pistol Collection, 1954, 1/1, $150-200.

H-1903 Sassy the Kitten "S", 1959-62, 1/1, $75-100.

Z-2000 The Cat in the Hat, 1959-61, $125-150.

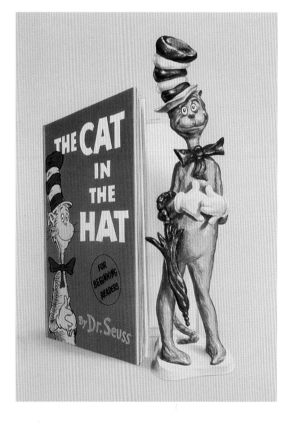

T-9002 Trackside Building Group, $30-40.

H-151 F9F-8 Cougar, 1960-63, 1/52, $30-35.

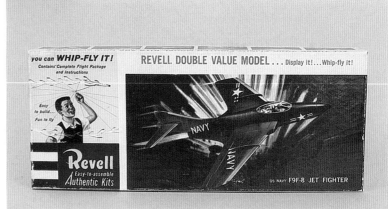

H-251 Lockheed F-104 Starfighter "S",
1957-58, 1/64, $30-40.

**H-241 A3D Skywarrior
"S",** 1/84, $30-40.

H-262 Boeing SST Prototype, 1967-70, 1/200, $75-100.
H-263 SST Pan Am Clipper, 1969-72, 1/200, $75-100.

G-293 3 WW I Dogfighters, 1968-70, 1/28, $100-120.

H-111 Martin B-26B Marauder "Flak Bait", 1966-69, 1/72, $10-15.

H-202 Avro "Dam Buster" Lancaster, 1964-68, 1/72, $20-30.

H-203 Consolidated B-24D "Blue Streak",
1964-79, 1/72, $15-25.

H-282 Supermarine Spitfire MK-I,
1967-70, 72-76, 1/32, $15-20.

H-287 Bell AH-1G Huey Cobra, 1967-80, 1/32, $15-20.

H-295 North American P-51B "Shangri-La",
1969-79, 1/32, $25-30.

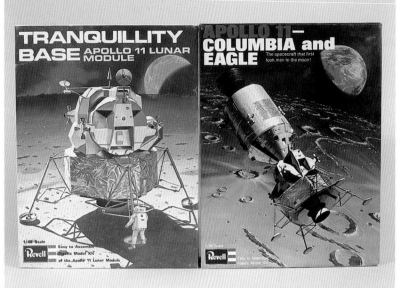

H-1861 Tranquility Base and Lunar Module, 1969-73, 1/48, $25-30. H-1862 Apollo II columbia and Eagle, 1969-73, 1/96, $40-50.

H-323 McHale's Navy PT-73, 1965-69, 1/72, $70-90.

H-334 SS Argentina, 1962-65, 1/400, $40-50. H-335 SS Dr. Lykes, 1962-65, 1/400, $40-50.

H-379 USS Burton Island, 1960-65, 1/292, $20-30.

H-427 USS Aaron Ward,
1962-67, 1/240, $30-40

H-324 Golden Hind with sails, 1965-71, 1/96, $20-30.

H-953 Morris 1000 Traveller, 1963, 1/46, $20-30.

H-957 Volkswagen Karman-Ghia, 1963, 1/41, $20-30.

H-958 Jaguar Mk II, 1963, 1/46, $20-30.

H-1274 Road Agent, 1964-68, 1/25, $175-200.

H-1282 Outlaw, 1962-68, 1/25, $60-80.

H-1286 Tweedy-Pie, 1963-66, 1/25, $180-200.

H-1302 Mother's Worry, 1963-65, 1/25, $100-120.

H-1303 Drag Nut with Rat Fink,
1963-65, 1/25, $100-120.

H-1306 Surfink, 1964-65, $110-130.

134

H-1255 Sunbeam Alpine Roadster, 1968-70, 1/32, $40-60.

H-1292 '57 Ford Fairlane, 1969-70, 1/32, $20-30.

H-1224 Tony Nancy's Roadster and Dragster, 1963-66, 1/25, $60-80.

H-1295 '69 Plymouth Barracuda Formula S, 1969-74, 1/32, $30-40.

H-1232 1959 Chevy Corvette Convertible, 1960-61, 1/25, $50-70.

H-1284 1957 Chevy Bel Air, 1963-70, 1/25, $40-50. Box art by Tom Daniel, who later designed model cars for Monogram.

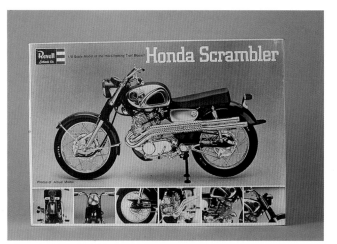

H-1235 Honda Scrambler, 1967-73, 1/8, $25-35.

H-1237 Harley-Davidson Hog, 1968-73, 1/8, $25-35.

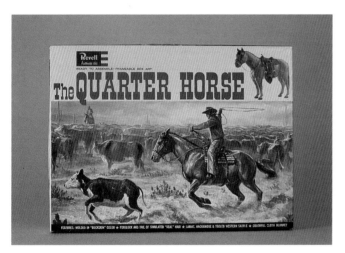

H-1922 Quarter Horse, 1963-66, 1/10, $45-55.

H-1924 Appaloosa, 1963-66, 1/10, $45-55.

H-222 P-51D Mustang & Ki-84 Hayate, 1970-72, 1/72, $10-15.
H-223 BF-109 & Hawker Tempest, 1970-72, 1/72, $10-15.

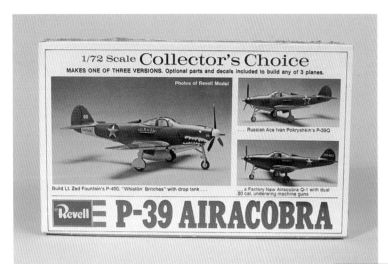

H-67 Bell P-39 Aircobra, 1975-76, 1/72, $5-8.

H-664 Air Racers!, 1976, 1/72, $20-25.

H-46 Curtiss P-40E, 1978-80, 1/72, $5-8.

H-145 North American OV-10A Bronco, 1970-77, 1/72, $8-10.

138

H-229 McDonald F4C Phantom II,
1972-76, 1/72, $6-9.

H-31 North American P-51D, 1978-80, 1/48, $10-12.

H-250 Messerschmitt Bf-110-G-4 "Destroyer",
1974-75, 1/32, $25-35.

H-275 Night Fighter Me-262 B-1a/U1, 1975-76, 1/32, $25-35.

H-279 Messerschmitt Bf-109G "Gustav", 1970-76, 1/32, $25-35.

H-580 Baa Baa Black Sheep Corsair, 1977-80, 1/32, $25-35.

H-354 USS Hornet +3, 1970-79, 1/538, $30-35.

H-384 German Sub U-47, 1975-80, 1/125, $20-30.

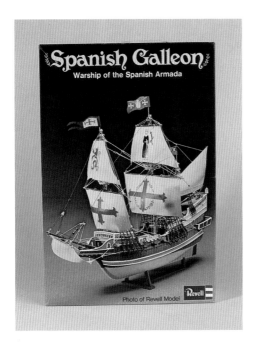

H-324 Spanish Galleon with sails (Quick Build),
1978-79, 1/96, $20-25.

H-435 USS Defiance, 1973, 1/130, $25-35.

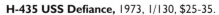

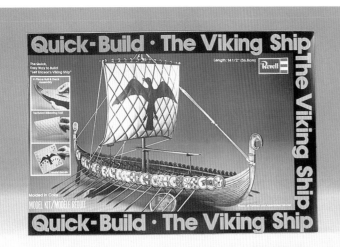

H-326 Viking Ship (Quick Build) with sail, 1977-79, 1/60, $25-30.

H-1362 Van, 1971-73, $50-60.

H-366 Mayflower with sails, 1970-79, 1/83, $12-15.

H-1272 1931 Cadillac Phaeton, 1978, 1/48, $10-15.

H-1203 '60 Chevrolet Corvette Convertible, 1977-79, 1/25, $15-20.

H-1310 VW Van "Rubber Duck", 1977-79, 1/25, $35-45.

H-1366 Baja Racer Valvoline VW, 1976, 1/25, $30-40.

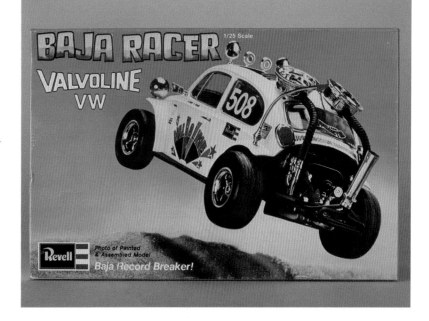

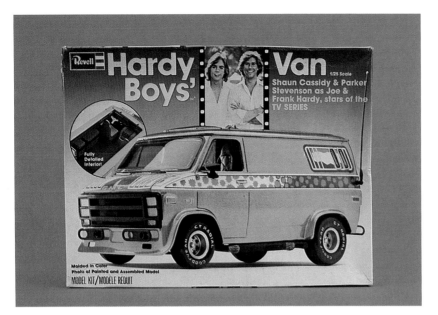

H-1398 1978 GMC Hardy Boys' Van,
1978-79, 1/25, $30-40.

H-1485 Grand Am "Revelleader" Funny Car,
1973-75, 1/16, $70-80.

H-1503 Husqvarna 400cc Moto-Cross,
1973-75, 1/12, $35-45.

H-1350, H-1351, H-1352, H-1353, The
Beatles, 1/8, $325-350

Jack Leynnwood painted this box illustration for a
three-plane set that was never issued. The Nieuport
28, Fokker Dr-1, and Sopwith Triplane.

1950s Kits

Aircraft

H-197 Sopwith Camel   1959-64   1/28 $30-50
Olive green, clear plastic windscreen not in later issues. Silver thread for rigging. British RFC decals. Pilot and ground crew figures. Box art by Lorenzo Ghiglieri. Reissued as: H-291 (1965); G-293 (1968); H-910 (1975); H-234 (1976); 3422 (1979) Advent.

H-198 North American X-15 "S"   1959-60   1/65 $60-80
Black, clear plastic. NASA decals. Removable canopy, rocket engine. Control surfaces, landing skids, air brakes move. Box art by Leynnwood. Reissued as H-164 (1961).

H-199 F-104 with Sidewinders "S"   1959-61   1/64 $45-55
Silver, clear plastic. Air Force decals. Wing-tip tanks from the first issue H-251 (1957) are replaced with Sidewinder missiles. Two trolleys hold four missiles. Pilot and three ground crew figures. Box art by Kishady. Reissued as: H-142 (1962); H-142 (1966); H-232 (1968).

H-201 Lockheed F-94C Starfire   1953   1/56 $80-100
Silver, clear plastic. Air Force decals. Packaged in one-piece box lacking full color. Desk model mounted on a stand. No landing gear, crew figure heads molded into the fuselage parts. Bulone model sculptor. This mold was modified and reissued as H-210 in 1954.

H-202 Chance Vought F7U-1 Cutlass   1953   1/59 $100-120
Dark blue, clear plastic. Navy decals. One-piece box lacking full color. Desk model mounted on simple stand. No landing gear, pilot figure head molded into the fuselage parts. A model of the early version Cutlass with an instrument boom on its nose. This mold was modified and reissued as H-211 in 1954.

H-203 Grumman F9F-6 Cougar   1953   1/52 $80-100
Dark blue, clear plastic. Navy decals. One-piece box lacking full color. Desk model mounted on a simple stand. No landing gear, pilot figure head molded into fuselage parts. A model of the early version Cougar with an instrument boom on its nose. This mold was modified and reissued as H-212 in 1954.

H-205 Convair B-36D   1954-61   1/184 $80-100
Silver, clear plastic. Air Force decals. Desk model without landing gear. First box art with blue sky by Eidson. For the second version, at the request of the sales department, Kishady repainted the sky yellow and added red trim to the aircraft. Reissued as: G-209 (1955); H-139 (1962); H-139 (1969).

H-206 Boeing B-47   1954-61   1/117 $60-80
Silver, clear plastic. Air Force decals. Desk model without landing gear. Bulone model sculptor. Box art by Eidson. Reissued as: G-209 (1955); H-140 (1962).

H-207 Boeing B-52   1954-61   1/175 $60-80
Silver, clear plastic. Air Force decals. Desk model without landing gear. Bulone model sculptor. Richard Kishady's first box art painting. Reissued as: G-209 (1955); G-195 (1959); H-162 (1961); H-273 (1966); H-253 (1968); 3351 (1979) Advent.

H-208 Boeing B-29   1954-61   1/135 $60-80
Silver, clear plastic. Army Air Corps decals. Desk model without landing gear. This would be one of Revell's most long-lived models, still appearing in the 1980 catalog. Box art by Kishady. Reissued as: H-141 (1962); H-239 (1966); G-209 (1955); H-159 (1974).

H-210 Lockheed F-94C Starfire   1954-59   1/56 $25-35
Silver, clear plastic. Air Force decals. This is a reissue of H-201 (1953). Modifications include: wings molded in two halves, crew figures separate from fuselage, landing gear added, rivets added. Mounted on new clear plastic swivel stand. Bulone primary model sculptor. Box art by Kishady. Reissued as: G-204 (1954); H-115 (1960); G-161 (1961); H-123 (1962).

H-211 Chance Vought F7U-3 Cutlass   1954-60   1/59 $50-70
Silver, clear plastic. Navy decals. This is a reissue of H-202 (1953). Modifications include: fuselage shape changed to –3 variant, nose instrument boom deleted, wings molded in two halves, pilot figure separate from fuselage, landing gear added, rivets added. Mounted on new clear plastic swivel stand. Box art by Kishady. Reissued as: G-204 (1954); H-171 (1961).

H-212 Grumman F9F-8 Cougar   1954-59   1/52 $50-70
Sea blue, clear plastic. Navy decals. This is a reissue of H-203 (1953). Modifications include: nose changed to –8 configuration with instrument boom deleted, wings molded in two halves, pilot figure separate from fuselage, landing gear added, rivets added. Mounted on new clear plastic swivel stand. Box art by Kishady. Reissued as: G-204 (1954); H-151 (1960); H-168 (1961).

H-213 Douglas D-558-2 Skyrocket   1955-59   1/54 $40-50
White, clear plastic. Navy decals. Heavy raised decal locater lines. *IPMS Journal* (November 1997, 33) says the model is accurate, except for a too tall, too narrow tail fin. Bulone primary model sculptor. Box art by Kishady. Reissued as: G-226 (1955); H-112 (1960); G-161 (1961); H-121 (1962).

H-214 Sikorsky S-55   1954-60   1/49 $40-60
Olive, clear plastic. Air Force decals. Engine doors open. Box art by Kishady. Reissued as: G-243 (1956); H-227 (1957); G-271 (1957); H-181 (1960); H-172 (1961); H-173 (1975).

H-215 Republic F-84F Thunderstreak   1955-59   1/54 $30-40
Silver, clear plastic. Air Force decals. Raised decal locater lines. Instrument boom in nose that will be deleted in future reissues. Box art by Kishady. Reissued as: G-226 (1955); H-152 (1960); H-125 (1962).

H-216 North American B-25C   1955-61   1/64 $40-50
Olive brown, clear plastic. "Flying Dragon" Army Air Corps decals. Charles Kishady primary model sculptor. Box art by Richard Kishady. Reissued as: G-226 (1955); H-136 (1962); H-238 (1966).

H-218 Consolidated B-24J   1955-61   1/92 $60-70
Light brown, clear plastic. "Buffalo Bill" Army Air Corps decals. Ten years after their issue, in 1965, Revell reported that the B-24 and B-25 were the best sellers among all the aircraft kits. Charles Kishady primary model sculptor. Box art by Richard Kishady. Reissued as: G-226 (1955); H-137 (1962); H-237 (1966).

H-219 Douglas DC-7 American "S"   1955-60   1/122 $90-110
Silver plastic (no clear parts). With pilot figure waving out cockpit window and passenger loading ramp. Recessed panel lines, rivets. Box art by Kishady. Reissued as: H-220 (1955); H-257 (1955); G-335 (1956); H-267 (1958); H-168 (1975).

H-219 Douglas DC-7 American "S"   1950s   1/122 $90-110
Silver plastic (no clear parts). Decal. Skyway Models of Los Angeles put mail order cards in American Airlines flight packs so that passengers could send in $1.00 to order a "souvenir of your flight." The kit came in a cardboard mailing box.

H-220 Douglas DC-7 United Flight 707   1955-57   1/122 $150-170
Silver plastic (no clear parts). One kit in each shipping carton was a display kit with the parts in a clear acetate tray (most valuable to today's collectors: $400). Includes truck, loading ladder to create an "Airport Scene." Also issued as H-219 (1955).

H-221 Northrop F-89D Scorpion "S"   1955-59   1/80 $40-50
Silver, clear plastic. Box art by Kishady. Reissued as: G-240 (1956); H-153 (1960); H-126 (1962).

H-222 Bell P-39B Airacobra "S"   1955-59   1/45 $50-70
Olive brown plastic. Early Army Air Corps decals. Box art by Kishady. Reissued as: H-155 (1960); H-144 (1962).

H-223 Piasecki H-16 "S"   1955-61   1/96 $40-60
Silver, clear plastic. Decals. Box art by Kishady. Reissued as H-138 (1962).

H-227 Sikorsky H-19 Air-Sea Rescue "S"   1956-60   1/72 $40-50
Silver, clear plastic. Rescue decals. This model is the Sikorsky H-19 (H-214) with a winch added to the fuselage above the side door and floats replacing wheels on the undercarriage. The added parts came from a separate auxiliary mold. This was one of Revell's most long-lived models, still appearing in the 1980 catalog. Box art by Kishady. Reissued as: H-214 (1954); G-243 (1956); G-271 (1957); H-181 (1960); H-172 (1961); H-173 (1975).

H-230 Martin B-57B "S"   1955-60   1/81 $50-70
Black, clear plastic. Air Force decals. Box art by Kishady. Reissued as: G-240 (1956); H-132 (1969); H-157 (1961); 3352 (1979) Advent.

H-231 McDonnell F-101A Voodoo "S"   1956-59   1/75 $30-40
Silver, clear plastic. Air Force decals. Three fuel tanks. Box art by Kishady. Reissued as: G-240 (1956); H-156 (1960); G-290 (1958); H-128 (1963).

H-232 Douglas A4D Skyhawk "S"   1956-58   1/51 $40-60
Light gray, clear plastic. Includes pilot figure and belly fuel tank. Box art by Kishady. Reissued as: G-243 (1956); H-299 (1959); G-271 (1957); H-179 (1961).

H-233 Convair F-102A "S"   1956-59   1/77 $30-40
Silver, clear plastic. Air Force decals. Box art by Kishady. Reissued as: G-240 (1956); H-116 (1960); H-124 (1962); G-290 (1958); G-161 (1961); H-130 (1969).

H-235 Ilyushin Il-38 Bison "S"   1957-59   1/169 $70-90
Green, clear plastic. Decals. Box art by Eidson. Reissued as H-182 (1960).

H-236 North American F-100C "S"   1956-59   1/70 $40-50
Silver, clear plastic. Box art by Kishady. Reissued as: G-240 (1956); H-117 (1960); H-127 (1962); G-290 (1958); G-161 (1961).

H-238 Convair R3Y-2 Tradewind "S"   1957-60   1/168 $70-90
Sea blue, plastic. Navy decals. Nose door hinged to open. Box art by Ghiglieri. Reissued as H-178 (1961).

H-239 Lockheed P2V-7 Neptune "S"   1957-60   1/104 $50-60
Silver, clear plastic. Navy decals. Box art by Kishady. Reissued as H-170 (1961).

H-241 Douglas A3D Skywarrior "S"   1957-60   1/84 $30-40
Light blue, clear plastic. Navy decals. Wing tips, tail fold. Box art by Leynnwood. Reissued as: H-177 (1961); H-256 (1968); 3355 (1979) Advent.

H-244 Martin P6M Seamaster "S"   1956-59   1/136 $40-50
First issue in light gray plastic; rare later issues in blue plastic with box art from Dawn Patrol (G-243). Navy decals. Later issues have minor changes, including rivets and more panel lines. Box art by Kishady. Reissued as G-243 (1956) and H-176 (1961).

H-245 Lockheed Super G Constellation "S" 1957-59 1/128 $90-110
Silver plastic (no clear parts). Eastern Airlines decals. This model was molded from the same basic tool used for the military radar picket aircraft, H-279 Warning Star (1958), with mold inserts to make the civilian version of the plane. Box art by Nixon Galloway. Reissued as H-167 (1975).

H-246 Boeing 707 American "S" 1958-61 1/140 $80-100
Silver plastic (no clear parts). This model had interchangeable fuselage blocks in the mold so that the plane could be produced with passenger windows for the airliner version or without passenger windows for the military version H-287 KC-135 (1958). This original issue of the 707 does not have fan-jet engines. Box art by Leynnwood. Reissued as: G-289 (1958); G-194 (1959); H-243 (1962); H-243 (1964); H-254 (1968).

H-246 Boeing 707 American 1950s 1/140 $100-120
Silver (no clear) plastic. Skyway Models of Los Angeles put mail order cards in American Airlines flight packs so that passengers could send in $1.00 to order a "souvenir of your flight." The kit came in a cardboard mailing box.

H-247 Lockheed C-130A Hercules "S" 1957-59 1/140 $50-70
Silver, clear plastic. Decals. Hinged rear cargo door with loading ramp. Includes fuel truck, mobile generator, and ground crew figure. This original issue had three-blade propellers that change to four in later issues. Leynnwood's first box illustration. Reissued as: H-183 (1960); H-230 (1968); H-148 (1974).

H-248 Douglas DC-8 United "S" 1959-63 1/143 $50-70
Silver (no clear) plastic. United decals. Engine cowls remove to show engines, passenger door can be fixed open, includes loading ramp. Side passengers' windows are represented by recessed rectangles in the fuselage. Has stand not included in later H-242 issue. Reissued as: G-194 (1959); H-242 (1964); H-270 (1970).

H-249 Grumman F11F-1 Tiger "S" 1957-60 1/55 $40-50
Light gray, clear plastic. Navy decals. Box art by Kishady. Reissued as: G-268 (1956); G-288 (1958); H-169 (1961).

H-250 LTV F8U-1 Crusader "S" 1957-59 1/67 $30-40
Light gray, clear plastic. Navy decals. Wing tips fold. Box art by Kishady. Reissued as: G-268 (1956); G-288 (1958); H-154 (1960); H-167 (1961); H-255 (1968); 3353 (1979) Advent.

H-251 Lockheed F-104 Starfighter "S" 1957-58 1/64 $30-40
Silver, clear plastic. This first issue has wing-tip tanks. Box art by Kishady. Reissued as: G-268 (1956); G-290 (1958); H-199 (1959).

H-252 Convair B-58 Hustler "S" 1958-61 1/94 $50-70
Silver, clear plastic. Three crew hatches can be fixed in open or closed positions. Box art by Leynnwood. Reissued as: G-289 (1958); H-143 (1962); H-272 (1966).

H-255 Lockheed Electra American "S" 1958-63 1/115 $150-175
Silver plastic (no clear parts). This mold was later retooled to become the H-163 P-3 Orion (1965). Box art by Leynnwood.

H-255 Lockheed Electra American 1950s 1/115 $100-120
Silver plastic (no clear parts). Skyway Models of Los Angeles put mail order cards in American Airlines flight packs so that passengers could send in $1.00 to order a "souvenir of your flight." The kit came in a cardboard mailing box.

H-255D Los Angeles "Dodgers" Electra II 1960s 1/115 $150-170
White plastic (no clear parts). The model was marketed as a mail-away premium and came in a corrugated cardboard shipping box.

H-256 Spad XIII "S" 1957-64 1/27 $40-50
Olive plastic with fabric texture. Includes silver rigging thread and clear windscreen not in later issues. Hat-in-the-Ring 94th Aero decals for Eddie Rickenbacker's plane. Pilot and two ground crew figures. Cowl lifts off to show engine. Box art by John Steel. Reissued as: H-290 (1965); H-235 (1976); G-293 (1968); 3423 (1979) Advent.

H-257 Douglas DC-7c Pan Am Airport Scene 1955 1/122 $500-700
Silver plastic (no clear parts). Pan Am decals. This is actually the standard DC-7a model (H-219). This kit was given away as part of a promotion, then sold in stores with a price sticker added.

H-258 PBM-5 Mariner "S" 1958-60 1/112 $40-50
Sea blue, clear plastic. Navy decals. Underwing bomb bay doors can be built closed or open to show bomb load. Box art by Ghiglieri. Reissued as H-175 (1961).

H-259 Douglas X-3 Stiletto "S" 1957-59 1/65 $40-50
White plastic, green-tinted clear canopy. Air Force decals. Includes tow tractor and driver figure, not in later reissues. Box art by Kishady. Reissued as: G-291 (1955); G-161 (1961); H-135 (1970); H-113 (1960); H-122 (1962).

H-267 DC-7c Swissair "S" 1958-59 1/120 $50-60
Silver plastic (no clear parts). Swissair decals. This is a modified reissue of the H-219 DC-7a from 1955. Changes to make it a DC-7c include: extended wing roots, taller tail fin, new side windows, different engine nacelles, and propellers with pointed spinners and rounded tips. Box art by Leynnwood.

H-269 Douglas AD-6 Skyraider "S" 1959-60 1/40 $30-40
Gray, clear plastic. Navy decals. Includes pilot and three ground crew figures. 500 pound bomb and twelve underwing rockets. Operating features include: folding wings, movable flaps and elevators, removable engine cowl, retractable landing gear, and sliding canopy. Ron Campbell sculpted the model prototype and was disappointed that the production model did not incorporate all his fine details. *Scale Modeler* (October 1970, 6) faults the kit for too short landing gear. Reissued as: H-260 (1962); H-261 (1966); H-260 (1974).

H-270 Fokker Dr-1 "S" 1957-64 1/27 $40-50
Red plastic with fabric texture. Includes clear windscreen not with later issues. Decals for Manfred von Richthofen's plane. Includes three figures. Box art by John Steel. Reissued as: H-292 (1965); H-233 (1976); G-293 (1968); 3421 (1979) Advent.

H-279 Lockheed WV-2 Warning Star "S" 1958-60 1/128 $60-80
Dark gray (no clear) plastic. This model was molded from the same basic tool used to mold the Super G Constellation (H-245) with mold inserts to make the military version of the plane. Added upper and lower radar domes, and the windows are circular rather than square. Box art by Gigliera. Reissued as H-174 (1961).

H-281 Convair F-102A Delta Dagger "S" 1959-68 1/49 $100-125
Silver, clear plastic. Air Force decals. Reissue of H-282 without airstrip accessories. Box art deletes original background and shows the plane against a yellow background. Damage to mold precludes further reissues. Box art by Leynnwood.

H-282 Convair F-102A Delta Dagger "S" 1958-59 1/49 $250-270
Silver, clear plastic for plane; yellow plastic for airstrip accessories. Decals. Includes four crew figures and ten airstrip accessories. Landing gear lowers when canopy is raised, flaps move, drag chute housing opens, engine can be removed and placed on service stand. Box art by Leynnwood. Reissued in 1959 as H-281 without the airstrip accessories.

H-285 Republic F-105 Thunderchief "S" 1958-61 1/75 $30-40
Silver, clear plastic. Air Force decals. Retractable refueling boom, opening canopy. With four underwing bombs. Box art by Kishady. Reissued as: G-290 (1958); H-166 (1961); H-166 (1978); H-231 (1968); 3354 (1979) Advent.

H-287 Boeing KC-135A "S" 1958-63 1/139 $40-60
Silver (no clear) plastic. Air Force decals. The model was produced from the same mold that made the 707 airliner (H-246), but mold insert parts were changed to those without side passenger windows and with an attachment under the tail for the movable refueling boom. Box art by Kishady. Reissued as H-275 (1966).

H-296 Yak-25 Flashlight "S" 1958-61 1/50 $50-70
Silver, clear plastic. Soviet decals. A very simple model. Box art by Kishady. Reissued as: H-158 (1961); H-274 (1966).

H-297 Fairchild F-27 "S" 1958-63 1/94 $30-40
Cream, clear plastic. Fairchild decals. Kit includes coupon that builders could mail in to get airline decals of their choice. Campbell model sculptor. Box art by Leynnwood.

H-298 Convair F-106A "S" 1959-60 1/67 $40-60
Silver, clear plastic. Air Force decals. Parachute doors open, control surfaces move. Box art by Kishady. Reissued as H-159 (1961).

H-299 A4D Skyhawk with Bullpups "S" 1959-60 1/50 $40-60
Gray, clear plastic. Navy decals. This kit was made from a modification of H-232. Two missiles, two trailers, and three ground crew figures added. Box art by Lorenzo Ghiglieri. Reissued as H-179 (1961).

Aircraft Gift Sets

G-194 Jet Airliner Gift Set 1959 $400-450
This gift set is a thin cardboard sleeve containing two regular boxed kits. H-246 Boeing 707 American; H-248 Douglas DC-8 United.

G-195 Man Into Space 1959 $400-450
Two regular boxed kits enclosed in a thin cardboard sleeve. H-198 X-15; H-207 B-52.

H-204 3 American Jet Fighters 1st issue 1953 $400-450
Planes diving box art by Eidson. H-201 Starfire; H-202 Cutlass; H-203 Cougar.

H-204 3 Jet Fighters 2nd issue 1954 $400-450
Planes climbing box art by Kishady. H-210 Starfire; H-211 Cutlass; H-212 Cougar.

H-209 Strategic Air Command 1954 $450-500
H-205 B-36; H-207 B-52; H-206 B-47; H-208 B-29.

G-209 Strategic Air Command 1955 $450-500
Reissue of H-209 in a larger box.

G-226 Sky Squadron 1955 $450-500
H-213 Skyrocket; H-215 F-84F; H-218 B-24; H-214 Sikorsky; H-216 B-25.

G-240 Air Power "S" 1956-57 $600-650
Box art by Kishady. H-221 F-89D; H-230 B-57D; H-231 F-101A; H-233 F-102A; H-236 F-100C.

G-243 Dawn Patrol "S" 1956 $450-500
H-227 HO4S-2 Rescue Helicopter (Blue plastic); H-232 A4D Skyhawk; H-244 P6M Seamaster (Blue plastic first issue; silver plastic second issue.).

G-268 Supersonic Jets "S" 1957 $450-500
Box art by Leynnwood. H-249 F11F-1; H-250 F8U-1; H-251 F-104.

G-271 Airborne Marines "S" 1957 $350-400
Box art by Gigliera. H-232 A4D Skyhawk; H-214 HRS-1 version in blue plastic.

G-288 Supersonic Marines 1958 $300-350
H-249 F11F-1 Tiger; H-250 F8U-1 Crusader.

G-289 Strategic Air Command   1958 $300-350
H-252 B-58 Hustler; H-287 KC-135 Tanker.

G-290 Century Series   1958 $400-450
Box art by Leynnwood. H-231 F-101A; H-233 F-102A; H-236 F-100C; H-252 F-104; H-285 F-105B.

G-335 Let's Take a Trip "S"   1956 $600-650
Tie-in with CBS-TV show "Let's Take a Trip." Two box versions: with and without "CBS" logo. Box art by Eidson. H-219 DC-7a American Airlines; H-312 SS United States; H-1200-6 1956 Cadillac Eldorado Convertible.

Missiles & Rockets

Revell's 1958-59 catalog introduced space age missiles from the front pages of the country's newspapers. Several model companies also entered the space race at the same time—and all discovered that the models were not good sellers.

G-541 Missile Combat Team   1959 $500-550
This set of four regular kits were packaged in a thin cardboard sleeve as a gift set. H-526 GI Battle Action Figures; H-1812 Tactical Missiles; H-1816 Lacrosse and Truck; H-1817 Hawk Battery.

H-1800 XSL-01 Manned spaceship "S"   1958-59   1/96 $350-370
Metallic blue plastic spaceship, silver engines, orange launch platform. Decals. First and second stage booster rockets can be jettisoned, and side of third stage can be removed to show interior. Fictional concept rocket to the Moon designed by Ellwyn Angle/Systems Laboratories. The final stage was reissued as H-1825. Box art by Leynnwood.

H-1801 Northrop Air Force SM-62 Snark "S" 1958-60   1/81 $40-50
Red plastic. Decals. With movable launch platform and two ground crew figures. Ghiglieri box art.

H-1803 US Army Redstone "S"   1959-60   1/110 $70-80
White plastic. Decals. With launch platform, support equipment, three ground crew figures. Box art by Leynnwood. Reissued with modifications in 1962 as H-1832.

H-1804 Douglas Army Nike-Hercules "S" 1958-65   1/40 $40-50
White plastic missile, olive drab launch platform with movable arm. Decals. With three ground crew figures. Box art by Leynnwood.

H-1805 Space Station "S"   1959-60   1/96 $800-900
Black, silver, orange, blue, clear plastic. Decals. Fictional orbital manned satellite designed by Ellwyn Angle/Systems Laboratories. With four space vehicles, ten crew figures, wall sections open to show detailed interior, sections rotate, radar dish turns. Mounted on a display stand. Box art by Leynnwood.

H-1806 Boeing Bomarc IM-99 "S"   1958-61   1/47 $70-90
Black plastic. Air Force decals. Includes movable launch pad and two ground crew figures. Box art by Leynnwood.

H-1808 Bendix Navy Talos "S"   1958-60   1/40 $60-80
White, olive green plastic. Box art by Leynnwood.

H-1810 USAF X-17 Research Rocket "S" 1958-60   1/40 $60-80
White, olive green plastic. Air Force decals. Three stages separate. Includes tracking scope and three crew figures. Box art by Leynnwood.

H-1812 Army Tactical Missiles Set "S" 1958-60   1/40 $40-60
White plastic missiles, olive drab launch platforms and guidance scope. Decals. Includes one Little John, four Darts, and six crew figures. Reissued as H-547 (1963).

H-1813 Convair USMC Terrier "S"   1958-60   1/40 $70-90
White plastic missiles, gray launch platform. Navy decals. Launcher turns and missiles elevate. Includes three crew figures. Leynnwood box art.

H-1814 Aerojet Aerobee-Hi "S"   1958-60   1/40 $50-70
White plastic missile, gray launch trailer. Decals. Includes movable launch arm and three ground crew figures. Leynnwood box art.

H-1815 Chance-Vought Regulus II "S" 1958-60   1/68 $50-70
Dark blue plastic. Navy decals. Leynnwood box art.

H-1816 Martin LaCrosse with Mobile Launcher 1958-60 1/40 $110-130
White plastic missile, olive drab truck, black tires. Army decals. Includes three figures. Missile is mounted on an Army M-35 truck. Reissued as H-549 (1963).

H-1817 Raytheon US Army Hawk "S"   1958-60   1/40 $90-110
White missiles, olive drab launch trailer, black tires. Army decals. Includes four crew figures and radar unit. Reissued as H-548 (1963).

H-1818 Firestone Corporal/Transporter "S" 1959   1/40 $130-150
White plastic missile, olive drab transporter. Army decals. Includes six figures, radar unit. Reissue of H-1820 with added transporter. Also reissued as H-543 (1960).

H-1819 Chrysler Jupiter "C" "S"   1959-65   1/110 $130-150
White, gray, red plastic. Army decals. Includes launch gantry, railroad base, seven figures. This rocket launched America's first earth satellite, the Explorer. C & H Sugar of San Francisco also offered this kit as a mail-away premium. Box art by John Steel.

H-1820 US Army Corporal "S"   1958-60   1/40 $70-90
White plastic missile, olive drab launch platform, radar unit, and three crewmen. Box art by Leynnwood. Reissued as H-1818 with transporter added.

H-1821 Honest John with Mobile Carrier "S" 1959-60 1/48 $130-150
White plastic Douglas missile, green trailer truck. Decals. Includes two figures. The truck is a modified version of the H-1403 Kenworth tractor-trailer. Box art by Leynnwood.

H-1822 Convair Atlas with Launch Pad "S" 1959-62   1/110 $180-200
White, yellow, gray plastic. Decals. Includes truck, launch pad with elevating tower, and six figures. Box art by Leynnwood. Reissued with modifications as H-1833 in 1963.

H-1823 Douglas Thor/Thor-Able "S"   1959-65   1/110 $200-220
White, dark blue plastic. Air Force decals. Includes launch platform, tank truck, pipe trailer, four figures. The missile can be built as a standard military Thor or, with an added second stage, as the research version Thor-Able. Uses same accessory parts as H-1824.

H-1824 Chrysler Jupiter with Truck "S" 1959-65   1/96 $100-120
White plastic missile, olive drab equipment. Army decals. Includes truck with crane, tractor trailer, launch platform, four figures. Uses same accessory parts as H-1823 Thor.

H-1825 Moonship "S"   1959-65   1/96 $160-180
Light blue plastic. Decals. This is the final stage of the fictional H-1800 Manned spaceship, mounted on a display stand. The fuselage opens to show the interior and three crew figures. Box art by Leynnwood. Reissued as G-291 (1965); H-1850 (1968).

H-1828 Convair Space Shuttlecraft "S" 1959-65   1/150 $200-220
Light blue plastic. Decals. Two-stage concept craft for shuttling from earth to satellites in orbit. Includes launching base, three ground crew, and removable fuselage panel to show five shuttle crew figures inside. Designed for Revell by Krafft Ehricke of Convair. Reissued with modifications in 1968 as Space Pursuit (H-1850).

H-1829 Helios Lunar Craft "S"   1959-65   1/160 $180-200
Metallic blue, white, clear plastic. Decals. Includes movable parts, six crewmembers. Designed for Revell by Krafft Ehricke of Convair. Leynnwood art. Reissued with modifications in 1968 as Atomic Space Explorer Solaris (H-1851).

Ships

Shipyard Ships in a Bottle

This line of miniature sailing ship models was introduced in the fall of 1952 by Gowland Creations of Santa Barbara, California, designers of the Highway Pioneers. Derek Brand, chief sculptor for the Highway Pioneers, also carved these models. The molds were cast beryllium-copper alloy.

Gowland developed, manufactured, and marketed these very small scale models down to the summer of 1954. They came in two versions: Ships in a Bottle, with a clear plastic, two-part "bottle," and Ships in Miniature, without the bottle. Both versions were water-line models that rested on an ocean surface base.

In the summer of 1954 Revell assumed distribution of the kits, but Revell marketed the ships just through 1955. Only the final two kits appeared in Revell packaging, with the Revell trademark.

In 1956 Gowland liquidated the leftover stock of these kits by selling remaining kits to Crafco, Inc., which packaged them in plastic bags and sold them under the "Mantle Models" trademark. Years later, in 1972 Addar Corporation of Brooklyn, New York, issued eight of the models (the *Golden Hind* did not reappear), and then the molds for the Ships in a Bottle disappeared.

Kits H-408 through H-414 were issued only in **Gowland** brand packaging and did not carry any letter or number kit designations on the box.

H-408 Santa Maria   1952-55 $20-25
Ivory plastic. Decal, paper flag sheet, rope ladders printed on clear plastic sheet.

H-409 Golden Hind   1952-55 $20-25
Ivory plastic. Decal, paper flag sheet, rope ladders printed on clear plastic sheet.

H-410 Mayflower   1952-55 $20-25
Ivory plastic. Paper flag sheet, rope ladders printed on clear plastic sheet.

H-411 Bon Homme Richard   1952-55 $20-25
Ivory plastic. Paper flag sheet, rope ladders printed on clear plastic sheet.

H-412 Frigate Constitution   1953-55 $20-25
Ivory plastic. Paper flag sheet, rope ladders printed on clear plastic sheet.

H-413 Revenue Cutter   1953-55 $20-25
Ivory plastic. Paper flag sheet, rope ladders printed on clear plastic sheet.

H-414 S. S. Savannah   1953-55 $20-25
Ivory plastic. Paper flag sheet, rope ladders printed on clear plastic sheet.

Kits H-415 and H-416 appear only in **Revell** brand packaging with just a small Gowland trademark in a corner of the box top.

H-415/HB-415 Flying Cloud   1955 $30-35
Ivory, dark brown plastic. Paper flag sheet, rope ladders printed on clear plastic
    sheet. HB-415 has the standard bottle and ocean base. H-415 has an added
    below-the-waterline hull part and a stand for the model to rest on.
H-416/HB-416 Charles W. Morgan   1955 $30-35
HB-416 has bottle. H-416 has hull and stand.

Modern Ships

HM-30 USS Missouri with motor   1954   1/535 $250-300
Gray plastic. Metal prop shafts. Electric motor, adjustable rudder. This kit was
    made from a second *Missouri* mold that has only very minor changes from the
    first mold. The most notable changes are a new more robust rudder and two
    bulges in the hull around the rudder where the propeller shafts come out. Also
    issued as H-309 in 1955. This mold is used to produce the non-motorized H-301
    Missouri kits after 1955 when the original H-301 mold was converted to the
    H-316 *New Jersey*. Box art by Kishady.
H-301 USS Missouri   1953-61 1/535 $60-80
Gray plastic. Paper signal flag sheet. First released in a narrow box; then in a standard
    flat box with new art. This may be Revell's all time best seller. In 1955 the mold
    used to produce this kit was revised and turned into the H-316 *New Jersey*. The
    mold formerly used to manufacture the HM-30 motorized *Missouri* was thereafter
    used to make the H-301 non-motor *Missouri* kits. Bulone model sculptor. Second
    flat box art by Eidson. Reissued as: HNF-6 Admiral's Fleet (1954); H-300 *Missouri*
    (1961); H-352 *Wisconsin* (1968); H-301 *Missouri* (1974).
H-302 Chris Craft Flying Bridge Cruiser 1954-70 1/56 $50-60
Brown plastic. Captain and two lady passenger figures. "Revell I, Los Angeles"
    decal. Bulone model sculptor. Box art by Eidson. This model was reissued with
    modifications as H-387 Balboa Marlin Fishing Boat (1961).
H-303 USS Nautilus   1953-54 1/305 $150-170
Dark blue, clear plastic. Decal. First issue has clear observation bridge and
    inscribed round portholes on front of the coning tower. Revell's model of the
    Nautilus was on hobby shop shelves months before the launching of the real
    vessel in January 1954. Packaged in one-piece box lacking full color. The *Nau-
    tilus* was among Revell's best selling ship models well into the 1960s. Bulone
    model sculptor. Reissued with modifications as H-308 in 1955. Also reissued
    as H-303 in 1961.
H-304 PT-212   1954-61 1/98 $50-60
Gray plastic. Decal, paper signal flag sheet. Three figures. Box art by Eidson.
    Reissued as: HNF-6 Admiral's Fleet (1954); G-311 Victory at Sea (1955); H-396
    Motorized *PT-212* (1961); H-421 *PT-212* (1962); H-306 *PT-207* (1966); H-421
    PT-212 (1972); H-464 *PT-211* (1975).
H-305 USS Sullivans   1954-59 1/301 $40-60
Gray plastic. Decal, paper signal flag sheet. Fletcher Class destroyer named for
    four brothers who died on a sinking ship in the Pacific in World War II. Box art
    by Eidson.
    Reissued as: HNF-6 Admiral's Fleet (1954); H-371 *Fletcher* (1960); H-307 (1966);
    G-311 (1955).
H-306 USS Los Angeles   1954-59 1/490 $100-120
Gray plastic. Decal sheet with numbers and names for all ships in this class. Balti-
    more Class heavy cruiser. Box art by Eidson. Reissued as: HNF-6 Admiral's Fleet
    (1954); H-370 *Helena* (1960); H-457 *Pittsburgh* (1967).
H-307 USS Franklin D. Roosevelt   1954-59 1/547 $60-70
Gray plastic. Includes 26 aircraft: Cougars, Skyraiders, Corsairs, and Piasecki
    copters. Midway Class aircraft carrier. Bulone primary model sculptor. Box art by
    Eidson. Reissued as: G-311 Victory at Sea (1955); H-373 *Midway* (1960); H-321
    Roosevelt (1961); H-399 *Coral Sea* motorized (1961); H-374 *Coral Sea* (1966);
    H-440 *Coral Sea* (1975); H-441 *Midway* (1975).
H-308 Guided-Missile Submarine Nautilus 1955-61 1/305 $60-80
Gray plastic. Reissue of H-303 with added deck hanger and missile. Clear observa-
    tion bridge part eliminated and inscribed round portholes are changed to square.
    The Navy experimented launching V-1 type "Loon" air-breathing missiles from
    the deck of a submarine—but not the *Nautilus*. Box art by Eidson. Reissued in
    HNF-6 (1954) and G-333 (1956).
H-309 USS Missouri with motor   1955   1/535 $250-300
Renumbered issue of HM-30. Electric motor.
H-312 SS United States   1955-61 1/602 $40-50
White plastic. Art by Kishady. Reissued as: G-335 (1956); H-332 (1961); H-332
    (1973).
H-314 Harbor Tug Long Beach "S"   1956-70 1/108 $40-50
Gray plastic. Decals. Charles Kishady model sculptor. First box art by Eidson;
    second by Steel. Reissued as: G-332 (1956); H-314 *Taurus* (1974); H-397 *Long
    Beach* (1961).
H-315 Hawaiian Pilot "S"   1956-59 1/400 $120-140
Light gray plastic. A model of a C-3 freighter. Box art by Eidson. Reissued as: G-332
    Merchant Fleet (1956); H-335 *Dr. Lykes* (1962); H-341 *Burleigh* (1964).
H-316 USS New Jersey "S"   1955-59 1/532 $50-70
Gray plastic. Includes instructions on how to paint a camouflage pattern [never

used on the real *New Jersey*], to distinguish this battleship model from Revell's
    already-issued *Missouri*. This kit was manufactured from the original mold used
    to make the H-301 *Missouri*. The only change was a switch from scout planes
    to helicopters on the fantail. Box art by Eidson. Reissued as H-369 *Iowa* (1960)
    and 2551 *Iowa* (1979) Advent.
H-320 USS Haven "S"   1956-59 1/500 $60-80
White plastic. Hospital ship. Helicopter landing platform on fantail. Box art by
    Eidson. Reissued as: H-381 *Repose* (1960); H-388 *Hope* (1961); H-458 *Repose*
    (1967).
H-322 Tanker J. L. Hanna "S"   1956-57 1/400 $50-70
Dull red plastic. Oil tanker of the Standard Oil of California line. Box art by Eidson.
    Reissued as H-342 *Mission Capistrano* (1964).
H-328 Robert E. Lee "S"   1956-59 1/275 $50-60
White plastic, decal, paper flag sheet. This first issue has boilers that are removed
    for the motorized issue H-402 (1961) and are not replaced in later non-motorized
    reissue H-323 (1973). Box art by Eidson.
H-329 USS Randall "S"   1956-59 1/376 $50-70
Gray plastic. Decal, paper signal flag sheet. An Arenae Class troop attack transport,
    the *Randall* landed Marines at Iwo Jima and in other World War II amphibious
    landings. The real ship starred in the 1956 movie *Away All Boats*, along with other
    Revell model ships used in a special effects shot. Box art by Eidson. Reissued as:
    H-380 *Montrose* (1960); H-452 *Montrose* (1968); H-452 *Montrose* (1972); 2503
    Montrose (1979) Advent.
H-331 USS Norton Sound "S"   1956-59 1/426 $80-100
Gray plastic. Guided missile experimental ship. Box art by Eidson. Reissued in
    G-333 (1956) and then reissued with modifications as H-362 USS *Pine Island*
    (1958).
H-334 USS Boston "S"   1956-59 1/480 $80-90
Gray plastic. Guided missile cruiser. Box art by John Steel. Reissued as: G-333 Mis-
    sile Fleet (1956); G-359 Naval Academy (1958); H-372 *Canberra* (1960); H-461
    Boston (1968); H-461 *Boston* (1972).
H-337 USCG Ice-Breaker Eastwind "S" 1957-59 1/285 $40-50
White, brown, mustard plastic. Decal, paper signal flag sheet. Includes Sikorsky
    HH-19G helicopter. Launched in June 1944, this icebreaker captured a German
    weather station and supply ship in Arctic waters late in World War II. Box art by
    Eidson. Reissued as: H-379 *Burton Island* (1960); H-453 *Eastwind* (1968); H-451
    Burton Island (1972); 2505 *Burton Island* (1979) Advent.
H-338 USCG Cutter Campbell "S"   1957-63 1/301 $40-50
White, mustard yellow, gray plastic. Coast Guard long-range cutter. Box art by
    Eidson. Reissued as: H-454 *Campbell* (1968); H-405 *Taney* (1976).
H-339 USS Forrestal "S"   1957-80 1/542 $60-80
Gray plastic. Box art by Eidson. Reissued as: G-359 Naval Academy (1958); H-385
    Saratoga (1961); H-360 *Ranger* (1962); H-359 *Independence* (1966); 2601 *Ranger*
    (1979) Advent.
H-346 SS Brasil "S"   1958-65 1/400 $60-80
White plastic. Blue metal foil for swimming pool. Box art by Eidson. Reissued as:
    H-346 *Brasil* (1962); H-334 *Argentina* (1962).
H-348 USS Arizona "S"   1958-74 1/426 $30-40
Gray plastic. Revell head engineer Charles Gretz traveled to Hawaii to gather
    material for this model. The kit was later used as part of the fund-raising pro-
    motion for the Arizona Memorial in Pearl Harbor opened in 1962. Box art by
    Eidson. Reissued as: H-398 Motorized *Arizona* (1961); H-302 *Arizona* (1975);
    H-422 *Pennsylvania* (1962).
H-352 USS Forrest Sherman "S"   1958-60 1/320 $50-60
Gray plastic. Decal. Paper flag sheet. Reissued as: G-359 (1958); H-309 *John Paul
    Jones* (1961); H-430 *Decatur* (1962); H-459 *Forrest Sherman* (1968); H-309 *John
    Paul Jones* (1972); H-463 *Forrest Sherman* (1973).
H-353 USS Essex "S"   1958-70 1/538 $50-60
Gray plastic. Essex Class aircraft carrier with post-World War II angled flight
    deck. Reissued as: H-384 *Bon Homme Richard* (1961); H-426 *Lexington* (1962);
    H-370 *Oriskany* (1968); H-375 *Wasp* (1968); H-354 *Hornet* (1970); H-442 *Bon
    Homme Richard* (1975); H-444 *Lexington* (1976); 2555 *Bon Homme Richard*
    (1979) Advent.
H-355 USCG Buckley "S"   1958-61 1/249 $40-60
Gray plastic. Destroyer Escort that rammed and sank a German U-boat in World
    War II. Reissued as: H-423 *Buckley* (1962); H-428 *Blessman* (1962); H-456 *Tai
    Chao* (1967); 2506 *Buckley* (1979) Advent.
H-362 USS Pine Island "S"   1958-60 1/424 $50-70
Gray plastic. Decal, paper signal flag sheet. Reissue of H-331 USS *Norton Sound*
    with missile deleted and Martin Mariner seaplane added. Reissued as: H-386
    Currituck (1961); H-455 *Pine Island* (1968); H-341 *Pine Island* (1973); 2504 *Pine
    Island* (1979) Advent.
H-365 USS George Washington "S"   1959-60 1/253 $60-70
Gray, black, light green plastic. Decals for interior. Right side of hull snaps off to show
    interior. The two forward missile tubes have opening hatches to launch missiles
    by metal spring power. Includes fold-out booklet by General Dynamics Corp.,
    The Story of Our Undersea Nuclear Navy. The first issue of the model inaccurately
    holds only eight missile launch tubes, but this is corrected to sixteen in later issues.

Reissued as: H-313 *Abraham Lincoln* (1961); H-425 Polaris Submarine (1962); H-433 *Patrick Henry* (1968); H-437 Polaris Submarine (1976).

H-366 N/S Savannah "S"   1959-61   1/380 $50-60
White plastic. Decals. Top removes to show nuke reactor. Reissued as H-333 (1962).

H-367 USS Olympia "S"   1959-65   1/232 $60-80
White, mustard yellow, tan plastic. Metal anchor chain. Decal. Paper flag sheet. Reissued as H-443 (1975) and 2552 (1979) Advent.

Historic Sailing Ships

H-319 "Old Ironsides" USS Constitution "S" 1956-70, 72-73   1/192 $30-40
Black, tan plastic. Pre-assembled threaded ratlines, with pattern on instruction sheet for trimming the ratlines. Paper flag sheet. No sails. First issue box does not have the "S" markings. Includes tube of cement. Hogg primary model sculptor. Box art by Eidson. Reissued as: G-358 Famous Sailing Ships (1958); H-329 (1968); H-320 (1973); H-303 (1977).

H-327 HMS Bounty without sails   1956-61   1/170 $30-40
Dark brown plastic. Preformed string ratlines. Twine for anchor cable. Spool of thread. Hogg primary model sculptor. Box art by Eidson. Reissued as: H-326 *Bounty* (1961); H-330 *Beagle* (1961); H-328 *Beagle* (1966); H-318 *Bounty* (1972); H-338 *Bounty* (1978).

H-336 Santa Maria "S"   1957-71   1/90 $20-60
Brown plastic. Vacuum-formed sails. Decal, paper flag sheet. Two colors of twine for rigging. Box art by Eidson. Reissued as H-358 (1958) and H-322 (1972).

H-344 Flying Cloud "S" with sails   1957-71   1/232 $20-60
Black, tan, white plastic. Angel figurehead. With vacuum-formed sails. Thread, preformed ratlines, decal, paper flag sheet. Launched in 1851 by Boston shipwright Donald McKay, this was the fastest clipper ship in the world. Hogg primary model sculptor. Box art by Eidson. Reissued as: G-358 Famous Ships (1958); H-325 *Stag Hound* (1962); H-343 *Yankee Clipper* (1973); H-344 *Flying Cloud* (1975); 2652 *Flying Cloud* (1979) Advent.

H-347 USCG Eagle "S"   1958-71   1/254 $40-60
White, rust, tan plastic. With vacuum-formed sails. Preformed string ratlines. Paper flag sheet. Coast Guard training ship; formerly the German *Horst Wessel*. Reissued as: H-382 *Seedler* (1960); H-331 *Seeadler* (1968); H-347 *Eagle* (1976); 2651 *Eagle* (1979) Advent.

H-363 HMS Victory with sails   1959-70, 72-74   1/146 $20-60
Brown, black, tan plastic. Vacuum-formed sails, preformed ratlines, thread, cement. Includes 24 page booklet *The Story of Ships*. Horatio Nelson's flagship. Box art by Philip Shelton. Reissued as H-363 (1972).

H-364 Cutty Sark "S"   1959-63   1/96 $60-120
Black, brown, white plastic. Pre-painted copper hull. Includes two spools of thread, two sizes of metal chain, cement. Steering wheel turns rudder. Twenty crew figures. Thirty inch model retailing for $9.95. This kit became the best seller in Revell's sailing ship line. Hogg primary model sculptor. Reissued as: H-390 *Thermopylae* (1960); H-394 *Cutty Sark* (1966); H-395 *Cutty Sark* (1966); H-399 *Pedro Nunes* (1967); H-399 *Cutty Sark* (1974); H-393 *Cutty Sark* (1978).

Ship Gift Sets

HNF-6 Admiral's Fleet   1954 $500-600
Released for Christmas, 1954. Contains paint set and tube of cement. H-301 *Missouri*; H-303 *Nautilus*; H-305 *Sullivans*; H-306 *Los Angeles*; H-304 *PT-212*.

H-311 Victory at Sea "S"   1955 $500-600
With cement. Released in the spring of 1955 as a Fathers Day gift set. This set was tied-in with the NBC-TV show "Victory at Sea." Box art by Kishady. H-304 *PT-212*; H-305 *Sullivans*; H-307 *Franklin D. Roosevelt*.

G-332 Merchant Fleet "S"   1956 $500-600
The Hawaiian Pilot and Tug Boat both have pre-painted red hulls below the waterline. Box art by Eidson. H-314 *Long Beach*; H-315 *Hawaiian Pilot*; H-322 *J. L. Hanna*.

G-333 Guided Missile Fleet "S"   1956 $500-600
This gift set was tied-in with the TV series "Navy Log" that aired on both ABC and CBS. The 1955 box has the CBS logo, and there are two different, very rare, 1956 ABC box versions. Box art by Eidson. H-308 *Nautilus*; H-331 *Norton Sound*; H-334 *Boston*.

G-335 Let's Take a Trip "S"   1956 $600-650
Tie-in with TV show "Let's Take a Trip." Two versions: with and without "CBS" logo. Art by Eidson. H-219 DC-7a American; H-312 *United States*; H-1200-6 Cadillac.

G-358 Famous Sailing Ships "S"   1958 $400-500
H-319 *Constitution*; H-336 *Santa Maria*; H-344 *Flying Cloud*.

G-359 US Naval Academy Gift Set "S"   1958 $700-800
With paints, brush, cement. Part of the proceeds from the sale of this gift set went to building Memorial Stadium at Annapolis. Box art by Eidson. H-360 *Ranger*; H-372 *Canberra*; H-352 *Forrest Sherman*.

Military Vehicles and Armor

Flexible vinyl rubber treads or tires. Some of the molds were owned by mold-maker Steve Adams and later were reissued by Adams, Athearn, Life-Like, SNAP, and UPC.

H-522 M4A1 Sherman Tank "S"   1956-59   1/40 $80-100
Olive plastic, silver vinyl treads. Army decals. Turret turns, cannon elevates. Includes tank commander and five soldiers. Box art by Kishady. Reissued as: H-544 (1960); H-554 (1972); H-554 (1968).

H-523 155mm Gun and Tractor "S"   1957-59   1/40 $130-150
Includes five figures. Box art by Kishady. The 155mm cannon was also issued separately as H-535, and the Tractor as H-536. The mold for this kit was owned by Adams.

H-524 M-20 Armored Combat Car "S"   1957-60   1/40 $80-100
Includes six figures. Box art by Kishady. The mold for this kit was owned by Adams.

H-525 Jeep and Trailer "S"   1957-60   1/40 $80-100
Windshield can be folded down. Includes three figures. Box art by Kishady. The mold for this kit was owned by Adams.

H-526 GI Battle Action Figures "S"   1957-60   1/40 $60-80
Thirty-six figures. Includes bazooka, mortar, machine gun, flame thrower, mine detectors. Box art by Kishady. The mold for this kit was owned by Adams.

H-527 Army Combat Team Gift Set "S"   1957-58   1/40 $500-600.
Box art by Kishady. H-522 Sherman Tank; H-523 M-2 Gun and Tractor; H-525 Jeep and Trailer; H-526 GI Battle Action Figures.

H-535 M2 155mm Long Range Cannon "S" 1958-59   1/40 $80-100
Gun elevates, recoils. 155mm Long Tom cannon. Box art by Kishady. Also issued in H-523. The mold for this kit was owned by Adams.

H-536 M4 High Speed Tractor "S"   1958-59   1/40 $250-280
Box art by Kishady. Also issued in H-523. The mold for this kit was owned by Adams.

H-537 US Army M-35 Truck "S"   1958-60   1/40 $70-90
Includes seven figures. Box art by Kishady. Reissued as: H-557 (1968); H-557 (1972).

H-538 Russian T-34 "S"   1958-60   1/40 $70-90
Olive green plastic. Includes five crew figures. Based on an Egyptian tank captured by the Israelis. Box art by Eidson. Reissued as H-546 (1961) and H-559 (1973).

H-539 105mm Howitzer "S"   1958-60   1/40 $70-90
Cannon elevates, recoil action. Includes four figures. Rests on earthen bunker base. Box art by Kishady. Reissued as H-555 (1968) and H-555 (1972).

H-540 M-56 Self-Propelled Gun "S"   1958-60   1/40 $70-90
Gun swivels, elevates, recoils. Includes four figures. Box art by Kishady. Reissued as H-556 (1968) and H-556 (1972).

1950s Cars
Revell/Gowland 1/16 Scale Cars
These three model car kits were also issued by Revell as pull-toys.

H-24 1910 Maxwell   1951-55   1/16 $60-70
Red, white, tan, bronze plastic; rubber tires, metal rods for axles, windshield and roof supports; sheet of clear acetate for windshield; paper pattern for roof; dashboard and license plate printed on instruction sheet. Converted from a pull-toy. This kit came in a white and orange box, without the kit number printed on it.

1960 Reissue   1960-63 $40-50
Red, white plastic; sheet of acetate for windshield, cut-out paper roof provided. This reissue comes in a colorful, turn-of-the-century art style box. The original-issue rubber tires are replaced with plastic wheel/tire parts.

H-51 1917 Ford Model T   1952-55   1/16 $50-60
Black, red, off-white, brown plastic. Rubber tires. Acetate sheet for windshield. This model came in a yellow and white box without the kit number on it.

1960 Reissue   1960-63 $40-50
Black, white, beige, silver plastic. Acetate sheet for windshield. This reissue comes in a colorful, turn-of-the-century art style box. The original-issue rubber tires are replaced with plastic wheel/tire parts.

H-59 1932 Ford Hot Rod   1953   1/16 $80-90
Red plastic. Metal axles. "77" decals. For the first time the Revell "Authentic Kit" motto is used on the box of this kit—a definitely unauthentic, crude model!

Highway Pioneers 1/32 Scale Cars
Some kits in this series come in boxes marked "Official Construction Kit" with the Boy Scouts or Cub Scouts insignias on them.

Series One

All five models in this series come in generic yellow boxes with pictures of all five cars in the series on the top. A rubber stamp on the box end indicates which car is inside.

H-32 1910 Ford Model T   1951-57   1/32 $15-20
Black plastic; metal windshield frame and metal rods for frame support. Over scale, two-part "Grandpa" driver figure. Converted from a pull-toy.
1954 "US Antique Series" Reissue
Black plastic; metal windshield replaced with plastic part. Proper scale, five-part driver figure added. The original "Action Miniature" rear axle and hole in the front end part are replaced with new parts. Hubcaps now hold on new wheels made just for this kit. The gas tank is now separated from the body part, and a trunk is added. "Ford" now appears on the radiator. Side lanterns and hood rivets added.
1960 Reissue   Black plastic   1960-63
H-33 1900 Packard   1951-55   1/32 $15-20
Dark red, black plastic. Over scale two-part driver. Converted from a pull-toy.
1960 Reissue   Light red plastic   1960-62
Proper-scale five part driver added. Chassis rails added to stabilize front and rear axles now that the "Action Miniature" axles have been replaced. Floorboard texture added. These changes were probably made earlier than 1960.
H-34 1909 Stanley Steamer   1951-57   1/32 $15-20
Dark green, black plastic. Over-scale three-part driver. Converted from a pull-toy.
1954 "US Antique Series" Reissue
Light green plastic. Proper-scale five-part driver. "Action Miniature" axles replaced. Hubcaps now hold on new wheels made just for this kit. New separate front axle, new headlights, new shift lever.
1960 Reissue   Light green plastic 1960-63
H-35 1903 Cadillac   1951-55   1/32 $15-20
Dark blue, black plastic. Converted from a pull-toy.
1960 Reissue   Blue plastic   1960-61
"Action Miniature" axles replaced. Hubcaps now hold on new wheels made just for this kit. Texture added to floorboard. Changes probably made prior to 1960.
H-36 1903 Ford Model A   1951-55   1/32 $15-20
Black plastic. This model was made from the same mold as the H-35 Cadillac—only the rear seat has been left off. Converted from a pull-toy and bearing the "Action Miniature" name on the underside of the chassis. (Some gift set models and kits marked with a star or with blank side panels, rather than the usual "Gowland" trademark, are in yellow plastic.) Beginning in 1953 a new mold was used to produce the Model A. The new model has two seats, wicker baskets on its sides, and a five-part driver. (AMT issued this model in 1953 as a built-up promo car for Ford dealers to commemorate the 50th anniversary of the Model A.)
1960 Reissue   Black plastic   1960-63

Series Two

All five models in this series come in generic orange boxes with pictures of all five cars in the series on the top.

H-38 1914 Stutz Bearcat   1952-57   1/32 $15-20
Yellow, black plastic.
1954 "US Antique Series" Reissue
Yellow plastic. Hubcaps now hold on new wheels made just for this kit. Spare tire added. Front axle springs now molded separately from axle.
1960 Reissue   Yellow plastic   1960-63
H-39 1910 Cadillac   1952-55   1/32 $15-20
Light blue plastic. Sheet of acetate for windows. The first car to have its own separately created wheels—rather than sharing the standard black wheels. But wheels are still attached by heating axle tips.
1954 "US Antique Series" Reissue
Light blue plastic.
H-40 1908 Buick Rumble   1952-55   1/32 $15-20
Red, black plastic. Bent iron rods for roof supports.
H-41 1910 Studebaker Electric   1952-55   1/32 $15-20
Dark green, black plastic. Sheet acetate for windshield.
H-42 1915 Ford Model T   1952-55   1/32 $15-20
Black plastic. Sheet of acetate for windows.
1960 Reissue   Black plastic   1960-63
"Ford" added to radiator. Hubcaps added. Changes probably made prior to 1960.

Series Three

All five models in this series come in generic green boxes with pictures of all five cars in the series on the top. All Series Three kits use the same five-part driver with his goggles pulled up on his cap.

H-44 1904 Olds Delivery Van   1953-55   1/32 $10-15
White plastic. Some kits came with black plastic wheels; others with white. "Gowland Bakery" decals. Beginning with Series Three, all cars come with hubcaps.
H-45 1907 Sears Buggy   1953-55   1/32 $15-20
Dark green plastic.
H-46 1911 Rolls Royce   1953-55   1/32 $15-20
Maroon, black plastic.
1954 "Foreign Antique Series" Reissue
Light green plastic.
1960 Reissue   Reddish brown plastic   1960-63
H-47 1904 Nash Rambler   1953-55   1/32 $15-20
Yellow plastic. Reissued with modifications as H-81 1906 Franklin.
1954 S Antique Series" Reissue
Yellow plastic.
H-48 1910 Pierce Arrow   1953-55   1/32 $15-20
Dark red plastic. Reissued with modifications as H-82 1910 Hudson.
1954 "U S Antique Series" Reissue
Red plastic.

Series Four "Foreign Cars"

All five models in this series first came in generic blue boxes with pictures of all five cars in the series on the top. In 1955 they were released in individualized boxes.

H-52 1953 MG-TD   1954-59   1/32 $20-25
Red plastic. Convertible top up. The first modern car in the series.
1960 Reissue   White plastic   1960-63
H-53 1907 Renault   1954-55   1/32 $15-20
Yellow plastic. Later release in brown plastic.
1960 Reissue   Brown plastic   1960-63
H-54 1913 Mercedes Benz   1954-55   1/32 $15-20
Dark green plastic.
1960 Reissue   Dark green plastic   1960-62
H-55 1915 Fiat Roadster   1954-55   1/32 $15-20
Dark red plastic.
H-56 1953 Jaguar XK-120   1954-59   1/32 $20-25
Pale green plastic. One-piece body shell.
1960 Reissue   Blue plastic   1960-63
H-60 1932 Ford Hot Rod   1954-59   1/32 $35-40
Red plastic. "US Modern Series." Teenage boy driver. "Ford" on hubcaps. Forty-four parts—the most complicated model in the series up to this time. Box art by Eidson. Reissued with modifications as H-80 Ford Jalopy.
1960 Reissue   Red plastic   1960-63

Non-Series Cars

Kits H-61 through H-82 were issued originally in boxes with illustrations for just one individual car, not a set of five cars, as with the earlier kits.

H-61 1893 Duryea   1954-55   1/32 $15-20
Black plastic. "US Antique Series."
H-62 1910 Auto Wagon   1954-55   1/32 $15-20
Yellow plastic. "U S Antique Series." International Harvester pick-up truck.
H-63 1929 4 1/2 Litre Bentley   1955   1/32 $15-20
Dark green plastic. "Foreign Classic Series."
H-72 1929 Duesenberg Model J   1955-57   1/32 $15-20
Light blue plastic. "U S Classic Series." Le Baron Phaeton with jaunty, pipe-smoking driver and "flapper" female passenger.
H-73 1936 Cord Phaeton   1955-57   1/32 $15-20
Dark blue plastic. "U S Classic Series." Male driver and female passenger figures—sitting so close together they are molded in one part.
H-74 1952 Ferrari 4.1 Litre   1955-59   1/32 $25-30
Red plastic. "Foreign Modern Series." Wheels split into two parts to create realistic spoked wheel effect. Helmeted and goggled driver, and standing flag man.
1960 Reissue   Red plastic, gray wheels   1960-63
H-80 1932 Ford Jalopy   1957-59   1/32 $30-35
Black plastic. Modified reissue of H-60. Roof, engine hood, front tow bar added. "Ford" erased from hub caps. Helmeted driver from H-63 Bentley replaced teenage driver.
1960 Reissue   Black plastic   1960-63
H-81 1906 Franklin   1956-57   1/32 $15-20
Green plastic. "U S Antique Series." Modified reissue of H-47 Nash. Lady passenger with umbrella added. Radiator changed to round shape. Top now folded down.
H-82 1910 Hudson   1956-57   1/32 $15-20
White plastic. "U S Antique Series." Modified reissue of H-48 Pierce Arrow. Flag waving boy passenger added. Top now folded down.

Highway Pioneers Gift Sets

Some issues of these "Gift Packs" come with paint, a brush, and cement. Revell issued these for Christmas and Father's Day as higher-priced items suitable for gifts. Often retail stores were sent holiday posters to promote the sets.

H-37 Highway Pioneers Gift Set, Series I   1951 $70-80
Contains all five Series I cars. H-36 Model A Ford comes in black or yellow plastic.

H-43 Highway Pioneers Gift Set, Series Two   1952 $70-80
Contains all five Series Two cars, and seven jars of paint, brush, thinner, and cement. Smaller box edition has no paint, cement.

H-49 Highway Pioneers Gift Set, Series Three 1953 $70-80
Includes all five Series Three cars

G-64 Foreign Car Series Gift Set   1955 $100-110
The same set at H-495.

G-66 Early American Gift Set   1955 $70-80
Includes H-34, H-36, H-44, H-45.

G-67 U S Antique Series Gift Set   1955 $70-80
Includes H-35, H-40, H-41, H-42.

G-69 Sports Cars Gift Set   1955 $200-250
Includes H-71, H-72, H-73, H-74. Packaged in cardboard sleeve and cellophane wrap.

G-79 Speedy Sportsters Gift Set   1956 $350-400
Includes: H-52 MG-TD, H-56 Jaguar XK-120, H-60 Ford Hot Rod, H-74 Ferrari.

H-395 Highway Pioneers Gift Set   1953-54 $100-110
Includes: H-32, H-33, H-34, H-35, H-36, H-41.

P-395 Highway Pioneers Gift Set   1954 $100-110
"American Cars." Includes H-32, H-33, H-34, H-35, H-36, H-41.

P-695 Highway Pioneers Gift Set   1954 $120-140
"Collectors Kit." Includes H-38, H-39, H-40, H-42, H-44, H-45, H-47, H-48. P-695 sets have only eight cars, with an "EIGHT" sticker placed over the "TEN" printing on the box.

H-795 10 Collectors Gift Set   1953 $140-160
P-795 10 Collectors Gift Set   1954
Includes all Series One and Series Two cars.

H-895 10 Collectors Gift Set   1953 $140-160
P-895 10 Collectors Gift Set   1954
Includes all Series Two and Series Three cars.

H-495 Highway Pioneers Gift Set   1954 $140-160
P-495 Highway Pioneers Gift Set   1954 $150-170
"Foreign Cars." Includes H-46, H-52, H-53, H-54, H-55, H-56. The same set as G-64. P-495 includes paint and cement.

Revell-AMT 1955-1956 Modern Cars

First issued as 1955 cars; then in late 1955 and early 1956 the models were modified to update them to Detroit's new 1956 releases. Since changes in the cars were modest, the kits were given a new look by molding them in plastic colors different from the 1955 issues and putting new figures with the cars.

Originally issued with the Revell-AMT trademark. In 1956 Revell bought-out AMT's interest, and thereafter the kits were issued with only the Revell trademark. None of the Revell-AMT model cars came with clear window glass parts, but they do have chrome parts.

H-1200 1955 Cadillac Eldorado Convertible "S" 1955   1/32 $70-90
Light blue plastic, metal axle rods. Man at the wheel, woman figure standing. Hood removes to show engine. AMT owned the mold for this model. Box art by Kishady.

H-1200-6 1956 Cadillac Eldorado Convertible "S" 1956-58 1/32 $70-90
Off-white plastic, metal axle rods. Man and woman figures in front seat. Box art by Leynnwood. Included in G-335 "Let's Take a Trip."

H-1201 1955 Chrysler New Yorker "S" 1955   1/32 $70-90
Off-white plastic, metal axle rods. Matron and her chauffeur figures. Hood can be removed to show engine. AMT owned the mold for this model. Box art by Kishady.

H-1201-6 1956 Chrysler New Yorker "S"   1956-58   1/32 $70-90
Black or light green plastic, metal axle rods. Man at driver's seat, woman and child standing. Box art by Leynnwood. Reissued in 1959 as H-1231 Customized Chrysler.

H-1202 1955 Ford Fairlane Convertible "S"   1955   1/32 $70-90
Blue-green plastic, metal axle rods. Man at wheel, mom, child. Hood can be removed to show engine. Box art by Kishady.

H-1202-6 1956 Ford Fairlane Convertible "S" 1955-58   1/32 $70-90

Light yellow plastic, metal axle rods. Woman at wheel and polo player. Reissued in 1959 as H-1229 Customized Ford. Box art by Kishady.

H-1203 1955 Buick Riviera "S"   1955   1/32 $70-90
Red plastic, metal axle rods. Man at wheel and woman standing. Hood removes to show engine. Box art by Kishady.

H-1203-6 1956 Buick Riviera "S"   1956-58   1/32 $70-90
Robin-egg blue plastic, metal axle rods. Man and woman standing. Box art by Kishady.
Reissued in 1959 as H-1230 Customized Buick.

H-1204 1955 Mercury Montclair "S"   1955   1/32 $70-90
Yellow plastic, metal axle rods. AMT owned the mold for this model. Box art by Kishady.

H-1204-6 1956 Mercury Montclair "S"   1956-58   1/32 $70-90
Orange plastic, metal axle rods. Two figures in front seat. Box art by Leynnwood. Reissued in 1959 as H-1233 Customized Mercury.

Customizing Kits

In 1959 Revell reissued four of the Revell-AMT car kits as "Customizing Kits" with some parts chrome plated and additional jazzy new parts like air scoops and side exhaust pipes. Also added was a sheet of decals with racing numbers and pin stripping. The figures that had accompanied the earlier issues were dropped.

H-1229 Ford Customizing Kit   1959-62   1/32 $60-80
Metallic blue plastic. Decals. Box art by Leynnwood. Reissue of H-1202-6.

H-1230 Buick Customizing Kit   1959-61   1/32 $80-90
Metallic maroon plastic; Revell hired full-sized custom car designer George Barris to develop this kit—making this the first of Barris' many custom models. Box art by Leynnwood. Reissue of H-1203-6.

H-1231 Chrysler Customizing Kit   1959-63   1/32 $80-90
Metallic black plastic. Box art by Leynnwood. Reissue of H-1201-6.

H-1233 Mercury Customizing Kit   1959-63   1/32 $80-90
Metallic purple plastic. Box art by Leynnwood. Reissue of H-1204-6.

G-1234 Car Customizing Gift Set   1959   1/32 $400-600
This gift set contains three regular boxed kits enclosed in a thin cardboard sleeve. H-1229 Ford; H-1230 Buick; H-1233 Mercury.

Revell-AMT Gift Sets

G-335 Let's Take a Trip "S"   1956 $400-500
Tie-in with TV show "Let's Take a Trip." Two box versions: with and without "CBS" logo. Box art by Eidson. H-219 DC-7a; H-312 *United States*; H-1200-6 Cadillac.

G-1206 Autorama Gift Set   1955   1/32 $350-450
H-1200 Cadillac; H-1202 Ford; H-1201 Chrysler; H-1203 Buick.

H-1211-6 Autorama Gift Set   1956   1/32 $450-550
H-1200-6 Cadillac; H-1201-6 Chrysler; H-1202-6 Ford; H-1203-6 Buick; H-1204-6 Mercury

G-1211 Autorama Gift Set   1956   1/32 $450-550
H-1201-6 Chrysler; H-1203-6 Buick; H-1202-6 Ford; H-1209 Continental

Modern Cars

H-1209 1956 Lincoln Continental Mk II "S" 1956-58   1/32 $55-65
Black plastic, metal axles. No clear window glass. Woman and doorman figures. Hood removes to show engine. Box art by Leynnwood.

H-1210 Lincoln Futura   1956-60   1/27 $100-125
Blue-green, clear, chrome plastic. Man and woman figures. No engine and little detail on underside. This was Lincoln's "dream car" for 1956. The actual car was later modified in the mid-1960s to become ABC-TV's Batmobile. Box art by Kishady.

H-1213 Pontiac Club de Mer   1957-62   1/25 $100-125
Blue-green, clear, chrome plastic. Man and woman figures. Trim decal. No engine and little detail on underside. Bud Anderson, later "The Kat from AMT," helped sculpt the pattern for this model. Box art by Kishady.

H-1214 Cadillac Eldorado "S"   1957-62   1/25 $125-150
Black, clear, chrome plastic. Box art by Leynnwood.

H-1217 1956 Austin-Healey 100-Six "S"   1959-63   1/25 $40-60
White, clear plastic. Seats tilt and hood opens. Reissued as: H-1244 (1961); H-1245 (1961); H-1202 (1977).

H-1220 1957 Ford Country Squire "S"   1957-60   1/25 $150-175
Dark brown, chrome, but no clear plastic. Cowboy and son figures. Opening tailgate, hood lifts to show engine. The mold for this kit was modified to create the H-1240 Ranchero (1960). Box art by Leynnwood.

H-1227 1959 Ford Fairlane Skyliner   1959-63   1/25 $100-120
Green, clear, chrome plastic. Metal axles. Includes two seated figures. Hardtop folds and retracts into trunk, hood opens. Box art by Leynnwood. Reissued as H-1333 (1976) and 3112 (1979) Advent.

H-1228 1957 Volkswagen Micro Bus   1959-63   1/25 $100-120

Red-orange, clear plastic. Includes three figures. Optional closed or open tops. Engine door and passenger doors snap on hinges to open and close. Classic 23-Window Micro Bus. Box art by Leynnwood. Reissued as: H-1267 Deluxe Station Wagon (1967); H-1202 "Bed Bug" (1970); H-1310 "Rubber Duck" (1977); 3144 Volkswagen Van (1979) Advent.

H-1238 1958 Porsche Carrera   1959-62   1/25 $40-50
White, chrome, clear plastic. Hood and trunk open. Reissued as: H-1246 (1961); H-1247 (1961); H-1204 (1977).

H-1239 1955 Mercedes Benz 190SL   1959-61   1/25 $30-40
Red, chrome, clear plastic. Hood opens, hardtop removes.

1/48 Scale Trucks
None of these truck models has clear or chrome parts.

H-1400 '56 Ford Pick-Up "S"   1956-57   1/48 $40-60
Blue plastic. Driver, policeman, and motorcycle. Box art by Leynnwood.

H-1401 1956 Chevy Stake Truck "S"   1956-57   1/48 $40-60
Green plastic. Two figures unloading cargo. Box art by Leynnwood.

H-1402 White Gas Truck "S"   1956-57   1/48 $40-60
Red plastic. Two figures. Box art by Leynnwood.

H-1403 Kenworth Bekins Van "S"   1956-57   1/48 $200-250
White plastic. "Bekins Moving" decal. Two figures. Kenworth 825 truck and Fruehauf trailer. Box art by Leynnwood. This truck was modified and used as the "Mobile Carrier" in the H-1821 Honest John Missile (1959).

Miniature Masterpieces
Miniature Masterpieces of Los Angeles was a partnership started by Revell's Lew Glaser, mold maker/manufacturer Steve Adams, and former Revell employee Ben Lench. The model prototypes were developed and created by Revell craftsmen Charles Gretz and Tony Bulone—and then Adams made the molds and produced the kits. Marketing was handled by the Miniature Masterpieces company, which was run by Lench. In the fall of 1954 Revell assumed production and distribution of the kits, but the tooling remained the property of Adams.

Early Miniature Masterpieces kits (H-500 through H-505) were packaged in old-fashioned two-color boxes and carry only the Miniature Masterpieces trademark. Models produced after the Revell take-over (H-506 through H-521) came in more colorful boxes and carry both the Revell logo and the Miniature Masterpieces name.

Revell discontinued sales of this line in 1956. Since then the molds for the Miniature Masterpieces have been used by six companies: Adams (1958), Boraxo (1950s-1960s), Athearn (1962), UPC (1965), Life-Like (1973), and Snap.

H-500 State Coach of England   1953-54   1/48 $50-70
Red plastic. This kit contains only the coach itself, without horses or figures. Reissued as H-506 in 1954.

H-501 Wells Fargo Stage Coach   1954-56   1/48 $30-40
Brown plastic, decal. With four horses, driver, and rifle-toting guard figure.

H-502 Lafayette Carriage   1954-56   1/48 $30-40
Dark brown plastic. With two horses, driver, lady with parasol, and the Marquis figures.

H-504 Roman Chariot   1954-56   1/48 $30-40
White plastic, decal. With four horses, driver, gladiator figures. With base part.

H-505 Covered Wagon   1954-56   1/48 $25-35
Brown plastic. With two oxen, husband on horseback, wife, and son figures. With base part.

H-506 State Coach of England   1954-56   1/48 $50-70
Red acetate plastic coach and white figures in early issues; brown and cream styrene plastic in later issues. With eight horses, four guide riders, Prince Philip, and Queen Elizabeth II figures. Reissue of H-500 in a more colorful box.

H-507 Chuck Wagon   1954-56   1/48 $30-40
Beige plastic. With two horses, two dogs, and three figures. With base part. Issued in a more colorful box, with both the Revell and Miniature Masterpieces logos.

H-509 Western Figures   1955-56   1/48 $30-40
Beige plastic, but two figures in dark brown plastic. With two oxen, two pack mules, three horses, a dog, and six figures. The first model kit in this series with full-color box art and only the Revell logo.

H-510 Ranch Wagon   1955-56   1/48 $30-40
Dark brown plastic. With four mules, a man, and boy figures. With base part.

H-513 Tally Ho Coach "A"   1955-56   1/48 $40-50
Gray plastic. "London, Birmingham, Tally Ho" decal. With four horses and nine figures. Box art by Eidson.

H-521 Medicine Wagon "S"   1955-56   1/48 $40-50
Tan plastic, "Doctor Brown's Snake Oil" decal. With two horses and seven figures. Box art by Eidson.

Miniature Masterpieces Gift Sets

G-508 Miniature Masterpieces Gift Set   1954   1/48 $150-200
H-501 Wells Fargo Stage; H-502 Lafayette Carriage; H-505 Covered Wagon.

H-511 Western Collection Gift Set "A"   1954   1/48 $150-200
H-501 Wells Fargo Stage; H-505 Covered Wagon; H-507 Chuck Wagon; H-510 Ranch Wagon.

G-511 Western Collection Gift Set "A"   1955   1/48 $150-200
H-501 Wells Fargo Stage; H-505 Covered Wagon; H-507 Chuck Wagon; H-509 Western Figures; H-510 Ranch Wagon.

G-518 3 Collectors Edition Gift Set   1955   1/48 $125-135
Sleeve type thin cardboard, open-front box into which any three kits could be slipped.

20 Mule Team   1954-1960s   1/48 $25-35
Light blue and dark brown plastic, cellophane packet of cement, silver thread. With three wagons, 20 mules, and two figures. The prototype for this model was developed and crafted by Revell's staff for Miniature Masterpieces, which produced it for Boraxo as a mail-away premium. By the late 1950s Adams Action Models had assumed production of this kit for Boraxo. Other Miniature Masterpieces western models that were offered by Boraxo as premiums were: Wells Fargo Stage Coach, Covered Wagon, Ranch Wagon.

American Firefighters
This series was introduced by Marlin Toy Company of New York City in the fall of 1952. Marlin sold just the first three kits, and packaged all three in a single generic box with the box contents indicated on one end panel. These models came without the horse and fireman figures.

In the summer of 1953 Revell took over distribution of the kits through a Revell subsidiary in Closter, New Jersey, called Collector's Kits. The models were repackaged in a single generic box with the Revell logo, and figures of firemen and horses were added to each model. In the summer of 1954 Revell assumed manufacturing of the models. However, production of the Firefighters stopped soon thereafter in the United States.

The first three models were later produced by Revell, Brazil. Reportedly, the tooling for the American Firefighters was lost at sea when the freighter returning them to the United States sank.

F-200 Steamer   1954-55   1/48 $30-50
Red, yellow, white plastic. Metal chain, flexible plastic tape for horse's reins. With two horses, two firemen, and a Dalmatian dog. Originally issued in 1952 by Marlin (100 FS) without the white plastic figures but with metal rods for handrails and twine for fire hose.

F-201 Chemical & Ladder   1954-55   1/48 $30-50
Red, bronze, white plastic. Metal chain. Two horses, two firemen, and a Dalmatian dog. Originally issued in 1952 by Marlin (101 FS) in red and yellow plastic without figures.

F-202 Hose Reel   1954-55   1/48 $30-50
Red, bronze, white plastic. Metal rods, thick twine for fire hose, flexible plastic tape for horse's reins. Two horses, two firemen, and a Dalmatian. Originally issued by Marlin (102 FS).

F-205 Aerial Ladder   1954-55   1/48 $50-60
Red, white, bronze plastic. Three horses, four firemen, and a Dalmatian dog. Released late in 1954 in a new individual box illustrating just this model.

H-706 American LaFrance Water Tower   1955-55   1/48 $100-120
Red, bronze, white plastic. Vinyl reins, brass chain. Three horses, three firemen, and a Dalmatian dog. This was the first Firefighters model designed and manufactured by Revell. Box art by Eidson.

Antique Guns

H-600 Pepperbox   1955-57   1/1 $25-35
Gunmetal gray, copper, brown plastic. Includes ivory plastic desk stand/wall mount.

H-601 Dueling Pistol   1955-57   1/1 $35-45
Silver, brown plastic. Includes ivory plastic desk stand/wall mount.

H-602 Derringer   1955-57   1/1 $25-35
Silver, dark brown plastic. Includes ivory plastic desk stand/wall mount. Mold designed and made at Paragon Tool of Los Angeles. Ernest Brown, who would later join Revell's staff, worked from a real gun.

H-603 Colt ".45" Peacemaker   1955-57   1/1 $30-40
Gunmetal gray, pearl plastic. Includes ivory plastic desk stand/wall mount.

H-606 Antique Pistol Collection   1954   1/1 $150-200
Contains paint, cement. H-600; H-602; H-603.

H-607 Pirate Blunderbuss "S"   1956-57   1/1 $25-35
Gunmetal gray, brown plastic. Includes wall bracket. Eighteen inches long.

H-609 Miquelet Arabian "S"   1956-57   1/1 $25-35
Gunmetal silver plastic. Includes wall bracket. Twenty-one inches long.

Wildlife Collection

Each kit came with a bottle of "S" liquid cement and three plastic packets of "fur" to be dusted over the model after it had been built and painted with cement.

H-1900 Perri the Squirrel "S" 1957-62 1/1 $75-100
Brown plastic, with transparent green plastic eyes. "S" cement, three packets of fur, brush, and spray bottle fur applicator (not included in the three later kits). Art by Eidson.

H-1901 Teddy the Koala Bear "S" 1958-62 1/2 $75-100
Brown, black plastic. "S" cement, three packets of fur, brush. Box art by Eidson.

H-1902 Friskie the Beagle Puppy "S" 1958-62 1/2 $75-100
Light beige, black plastic, with clear plastic and decals for eyes. "S" cement, three packets of fur, brush. Box art by Eidson.

H-1903 Sassy the Kitten "S" 1959-62 1/1 $75-100
Off-white plastic. Transparent blue eyes. Orange, brown, white fur. Box art by Eidson.

Dr. Seuss Zoo Animals

This collection of figure kits was based on the characters in the book *If I Ran the Zoo* and other books by Theodore Geisel—Dr. Seuss. The kits were designed as play toys for young children and most featured parts that could be snap-assembled and disassembled. Parts from one model were interchangeable with parts from another. The eyes were pre-painted on each character. The first six of these models were issued in regular kit boxes in 1959; the second issues came out in 1960 in boxes with a cellophane window.

Z-2000 The Cat in the Hat 1959-61 $125-150
Blue, red, white plastic. Includes cement. This 12 inch tall model is designed to be cemented together. "Beginner Hobby Kit."

Z-2001 Tingo the Noodle Topped Stroodle 1959 & 1960-61 $80-100
Red, blue, yellow, orange plastic. Second issue of this kit comes in a pink box with a cellophane window and has two fewer neck segment parts.

Z-2002 Gowdy the Dowdy Grackle 1959 & 1960-61 $80-100
Yellow, brown, red, blue plastic. Second issue in a green window box.

Z-2003 Norval the Bashful Blinket 1959 & 1960-61 $80-100
Yellow, blue, brown, red plastic. Second issue in purple cellophane window box.

Z-2004 Roscoe the Many Footed Lion 1959 & 1960-61 $80-100
Yellow, orange, blue plastic. Second issue in blue cellophane window box with one fewer body segments.

Z-2005 Grickily the Gractus 1960-61 $80-100
Yellow, white, brown plastic. Only issued in orange cellophane window box.

Z-2006 Busby the Tasse, Tasseated Afghan Spaniel Yak 1960-61 $80-100
Brown, white, green plastic. Only issued in blue cellophane window box.

Z-2050 Cat in the Hat with Thing 1 & 2 1960-61 $100-120
Reissue of Z-2000 with new box art and two new small character figures. Converted from a glue kit to a snap-together kit. "Beginners Hobby Kit."

Z-2051 Birthday Bird 1960-61 $100-120
Red, yellow, white plastic. This kit is designed to be cemented together. Includes cement. The Bird rests on a cloud base, holding a "Happy birthday" cake. Comes with an assortment of letters to spell a child's name on the cake. "Beginners Hobby Kit."

Z-2052 Horton the Elephant 1960-61 $100-120
Gray, yellow, white plastic. This kit is designed to be cemented together. Includes cement. Horton sits on a nest holding an egg. "Beginners Hobby Kit."

G-2080 Dr. Seuss Zoo Set 1959 $200-240
Pink box. Z-2001 Tingo; Z-2002 Gowdy; Z-2003 Norval.

G-2080 Dr. Seuss Zoo Set #1 1960-61 $200-240
Blue box. Z-2001 Tingo; Z-2002 Gowdy; Z-2003 Norval.

G-2081 Dr. Seuss Zoo Set #2 1960-61 $200-240
White box. Z-2004 Roscoe; Z-2005 Grickily; Z-2006 Busby.

Z-2100 The Game of Yertle 1960 $100-120
This is a board game that requires players to balance many small turtle pieces on a three-platform base.

Model Train Structures

Revell began selling HO Scale model trains in the mid-1950s, and in 1958 introduced a line of plastic assembly kits to provide realistic landscape structures for train layouts. Each kit was molded in three colors of plastic, with very intricate detail. Kits included decals and sheets of acetate for window glass. Revell also issued some HO Scale (1/87) trucks and cars. In the early 1960s Revell got out of the model train field, but in 1977 some of the structure kits were reissued. Alan Armitage, a veteran model railroad buff, was the primary model sculptor for the railroading kits. The tooling for these kits is currently owned by Con-Cor.

T-6018 Global Van Lines Truck $30-40
T-6019 Converta-Car Kit $50-70

Seven Chrysler cars with styling suggestions provided by Ed Roth and *Rod & Custom Magazine*.

T-6021 Ford Auto Transport $30-40
T-9001 Small Town Station $25-35
Reissued as H-985 (1977). Also issued as T-9036 Country School House.

T-9002 Trackside Building Group $30-40
Reissued as H-988 (1977).

T-9003 Farmhouse Building Set $30-40
Reissued as H-987 (1977).

T-9004 Interlocking Tower $30-40
T-9005 Water Tower $25-35
T-9006 Elevated Switchman Shanty $25-35
T-9008 Crossing Tender's Shack $25-35
T-9009 Farmhouse & Privy $30-40
Reissued in modified form as T-9034 Suburban House.

T-9010 Garage $25-35
T-9011 Chicken Coop $25-35
T-9015 Barn Group $30-40
Reissued as H-989 (1977).

T-9016 Barn $25-35
Also issued in modified form as T-9035 Summer Stock theater.

T-9017 Farmyard Buildings $30-40
T-9020 Freight Station $40-60
T-9022 Maintenance Shed $25-35
T-9028 Operating Engine House $40-50
Reissued as H-995 (1977). Also issued with new front facades and modified details as T-9038 Weekly Herald and T-9037 Superior Bakery.

T-9029 Sand & Pump House with Fuel Tank $25-35
T-9030 Sand & Pump House $25-35
T-9031 Fuel Tank $25-35
T-9032 Yardmaster's Office $25-35
T-9033 Crew Shanty $25-35
T-9034 Suburban House $30-40
Reissue of T-9009 Farm House with the porch deleted and a garage replacing the privy.

T-9035 Summer Stock theater $30-40
Also issued in modified form as T-9016 Barn.

T-9036 Country Schoolhouse $30-40
Reissued as H-986 (1977). Also issued in modified form as T-9001 Small Town Station.

T-9037 Superior Bakery $30-40
Reissued as H-997 (1977). Also issued in modified form as T-9028 Engine House.

T-9038 Weekly Herald $30-40
Reissued as H-966 (1977). Also issued in modified form as T-9028 Engine House.

H-1550 Westinghouse Atomic Power Plant 1959-63 1/192 $450-500
Gray, yellow, olive green, black plastic. Half reactor dome removes to show interior. Gantry, cranes, hoists move. Includes ten figures and service truck. Also booklet on atomic power. Rare second 1961 issue box has photo of built model. Includes thin plastic sheet with grass and parking spaces printed on.

1960s Kits

1960s Aircraft

G-161 Supersonic Gift Set – 6 Famous Planes 1961 $400-450
H-111 Saab J-35 Draken; H-210 Lockheed F-94C; H-213 Douglas Skyrocket; H-233 Convair F-102A; H-236 F-100C; H-259 Douglas X-3 Stiletto.

H-1551 Allison Prop Jet Engine 1960-63 1/11 $75-100
Light metallic blue, black, silver, orange plastic. Non-motor version of H-1552.

H-1552 Allison Prop Jet Engine with motor 1960-63 1/11 $75-100

Air Cadet Series

These six kits were issued in 1960 in plastic bags with cardboard header cards for hanging from a peg board. Each sold for 49 cents.

H-111 SAAB J-35 Draken 1960 1/71 $15-25
Silver, clear plastic. Swedish decals. This kit was issued for the first time in this series. Reissued as G-161 (1961) and H-131 (1970).

H-112 Douglas D-558-2 Skyrocket 1960 1/54 $15-25
White, clear plastic. Decals. Reissue of H-213 (1955).

H-113 Douglas X-3 Stiletto 1960 1/64 $15-25
White, clear plastic. Decals. Reissue of H-259 (1957).

H-115 Lockheed F-94C Starfire 1960 1/56 $15-25
Silver, clear plastic. Decals. Reissue of H-210 (1954).

H-116 Lockheed F-102A 1960 1/77 $15-25
Silver, clear plastic. Decals. Reissue of H-233 (1956).
H-117 North American F-100 1960 1/70 $15-25
Silver, clear plastic. Decals. Reissue of H-236 (1956).
H-1830 German V-2 Rocket 1960 1/69 $30-40
Olive green plastic. This bagged kit was a special order for a hobby dealer. Also issued as H-1830 (1960) in a regular box.

Academy Series

This series of kits was issued in 1962. The side panels of the boxes had a picture of the Air Force Academy falcon and various sets of aviator wings. These reissues of 1950s kits sold for 79 cents.

H-121 Douglas D-558-2 Skyrocket 1962-63 1/54 $15-25
White, clear plastic. Navy decals. Reissue of H-213 (1955).
H-122 Douglas X-3 Stiletto 1962-63 1/65 $15-25
White, clear plastic. Air Force decals. Reissue of H-259 (1957).
H-123 Lockheed F-94C Starfire 1962-63 1/55 $15-25
Silver, clear plastic. Air Force decals. Reissue of H-210 (1954).
H-124 Lockheed F102A 1962-63 1/77 $15-25
Silver, clear plastic. Air Force decals. Reissue of H-233 (1956).
H-125 Republic F-84F Thunderstreak 1962-63 1/54 $15-25
Silver, clear plastic. Air Force decals. Reissue of H-215 (1955).
H-126 Northrop F-89D Scorpion 1962-63 1/80 $15-25
Silver, clear plastic. Air Force decals. Reissue of H-221 (1955).
H-127 North American F-100 1962-63 1/70 $15-25
Silver, clear plastic. Air Force decals. Leynnwood box art. Reissue of H-236 (1956).
H-128 McDonnell F-101A Voodoo 1962-63 1/75 $15-25
Silver, clear plastic. Air Force decals. Reissue of H-231 (1956).

Strategic Air Power Series

These 1950s vintage kits were reissued in 1969 in the "Strategic Air Power" series.

H-130 Lockheed F-102A 1969-80 1/77 $15-25
Light gray, clear plastic. Air Force/Air National Guard decals. Reissue of H-233 (1956).
H-131 SAAB J-35 Dragon 1969-77 1/71 $15-25
Dark green, clear plastic. Swedish Air Force decals. Reissue of H-111 (1960).
H-132 Martin B-57B Intruder 1969-77 1/85 $20-30
Dark green, clear plastic. Air Force decals. Canopy is US "B" version canopy used in original H-230 (1955) issue.
H-133 A7D Corsair II 1969-78 1/72 $10-15
Olive green, clear plastic. Air Force decals. Reissue of H-114 (1968).
H-134 North American A-5A Vigilante 1969-76 1/82 $15-25
Light gray, clear plastic. Navy, VAH-7 decals. Reissue of H-196 (1960).
H-135 Douglas X-3 Stiletto 1969-77 1/65 $15-25
White, clear plastic. Decals. Reissue of H-259 (1957).

Air Power Series

These eight 1950s kits were reissued in 1962 in the "Air Power" series. Some continued in the catalog under the same kit number after the Air Power series ended.

H-136 North American B-25C 1962-68 1/64 $20-30
Olive, clear plastic. Air Force decals. Reissue of H-216 (1955).
H-137 Convair B-24 1962-68 1/92 $25-35
Light olive, clear plastic. Air Force decals. Reissue of H-218 (1955).
H-138 Piasecki H-16A 1962-69 1/96 $20-30
Silver, clear plastic. Air Force decals. Leynnwood box art. Reissue of H-223 (1955).
H-139 Boeing B-36D 1962-69 1/184 $35-45
Silver, clear plastic. Air Force decals. Reissue H-205 (1954).
H-140 Boeing B-47 1962-69 1/117 $25-35
Silver, clear plastic. Air Force decals. Reissue of H-206 (1954).
H-141 Boeing B-29 1962-68 1/135 $35-40
Silver, clear plastic. Air Force decals. Reissue of H-208 (1955).
H-142 Lockheed F-104 1962-68 1/64 $20-30
Silver, clear plastic. Air Force decals. Reissue of H-199 (1959). Also issued by AHM, American importer of Fujimi kits, in an AHM box with new box art.
H-143 Convair B-58 Hustler 1962-63 1/94 $25-35
Silver, clear plastic. Air Force decals. Reissue of H-252 (1958).

Whip-Fly It Series

This series of kits was issued in 1960-61. These reissues of 1950s kits were modified with the addition of clay to weight the nose, a length of line, and a plastic handle. There was a hole in one wingtip to attach the "control line," and then a kid could swing it round-and-around.

H-151 F9F-8 Cougar 1960-63 1/52 $30-35
Dark blue, clear plastic. Navy decals. Reissue of H-212 (1954).
H-152 F-84F Thunderstreak 1960-63 1/54 $30-35
Silver, clear plastic. Air Force decals. Reissue of H-215 (1955).
H-153 F-89D Scorpion 1960-63 1/80 $40-50
Silver, clear plastic. Air Force decals. Reissue of H-221 (1955).
H-154 F8U-1 Crusader 1960-63 1/67 $30-35
Light gray, clear plastic. Navy decals. Reissue of H-250 (1957).
H-155 P-39 Airacobra 1960-63 1/45 $35-40
Olive brown, clear plastic. Army Air Corps decals. Reissue of H-222 (1955).
H-156 F-101A Voodoo 1960-62 1/75 $35-40
Silver, clear plastic. Air Force decals. Reissue of H-231 (1956).
H-157 British Canberra Bomber 1961-63 1/81 $45-55
Silver, clear plastic. RAF decals. New "bubble" canopy used for this British B-6 version of the Martin B-57. Decal locater lines eliminated. With added plastic "whizzer" for sound. Reissue of H-230 (1955).
H-158 Yak-25 Flashlight 1961-63 1/50 $40-50
Silver, clear plastic. With added "whizzer" for sound. Reissue of H-296 (1958).
H-159 Lockheed F-106A 1961-63 1/67 $35-40
Silver, clear plastic. Air Force decals. With added "whizzer" for sound. Box art by Bart Doe. Reissue of H-298 (1959).

Famous Artist/Famous Aircraft Series

These 1950s kits were reissued in 1961 as the "Famous Artist" series, but by the fall of that year the series box texts had been changed to "Famous Aircraft." The "Famous Artist" issues are more valuable. Each kit came with a "collector stamp." These models celebrated fifty years of Naval aviation.

H-167 F8U-1 Crusader 1961-63 1/67 $25-40
Gray, clear plastic. Navy decals. Includes sidewinder missiles. Art by George Akimoto. Reissue of H-250 (1957).
H-168 F9F-8 Cougar 1961-63 1/52 $25-40
White, clear plastic. Navy and Marine decals. Art by Bart Doe. Reissue of H-212 (1954).
H-169 F11F-1 Blue Angels Tiger 1961-66 1/55 $25-40
Blue, clear plastic. Blue Angels decals. Art by Don Wilson. Reissue of H-249 (1957).
H-170 P2V-7 Neptune 1961-63 1/104 $40-60
Dark blue, clear plastic. Navy decals. Art by Jack Leynnwood. Skis added to wheels to create "Operation Deep Freeze" Antarctic survey plane. Mold changes were permanent. Reissue of H-239 (1957).
H-171 F7U-3 Cutlass 1961-63 1/59 $25-40
Light gray, clear plastic. Navy decals. Art by Chuck Coppock. Four underwing missiles. Reissue of H-211 (1954).
H-172 Sikorsky H04S-1 1961-70 1/49 $25-40
Orange, clear plastic. Navy decals. Art by Jack Leynnwood. Reissue of H-214 (1954).
H-174 Lockheed WV-2 Radome 1961-63 1/128 $40-60
Gray (no clear) plastic. Navy decals. Art by Al White. Reissue of H-179 (1958).
H-175 Martin PBM-5 Mariner 1961-63 1/118 $40-60
Dark blue, clear plastic. Navy decals. Art by George Akimoto. Reissue of H-258 (1958).
H-176 Martin P6M Seamaster 1961-63 1/136 $40-60
Light gray, clear plastic. Navy decals. Art by Jack Leynnwood. Reissue of H-244 (1957).
H-177 Douglas A3D Skywarrior 1961-63 1/84 $25-40
Light gray, clear plastic. Navy decals. Art by Chuck Coppock. Reissue of H-241 (1957).
H-178 Convair R3Y-2 Tradewind 1961-63 1/168 $40-60
Dark blue, clear plastic. Navy decals. Art by Ken Smith. Reissue of H-238 (1957).
H-179 A4D Skyhawk 1961-66 1/51 $25-40
Light gray, clear plastic. Navy decals. Art by Bart Doe. Reissue of H-299 (1959).

Picture Plane Series

These three 1950s kits were reissued in 1960 in the "Picture Plane" series with new box art by Jack Leynnwood. These kits were the first to use the new box layout adopted in the 1960s with a panel on the left side of the box top containing the kit name and kit series.

H-181 Sikorsky HRS-1 Marine Helicopter 1960-70 1/49 $35-45
Dark blue, clear plastic. Marines decals. Reissue of H-214 (1954).
H-182 Ilushin Il-38 Bison 1960-63 1/159 $40-60
Dark green, clear plastic. Russian decals. Reissue of H-235 (1956).
H-183 Lockheed C-130A Hercules 1960-66 1/140 $35-45
Silver, clear plastic. Air Force decals. Includes fuel truck, mobile generator, and ground crew figure. Three-blade prop s. Leynnwood box art. Reissue of H-247 (1957).

Air Commando Series

These 1950s kits were reissued in 1967 in the "Air Commando" series.

H-229 McDonald F4C Phantom II   1967-71   1/72 $8-10
Dark green, clear plastic. Air Force decals. Includes four Sparrow missiles and two extra fuel tanks. Reissue of H-110 (1965).

H-230 Lockheed C-130B Herky Bird   1967-69   1/140 $15-20
Dark green, clear plastic. Air Force decals. New four-blade propellers replace original three-blade props, and original ground equipment deleted. Reissue of H-247 (1957).

H-231 Republic F-105 Thunderchief   1967-76   1/75 $8-10
Tan, clear plastic. Air Force decals. Hinged canopy. Reissue of H-285 (1958).

H-232 Lockheed F-104   1967-70   1/67 $10-15
Dark green, clear plastic. Air Force decals. With four figures, four Sidewinders, and missile loading cart. Reissue of H-199 (1959).

Pacific Raiders Series

These three 1950s kits were reissued in 1965 as World War II Pacific Theater aircraft.

H-237 B-24J "Jolly Roger"   1965-70   1/92 $30-35
Dark olive, clear plastic. Army Air Force decals, 90th Bombardment Group, 17th Air Force. Reissue of H-218 (1955).

H-238 B-25 "Doolittle Raider"   1965-70   1/64 $30-35
Olive, clear plastic. Early Army Air Corps decals. Reissue of H-216 (1955).

H-239 B-29 "Dauntless Dotty"   1965-70   1/135 $30-35
Silver, clear plastic. Army Air Force decals. Reissue of H-208 (1954).

Airliners/Jet Horizon Series

These older airliner kits were reissued in the 1960s and in 1968 most came in new packaging in the "Jet Horizon" series.

H-241 SE-210 SAS Caravelle   1966   1/96 $20-30
Off white (no clear) plastic. Scandinavian Airlines system decals. Does not come with the stand that was included with the first issue H-184 (1961).

H-242 DC-8 United Jet Mainliner   1964-70   1/143 $30-40
Silver (no clear) plastic. United decals. Cowlings remove to show engines. Includes loading ramp. Does not include stand as in original issue H-248 (1959).

H-243 Boeing 707 Astrojet American   1962-70   1/140 $30-40
Silver (no clear) plastic. American Airlines decals. With updated fan-jet engines and taller tail fin. Reissue of H-246 (1958).

H-244 Convair 990 Coronado Swissair   1964-68   1/135 $60-70
Silver (no clear) plastic. Swissair decals. Reissue of H-254 (1962).

H-245 Boeing 727-100 American Astrojet   1964-70   1/144 $30-40
Silver (no clear) plastic. American Airlines decals. No "Jet Horizon" marking on box.

H-246 Douglas DC-9   1966-70   1/120 $20-30
White (no clear) plastic. Douglas decals, but decals for eight airlines were available from Revell for 25 cents each. R & D planned this kit for standard 1/144 scale, but engineering changed it to 1/120 to make the model "fit the box." No "Jet Horizon" marking on box. Reissued as H-247 (1967).

H-247 Douglas DC-9 Delta Fan Jet   1967-70   1/120 $20-30
White (no clear) plastic. Delta decals. Includes three-view collector drawings. No "Jet Horizon" marking on box. Reissue of H-246 (1966).

Jet Commando Series

In 1968 these 1950s kits were reissued in the "Jet Commandos" series.

H-253 Boeing B-52C   1968-76   1/175 $15-20
Black, clear plastic. New arrowhead-shaped stand. Decals. Reissue of H-207 (1954).

H-254 MAC C-135B   1968-70   1/139 $15-20
Silver (no clear) plastic. Military Airlift Command decals. Reissue of H-246 (1958).

H-255 LTV F-8E Crusader   1968-73   1/67 $10-15
Light gray, clear plastic. Navy decals. Reissue of H-250 (1957).

H-256 A-3B Skywarrior   1968-70   1/84 $15-20
White, clear plastic. Navy decals. Reissue of H-241 (1957).

Jet Command Series

These 1950s kits were reissued in 1964 with new box art and graphics.

H-272 Convair B-58 Hustler   1966-69   1/94 $20-25
Silver, clear plastic. Reissue of H-252 (1958).

H-273 Boeing B-52 with X-15   1965-69   1/175 $40-50
Silver, clear plastic. B-52 with long nose and without molded-in stand ball. Reissue of H-207 (1954).

H-274 Yakovlev Yak-25 Flashlight   1966   1/50 $40-50
Silver, clear plastic. Reissue of H-296 (1958).

H-275 Boeing KC-135   1966-67   1/139 $20-30
Silver, clear plastic. Reissue of H-287 (1958).

Non-Series Kits

Non-Standard Scale Kits

H-144 Cobra II   1962-66   1/45 $20-30
Yellow orange, clear plastic. Bell P-39 with permanent mold changes, most notably a new four-blade propeller. 1946 Thompson Trophy winner. Reissue of H-222 (1955).

H-162 B-52 with X-15   1961-63   1/175 $30-35
Silver, clear plastic. B-52 has original short nose and molded-in ball for stand. Also has 1950s clear globe stand with B-52/X-15 decal. Reissue of H-207 (1954).

H-163 Lockheed P3A Orion   1965-68   1/115 $20-30
Gray, clear plastic. Navy decals. Reissue of the H-255 Lockheed Electra (1958) with major, permanent mold revisions. Some revisions: side windows deleted, tail cut off and tail radar boom part added, fuselage forward of wings shortened, and nose made more pointed. Propellers retain their squared-off tips, but should have rounded tips.

H-164 North American X-15   1961-69   1/65 $20-30
Black, clear plastic. NASA decals. Nose boom removed. Reissue of H-198 (1959).

H-165 North American A3J Vigilante   1961-66   1/82 $20-30
Light gray, clear plastic. Navy decals. Reissue of H-196 (1960).

H-166 Republic F-105B Thunderchief   1961-68   1/75 $15-20
Silver, clear plastic. Retractable fuel boom. Four underwing bombs. Leynnwood box art. Reissue of H-285 (1958).

H-169 F11F-1 Blue Angels Tiger   1966-69   1/55 $20-30
Blue, clear plastic. Blue Angels decals. Reissue of H-169 (1961).

H-184 SE-210 Caravelle SAS   1961-63   1/96 $30-40
Silver (no clear) plastic. Scandinavian Airlines System decals. Came with a stand not included in "Jet Horizon" reissue H-241 (1964).

H-185 Fairey Rotodyne   1961-63   1/78 $50-70
Silver, clear plastic. Fairey decals. Includes ten figures. Right side panel removes to show interior, rear cargo door hinged to open, passenger door opens. Ron Campbell primary model sculptor. Leynnwood box art.

H-187 Bell X-5   1960-63   1/40 $25-35
Cream, clear plastic. Wings move to sweptback position, landing gear retracts, air brakes and control surfaces move.

H-196 North American A3J Vigilante "S"   1960   1/82 $45-55
Gray, clear plastic. Removable jet engines, tail fins pivot, canopies open. The last kit to bear the "S" mark on its box. Reissued as: H-165 (1961); H-134 (1970); 3356 (1979) Advent.

H-243 Boeing 707 Astrojet American   1962   1/140 $40-50
Silver (no clear) plastic. With updated fan-jet engines and a taller tail. This kit comes in an "Air Mail" box with red and blue slashes on the box edges, like an air mail envelope. Reissue of H-246 (1958).

H-254 Convair 990 Coronado Swissair   1962-63   1/135 $70-80
Cream, clear plastic. Swissair and SAS decals. Cowlings remove to show engines. Reissued as H-244 (1964).

H-260 Douglas AD-6 Skyraider   1961-65   1/40 $20-30
Blue, clear plastic. Navy decals. Reissue of H-269 (1959).

H-261 Douglas A-1 Skyraider   1966-70   1/40 $15-20
Gray, clear plastic. Navy and South Vietnam AF decals. Reissue of H-269 (1959).

H-262 Boeing SST Prototype   1967-70   1/200 $75-100
Mustard yellow, clear plastic. Boeing decals. The kit contains two 18-inch models mounted on the same base. One version shows the plane in its swing-wing, supersonic mode and the other depicts it in its wings-out, nose down configuration. R & D originally planned this as one model with moving wings and nose. Reissued as H-263 (1969).

H-263 SST Pan American Clipper   1969-72   1/200 $75-100
White, clear plastic. This is the same kit as H-262, but with Pan American decals.

H-285 North American B-25B "Doolittle Raider" 1968-72 1/48 $25-35
Olive, clear plastic. Army Air Force decals. Builds to either the B or C variant. Three crew figures. Bomb bay doors open to show four 500 pound bombs. Based on a B-25C owned by reclusive millionaire Howard Hughes and preserved in a hanger one mile from the Revell plant. Reissued as H-285 (1977).

H-290 Frank Luke Spad XIII   1965-76   1/27 $25-35
Olive plastic. Decals for Frank Luke's plane. No figures or rigging thread as in first issue. Reissue of H-256 (1957).

H-291 William Barker Sopwith Camel   1965-76   1/28 $25-35
Medium green plastic. Decals for William Barker's Camel. No figures or rigging thread as in first issue. Reissue of H-197 (1959).

H-292 Werner Voss Dr-1 Fokker Triplane   1965-76   1/27 $20-25
Light blue plastic. Decals for Werner Voss's triplane. No figures or rigging thread as in first issue H-270 (1957).

G-293 3 WW I Dogfighters   1968-70   1/28 $100-120
H-290 Spad XIII in tan plastic with French markings decals used only with this issue. H-291 Camel in green plastic with Roy Brown decals.

H-292 Fokker Dr-1 in red or blue plastic with Voss decals, although the box illustration shows the "Red Baron" plane.

1/72 Aircraft Scale Kits

H-110 McDonnell F4B Phantom II 1965-70 1/72 $8-10
Gray, clear plastic. Navy decals. Reissued as: H-129 (1968); H-229 (1968); H-186 (1972); H-229 (1972); H-195 (1974); H-179 (1977).

H-111 Martin B-26B Marauder "Flak Bait" 1966-69 1/72 $10-15
Olive, clear plastic. Army Air Force decals. Includes three crew figures. Removable engine cowls. Nose cone is too pointed and canopy is wrong shape. Model developed in the US, but mold made in England. This is a model of the B-26 preserved in the Smithsonian. Reissued as H-147 (1973).

H-112 Heinkel He-219 Owl 1967-69 1/72 $8-12
Light gray-blue, clear plastic. Hinged access panels. Decals. Mold made in England and first released there. Reissued as H-160 (1974).

H-113 Junkers Ju-88 1968-69 1/72 $8-12
Light gray, clear plastic. Decals. Can be built into A-4 bomber or D-1 reconnaissance versions. Includes three crew figures and four 550 lb. bombs. Based on a plane in the Air Force Museum, Dayton, Ohio. Reissued as H-165 (1975).

H-114 Vought A7A Corsair II 1968-70 1/72 $8-10
Light gray, clear plastic. Includes underwing fuel tanks, Sidewinders, bombs. Reissued as H-133 (1969, 1973). Also issued by AHM, American importer of Fujimi kits, in AHM box with new box art.

H-115 Douglas A-20C Havoc/Boston III 1968-69 1/72 $10-15
Light gray, clear plastic. Alternate USAF or RAF decals. Removable cowlings. Based on a plane owned by Howard Hughes, preserved in a hanger one mile from the Revell plant. Reissued as H-156 (1974) and H-232 (1975).

H-129 McDonnell F-4K Phantom 1968-69 1/72 $10-15
Blue, clear plastic. British Royal Navy decals. Reissue of H-110 (1965).

H-201 Boeing B-17F "Memphis Belle" 1962-79 1/72 $15-30
Olive green, clear plastic. Army Air Force decals. Wheels retract, bomb bay doors open and close. Heavy riveting. Revell's first 1/72 scale model. Reissued as H-209 (1968) and H-228 (1974).

H-202 Avro "Dam Buster" Lancaster 1964-68 1/72 $20-30
Black, clear plastic. REF decals. The mold used to produce this model had "change block" sections that could be switched to also make the standard H-207 Lancaster (1965). This kit includes externally carried cylinder skip bomb, modified bomb bay, and longer wheel struts. Reissued as H-202 (1972); 3413 (1979) Advent.

H-203 Consolidated B-24D "Blue Streak" 1964-79 1/72 $15-25
Olive green, clear plastic. Army Air Force decals. Reissued as H-205 (1965).

H-204 Focke Wulf Fw-200C Condor 1966-69 1/72 $15-25
Baby blue, clear plastic. German decals. Movable flaps, bomb bay doors. *Scale Modeler* (March 1965, 52) praised the model, but said some seams would need filling, the rivets were too heavy, and there was no swastika on the decal sheet. Model designer Lloyd Jones complained that the English tool maker did not follow his instructions to make flush aileron attachments, as on the real plane. Reissued as H-204 (1972).

H-205 Consolidated PB4Y-1 1965-69 1/72 $20-30
Dull blue, clear plastic. Navy decals. The parts in this kit are unchanged from the original issue Army Air Force H-203 B-24D (1964). Reissued as H-205 (1974).

H-206 Lockheed YF-12A (A-11) Interceptor 1966-70 1/72 $15-20
Black, clear plastic. Air Defense Command decals. Nose cone removes to show radar dish. This is a model of the interceptor version of the "Blackbird." Features of this model deleted in the H-212 SR-71 reissue (1967) include: two right-side missile bays that can be built in open position to show Hughes AIM-47A air-to-air missiles, two underwing camera pods, two underwing ventral fins, and large fuselage ventral fin that can be built in either extended position for flight or folded position for landing. Also issued by AHM.

H-207 Avro Lancaster MK I "Sugar" 1965-69 1/72 $15-25
Olive, clear plastic. RAF decals. This model was produced from the same mold used to make the Dam Buster Lancaster, but a "change block" in the mold was switched to make a standard Lancaster. Leynnwood box art. Reissue of H-202 (1964).

H-208 F-111 Tactical Fighter (TFX) 1966-77 1/72 $15-20
Light gray, clear plastic. Air Force/Navy decals. Retractable landing gear, removable nose cone to show radar dish, movable swept wings. Can be built to A or B version with alternate nose, wing tip, elevator, and control surfaces (but no tail hook for Navy version). Controversial General Dynamics multi-purpose jet. *Scale Modeler* (November 1966, 11) "Without a doubt, this is the most sophisticated jet kit to ever appear on the market. Revell must be applauded for its engineering know-how." Reissued as H-210 (1968).

H-209 8th Air Force B-17F "Lady Luck" 1968-70 1/72 $15-25
Gray, clear plastic. Two position landing gear, opening bomb bay doors, movable control surfaces. Reissue of H-201 (1962).

H-210 Royal Australian Air Force F-111C 1968-69 1/72 $20-30
Tan, clear plastic. Australian Air Force decals. Reissue of H-208 (1966).

H-211 Catalina PBY-5A Black Cat 1969-72 1/72 $15-20
Black, clear plastic. Wing-tip floats fold up. Includes landing gear. *Scale Modeler* (July 1969, 32) called it the best PBY model ever offered for sale. Reissued as: H-277 (1972); H-576 (1977); 3412 (1979) Advent.

H-212 Lockheed SR-71 Secret Spy Plane 1967-77 1/72 $10-15
Black, clear plastic. Air Force decals. Several parts deleted from the H-206 Interceptor issue (1966) and tail instrument cone added. Reissued as 3411 (1979) Advent.

H-258 Sikorsky CH-54A Sky Crane 1969-76 1/72 $15-20
Olive, clear plastic. Combat or medic decals. Includes detachable cargo pod, 105 gun.

H-611 Spitfire 1963-68 1/72 $6-8
Brown, clear plastic. Brian Knight box art. Reissued as: H-682 (1967); H-221 (1970); H-611 (1972); H-663 (1976); H-50 (1978).

H-612 Messerschmitt Bf-109E 1963-68 1/72 $6-8
Light blue or light gray, clear plastic. Knight box art. Reissued as: H-682 (1967); H-684 (1967); H-223 (1970); H-612 (1972); H-63 (1974); H-663 (1976); H-49 (1978).

H-613 Republic P-47D 1963-68 1/72 $6-8
Light olive, clear plastic. Knight box art. Reissued as: H-684 (1967); H-224 (1971); H-66 (1975); H-69 (1976); H-48 (1978).

H-615 Focke Wulf Fw-190 1963-68 1/72 $6-8
Brown, clear plastic. Leynnwood box art. Reissued as: H-226 (1971); H-62 (1974); H-661 (1976); 3305 (1979) Advent.

H-616 Hawker Hurricane 1963-68 1/72 $6-8
Green, clear plastic. RAF decals. *Scale Modeler* (July 1965, 21) reviewer writes that the model is well molded and fits together well, but lacks detail. Reissued as: H-682 (1967); H-226 (1971); 3306 (1979) Advent.

H-617 Mitsubishi A6M5 Zero 1963-68 1/72 $6-8
Gray, clear plastic. Reissued as: H-220 (1970); H-617 (1972); H-662 (1976); 3304 (1979) Advent.

H-619 North American P-51D 1963-68 1/72 $6-8
Silver, clear plastic. An inaccurate model tooled and first released in England. Knight box art. Reissued as: H-686 (1967); H-222 (1970); H-72 (1976); H-666 (1976); H-664 (1976); H-47 (1978).

H-620 Hawker Tempest V 1963-68 1/72 $6-8
Olive green, clear plastic. Knight box art. Reissued as H-223 (1970) and H-620 (1972).

H-621 Kawasaki Ki-61-IA Hein Tony 1963-68 1/72 $8-10
Silver, clear plastic. Reissued as: H-686 (1967) and H-224 (1971).

H-623 P-40E Warhawk 1964-68 1/72 $6-8
Silver, clear plastic. Reissued as: H-623 (1972); H-60 (1974); H-46 (1978).

H-624 Messerschmitt Me-262 1965-68 1/72 $6-8
Light gray plastic. Decals. *Scale Modeler* (February 1970, 16) "Perhaps the best 72nd scale model on the market." Reissued as: H-221 (1970); H-624 (1972); H-56 (1978); 3307 (1979) Advent.

H-625 Chance Vought F4U-1D Corsair 1965-68 1/72 $6-8
Silver, clear plastic. Leynnwood box art. Reissued as: H-225 (1971); H-61 (1974); H-45 (1978).

H-627 Spad XIII 1963-68 1/72 $6-8
Tan plastic. Rickenbacker decals. Eldon of Japan copied this model in 1968. Reissued as: H-683 (1967); H-627 (1972); H-68 (1975); H-665 (1976).

H-628 Sopwith Camel 1963-68 1/72 $6-8
Tan plastic. Roy Brown decals. Hansen says struts are too long. Eldon copied this model. Reissued as: H-676 (1968); H-628 (1972); H-64 (1975); H-51 (1978).

H-629 Albatros D-III 1963-68 1/72 $6-8
Red plastic. Richthofen decals. Hansen says fuselage too pointed at both ends, top wing wrong shape. Eldon copied this model. Reissued as H-685 (1967) and H-74 (1976).

H-631 Nieuport 17c 1964-68 1/72 $8-10
Olive plastic with matte finish to simulate fabric. French decals. Eldon copied this model. Reissued as H-685 (1967).

H-632 Fokker D-VII 1964-68 1/72 $6-8
White plastic with matte finish. Herman Goring decals. Hansen rates this one of the most accurate in the set. Eldon copied this model. Reissued as H-683 (1967) and H-71 (1975).

H-633 SE-5a 1964-68 1/72 $6-8
Olive plastic with matte finish. RFC decals. Eldon copied this model. Reissued as H-683 (1967) and H-69 (1975).

H-635 Polikarpov Po-I-16 1965-68 1/72 $8-10
Green, clear plastic. Knight art. Reissued as H-678 (1968).

H-636 Brewster F2A Buffalo 1965-68 1/72 $6-8
Silver, clear plastic. Navy decals. Reissued as H-684 (1967) and 3302 (1979) Advent.

H-637 Nakajima Ki-84 Frank 1965-68 1/72 $8-10
Green, clear plastic. Decals. *Scale Modeler* (July 1965, 20): "Revell's new program of bringing out the more obscure fighters is refreshing. It will wake up the public to the fact that not all Japanese fighter planes were Zeroes." Reissued as H-686 (1967).

H-639 Grumman F4F-4 Wildcat   1965-68   1/72 $6-8
Gray-blue, clear plastic. Reissued as: H-681 (1967); H-220 (1970); H-639 (1972);
  H-662 (1976); H-73 (1976); 3303 (1979) Advent.

H-640 Bell P-39 Aircobra   1965-68   1/72 $6-8
Olive, clear plastic. Removable engine panel. Reissued as: H-681 (1967); H-67
  (1975); H-664 (1976); 3301 (1979) Advent.

H-641 Nakajima Ki-43 Hayabusa Oscar   1965-68   1/72 $8-10
Silver, clear plastic. Decal. Knight box art. Reissued as H-681 (1967) and H-225
  (1971).

H-643 DeHavilland DH-2   1966-68   1/72 $8-10
Tan plastic with matte finish. RAF decals. Reissued as H-685 (1967).

H-644 Morane-Saulnier N   1965-68   1/72 $8-10
Silver plastic with matte finish. Russian decals. Reissued as H-676 (1968).

H-645 Fokker E-III   1965-68   1/72 $8-10
Tan plastic with matte finish. Reissued as H-676 (1968).

H-647 PZL-11c   1967-68   1/72 $8-10
Olive, clear plastic. Polish AF decals. Reissued as H-678 (1968).

H-648 Fiat C. R. 42 Falco   1967-68   1/72 $8-10
Light brown plastic. Leynnwood box art. Reissued as H-678 (1968).

H-649 Boeing PT-13D Kaydet   1967-68   1/72 $10-15
Silver, clear plastic. Navy decals.

H-652 Fokker Dr-I   1966-68   1/72 $6-8
Light blue plastic with matte finish. Werner Voss decals. The mold for this kit was
  cut in Great Britain, and the first run of the kit was made there. This first English-
  issue kit had a headrest behind the cockpit and an incorrectly shaped fuselage
  that caused poor fit with the cowl. Later issues of the kit corrected the first issue
  errors. Reissued as: H-65 (1975); H-665 (1976); H-52 (1978).

H-653 Nieuport 28   1967-68   1/72 $8-10
Light blue plastic with matte finish. Decals. Reissued as H-70 (1975).

H-654 Sopwith Triplane   1966-68   1/72 $8-10
Tan plastic with mate finish. Decals for the Royal Navy. Reissued as H-75 (1976).

H-676 3 Famous Fighters of WWI   1968-69   1/72 $20-25
H-628 Camel in olive plastic with RAF decals.
H-644 Morane-Saulnier in silver plastic with Frenchman Roland Garros decals.
H-645 Fokker E-III in dark gray plastic with Turkish AF decals.

H-677 3 Pioneer Fighters of WW II   1968-69   1/72 $20-25
This kit included three models not issued separately in the US.
H-656 Curtiss P-26A with Army Air Force decals.
H-657 Macchi MC 200 Saetta with Italian AF decals.
H-658 Curtiss P-36A Hawk with Army Air Force decals.

H-678 3 Freedom Fighters of WW II   1968-69   1/72 $20-25
H-635 Polikarpov I-16 with Republic of China decals.
H-647 PZL P-11c with Polish AF decals.
H-648 Fiat CR-42 with Swedish decals.

H-681 3 Pacific Sky Fighters   1967-69   1/72 $20-25
H-639 Grumman F4F-4 Wildcat with Navy decals.
H-640 Bell P-39Q Aircobra with Army Air Force decals.
H-641 Nakajima Ki-83 Hayabusa Oscar with Thai AF decals.

H-682 3 Battle of Britain Fighters   1967-69   1/72 $20-25
H-611 Spitfire with RAF decals.
H-612 Messerschmitt Bf-109E with German decals.
H-616 Hawker Hurricane with RAF decals.

H-683 3 Fighter Aeroplanes of World War I 1967-69   1/72 $20-25
H-627 SPAD XIII in green plastic with US 22nd Aero Squadron decals.
H-632 Fokker D-7 in red plastic with Ernst Udet decals.
H-633 SE-5a in tan plastic with US 25 Aero Squadron decals.

H-684 Air Aces of World War II   1967-69   1/72 $20-25
H-612 Messerschmitt Bf-109E with Werner Molders decals.
H-613 Republic P-47D with Glenn Eagleston decals.
H-636 Brewster F2A with Finland's Eino Luukkanen decals.

H-685 Air Aces of World War I   1967-69   1/72 $20-25
H-629 Albatros D-III in light blue plastic with Werner Voss decals.
H-631 Nieuport 17c in gray plastic with George Guynemer decals.
H-643 DeHavilland DH-2 in tan plastic with Lanoe Hawker decals.

H-686 Fighters of the Pacific   1967-69   1/72 $20-25
H-619 North American P-51D
H-621 Kawasaki Ki-61 Hein Tony
H-637 Nakajima Ki-84 Frank

1960s 1/32 Scale Kits

H-259 Bell UH-1D Huey Attack Helicopter 1968-80   1/32 $15-25
Olive, clear plastic. Army Air Cavalry decals. Doors open. Includes pilot and
  gunner figures. Three interchangeable weapons systems: SS-11 missile system,
  M-6 machine guns with 2.75" rockets, 7.62 mm mini-guns. Leynnwood box art
  . Reissued as: H-286 (1968); H-801 (1978); H-274 (1979); H-801 (1979).

H-265 Mitsubishi A6M5 Zero   1968-70, 72   1/32 $25-30

Green, clear plastic. Japanese Navy decals. Cowl removes to show engine. Canopy
  slides open. Pilot figure. *Scale Modeler* (October 1968, 12) "The best rendition
  yet offered by anyone, anywhere ... almost without flaw." Reissued as H-581
  (1978).

H-282 Supermarine Spitfire MK-I   1967-70, 72-76   1/32 $15-20
Light gray-blue, clear plastic. RAF 610 Squadron, Biggin Hill decals. Pilot figure.
  Canopy slides open. Wheels retract. The first of Revell's 1/32 scale aircraft kits
  to be issued. *Scale Modeler* (July 1968, 55) noted that the kit was based on the
  book *Superscale Drawings*. Nice flush riveting. Reissued as: G-288 (1968); H-294
  (1970); H-281 (1976).

H-283 Curtiss P-40E Flying Tiger   1967-79   1/32 $30-40
Gray, clear plastic. "Flying Tiger" Nationalist China decals. Sliding canopy, removable engine panel, detailed Allison engine, retractable landing gear, movable
  control surfaces. Pilot figure. *Scale Modeler* (October 1967, 55) rated this kit
  more highly than the Spitfire and Messerschmitt Bf-109F. "It really is a work of
  art." Reissued as H-271 (1970).

H-284 Messerschmitt Bf-109F   1967-70, 72-74   1/32 $25-30
Light gray, clear plastic. Retractable landing gear, hinged canopy, removable engine
  cowl, movable control surfaces. Pilot figure. Decals for Werner Molders' plane
  flown in the Battle of Britain. Based on a Bf-109G in the Ontario, California, air
  museum. Thus some aspects of the model are wrong: type of engine, cockpit
  layout, canopy. Reissued as G-288 (1968) and H-279 (1970)

H-286 Bell UH-1D "Huey"   1967-78   1/32 $15-20
Olive, clear plastic. Army decals. Removable cowling, doors open. Detailed jet
  engine. Two pilot figures. Can be built in armed or unarmed version with troop
  seats and cargo. Reissued as: H-259 (1968); H-801 (1978); H-274 (1979); H-801
  (1979).

H-287 Bell AH-1G Huey Cobra   1967-80   1/32 $15-20
Olive, clear plastic. Army decals. Removable cowling, detailed engine, hinged
  canopies, two crew figures, rotating gun turret, rocket launchers, mini-gun pods,
  grenade launcher.

G-288 2 Battle of Britain Fighters   1968   1/32 $130-150
Light gray, clear plastic. H-282 Spitfire I; H-284 Messerschmitt Bf-109F.

H-295 North American P-51B "Shangri-La" 1969-79   1/32 $25-30
Olive, clear plastic. Army Air Force decals. Based on an aircraft in the Tallmantz
  Movieland of the Air Museum. *Scale Modeler*'s reviewer (February 1970, 38)
  found the part fit well, but the shape of the nose was too tapered, the propeller
  blades too thin, the landing gear flimsy, and the tires too wide. Reissued as: H-152
  (1972); H-274 (1973); H-272 (1974).

H-296 Republic P-47D Thunderbolt   1969-77   1/32 $40-50
Silver, clear plastic. Army Air Force decals. The mold for this kit was designed with
  a "change block" fuselage insert that allowed molding of either this bubble top
  version or the razorback variant, issued in 1972 as H-151.

H-298 Junkers Ju-87B Stuka   1969-80   1/32 $25-30
Gray, clear plastic. *Scale Modeler* (June 1970, 40) describes this model as accurate and detailed ... "magnificent." This is a 1941 desert theater version. Revell
  staffer Dave Fisher climbed into the rafters of the Chicago Museum of Science
  and Industry to take photos of this plane hanging from the ceiling. Reissued as
  H-153 (1972).

H-299 Grumman F4F-4 Wildcat   1969-78   1/32 $25-30
Blue, clear plastic. Wings fold, canopy slides open, removable engine access panel.

1960s Missiles and Space Kits

G-291 Space Age Gift Set   1965 $200-250
H-111 Saab J-35 Draken; H-221 Northrop; F-89D Scorpion; H-259 Douglas; X-3
  Stiletto; H-1825 Moonship.

H-543 Firestone Corporal with Transporter "S" 1960-65 1/40 $100-130
White plastic missile, olive drab transporter. Army decals. Includes six figures, radar
  unit. Issued as H-1818 Corporal with Transporter in 1959.

H-547 Army Tactical Rockets Set   1963   1/40 $25-35
Light brown plastic. Reissue of H-1812 (1958).

H-548 Hawk Missile Battery   1963   1/40 $30-40
Olive plastic. Reissue of H-1817 (1958).

H-549 LaCrosse and Truck   1963   1/40 $80-100
Olive plastic. Reissue of H-1816 (1958).

H-1830 German V-2 Rocket   1960-66   1/69 $60-80
Olive green plastic. Includes launch trailer, hinged to raise rocket, launch platform,
  and three ground crew. Hull half removes to show fuel tanks and motor. John Steel
  box art. Reissued as H-1830 (1960) Air Cadet series and H-560 (1973).

H-1832 Mercury Redstone   1962-69   1/105 $100-120
Off-white plastic. US decals. Includes three ground crew and launch equipment.
  This is a modified reissue of the H-1803 Redstone (1959) with a Mercury capsule
  on top.

H-1833 Mercury/Atlas "Everything is GO" 1963-70 1/110 $50-60
Light gray, silver, orange plastic. "Friendship 7" decals. This is a reissue of the H-1822
  Atlas and launch pad (1959) with John Glenn's Mercury capsule on top.

H-1834 Mercury/Gemini   1964-70   1/48 $40-50

Gray plastic. The Mercury capsule comes on a stand and has a side panel that removes to show the astronaut inside. Decals for five different Mercury missions. The Gemini has hinged doors that open to show two astronaut figures. It is displayed on a stand and has a detachable launch module. Reissued in H-1847 (1969).

H-1835 Gemini Capsule   1965-70   1/24 $50-60
Dark gray plastic. NASA decals. Includes two figures. Hinged doors open, equipment module detaches. Comes with a stand. Includes eight-page booklet on the space program. Revell claimed that this was its best selling kit for 1966. The model is based on an actual Gemini capsule that Revell acquired and then gave away in its annual sweepstakes contest. Leynnwood box art. Reissued in H-1839 (1968) and H-1855 (1970).

H-1836 Apollo Spacecraft   1967-70   1/96 $30-40
White plastic. NASA decals. Detaches into three sections. Command module is mounted on a stand. Lunar lander rests on a moon terrain base. Three astronaut figures. Reissued in H-1843 (1969) and H-1862 (1969).

H-1837 Gemini Astronaut   1967-70   1/6 $40-50
White plastic. Gold tinted visor plastic. NASA decals. Figure has movable arms. Base is a section of the Gemini capsule. Based on Ed White's 1965 space walk. H-1841 is a half-size copy of this model. Reissued as H-1839 (1968) and H-1855 (1970).

H-1838 Apollo Lunar Spacecraft   1967-73   1/48 $80-90
White, clear plastic. US decals. Fully assembled model is twenty-one inches tall. Includes command module, service module, lunar lander, LES tower, and adapter shroud. Five astronaut figures. Legs of lunar lander fold to enclose in adapter section. Removable panels to show interiors of service and command module.
Lunar lander only reissued in H-1842 (1969) and H-1861 (1969).
Command and service module reissued in: H-1839 (1968); H-1847 (1969); H-1855 (1970).

H-1839 American Space Program   1968-70 $150-170
"Collector's Set." Three earlier space kits were repackaged together, along with cement, paint, and brush. H-1835 (1965); H-1837 (1967); H-1838 (1967).

H-1841 Astronaut in Space   1968-70   1/12 $30-40
White, gold-tinted visor plastic. NASA decals. This model is a half-scale copy of the Gemini Astronaut (H-1837).

H-1842 Apollo Lunar Module   1968-70   1/48 $30-40
White, clear plastic. US decals. Ascent stage separates from the descent stage; landing gear folds. Two astronaut figures. Reissued in H-1861 (1969).

H-1843 Apollo Saturn V Moon Rocket 1969-73   1/96 $150-170
White, silver plastic. NASA decals. Builds to a model almost four feet tall. Fuel tank sections are formed from sheets of plastic with pre-painted details that are rolled into cylinders and held in place by top and bottom rings. Command module, service module, and lunar lander are from H-1836.

H-1844 Russia's First Spacecraft: Vostok 1969-70   1/24 $40-50
Silver, clear plastic. USSR decals. Model comes with stand. The assembly of descent capsule, crew module, and two upper rocket stages is fifteen inches long. Based on photos of the real spaceship then on display in Toronto.

H-1847 American Space Pioneers   1969-70   1/48 $130-150
Gemini and Mercury capsules in gray plastic from H-1834.
Apollo command and service modules in silver plastic from H-1838.

H-1850 Space Pursuit   1968-70 $110-130
This pop art styled reissue of two 1950s vintage models offered a futuristic combination of a space pirate and a space police cruiser. Psychedelic decals. Moonship (H-1825) in metallic red plastic. Space Shuttle (H-1828) in black plastic.

H-1851 Atomic Space Explorer Solaris 1968-70 1/160 $110-130
Metallic blue, white, silver plastic. Pop art decals. This kit is an updated reissue of the Helios Lunar Landing Craft (H-1829) from 1959.

H-1861 Tranquility Base and Lunar Module 1969-73 1/48 $25-30
Gray, clear plastic. Gold foil. NASA decals. The Apollo 11 lunar module (H-1842) resting on a moon base. One astronaut on the stairs, another holds an American flag. Reissued as: H-1855 (1970); H-1861 (1976).

H-1862 Apollo 11 Columbia and Eagle 1969-73   1/96 $40-50
Silver plastic. NASA decals. Gold foil covering for service module. Three astronaut figures. The Eagle rests on a moon base, and a clear plastic stand supports the Columbia command ship overhead. This kit is a reissue of H-1836 from 1968. Detaches into three sections. Reissued as H-1862 (1976).

1960s Ships

Modern Ships

H-300 USS Missouri   1961-73   1/535 $15-30
Gray plastic. Decal. Paper flag sheet. Revised reissue of HM-30/H-309 Motorized *Missouri* (1954) with added one-inch "miniature replica" of the circular plaque on the deck of the *Missouri* indicating the spot where the instrument of surrender was signed in 1945. Part of the Picture Fleet series in 1961.

H-302 Flying Bridge Cruiser   1954-70   1/56 $30-35

Brown plastic. Part of the Coastal Series in 1964.

H-303 Nautilus   1961-72   1/305 $30-35
Gray plastic. Part of the Nuclear Fleet in 1961. Reissue of H-308 (1955) without the deck hanger and missile.

H-306 Mosquito Boat PT-207   1966-70   1/98 $20-30
Gray plastic. Decal. Reissue of H-304 *PT-212* (1954). Jack Leynnwood art.

H-307 USS Sullivans   1966-70   1/301 $20-30
Gray plastic. Decal. Paper flag sheet. Reissue of H-305 (1954).

H-309 USS John Paul Jones   1961-67   1/320 $20-30
Gray plastic. Decal. Paper flag sheet. Part of the Picture Fleet series and the Commander Series. Reissue of H-352 *Forrest Sherman* (1958).

H-310 PT-109   1963-80   1/72 $15-35
Olive green plastic. Decals. With four torpedo tubes, four figures, including Lt. Kennedy. Original Steel box art replaced by Leynnwood in 1970s. Reissued as: H-312 *PT-190* (1966); H-342 *PT-167* (1973).

H-311 RMS Queen Mary   1961-67   1/568 $25-35
White plastic. Decal. Twenty inches long. Includes twelve page booklet *The World's Wonder Ships*, a promotion for the Cunard Lines. Launched in 1934. John Steel box art. Reissued as: H-311 (1972); 2603 (1979) Advent.

H-312 PT-190   1966-68   1/72 $20-30
Gray plastic. Decals. Revised reissue of H-310 *PT-109* (1963) with four torpedoes on racks rather than in tubes.

H-313 USS Abraham Lincoln   1961   1/253 $50-60
Gray, black, light green plastic. Decals. Spring-loaded missiles fire from two forward tubes. Includes booklet on US subs. A reissue of H-365 *George Washington* (1959).

H-313 USS North Carolina   1969-80   1/570 $15-20
Gray plastic. Two Kingfisher scout planes. North Carolina Class battleship. Reissued as: H-401 *Washington* (1971); 2602 *North Carolina* (1979) Advent.

H-321 USS Franklin D. Roosevelt   1961-74   1/547 $25-35
Gray plastic. Decals. Part of the Picture Fleet in 1961. Reissue of H-307 (1954).

H-323 McHale's Navy PT-73   1965-69   1/72 $70-90
Gray plastic. Decal. Includes McHale and three other crew figures. Model based on a British Vosper MTB acquired by ABC-TV to play the role of a US PT boat in the 1962-66 series starring Ernest Borgnine. Reissued as H-335 Vosper MTB (1968).

H-332 SS United States   1962-76   1/602 $30-40
White plastic. Issued in 1962 as part of the Passport to Pleasure series in a white box with photo illustration—later issue boxes in full color. Reissue of H-312 (1955).

H-333 NS Savannah   1962-68   1/380 $40-50
White plastic. Part of the Passport to Pleasure series in 1962 in a white box with photo illustration ($100-120)—later issue boxes in full color. Reissue of H-366 (1959).

H-334 SS Argentina   1962-65   1/400 $40-50
White plastic. Paper flag sheet. Issued in 1962 as part of the Passport to Pleasure series in a white box with photo illustration. Reissue of H-346 *Brasil* (1958).

H-335 SS Dr. Lykes   1962-65   1/400 $40-50
White plastic. Issued in 1962 as part of the Passport to Pleasure series in a white box with photo illustration. Reissue of H-315 *Hawaiian Pilot* (1956).

H-335 British Vosper MTB   1968   1/72 $25-35
White plastic. Decals. Revised issue of H-323 McHale's Navy (1966) with radar removed and some other changes. Includes original McHale figure and three crewmen.

H-341 USS Burleigh   1964-67   1/400 $30-40
Gray plastic. Part of the Commander series in 1964. Reissue of H-315 *Hawaiian Pilot* (1956) as World War II freighter with added anti-aircraft guns.

H-342 USS Mission Capistrano Fleet Oiler 1964-67 1/400 $40-50
Gray plastic. Issued in 1964 in Commander Series. Reissue of H-322 *J. L. Hanna* (1956) as World War II refueling ship with added anti-aircraft guns.

H-349 USS New Jersey   1966-80   1/532 $20-30
Gray plastic. Decal. Paper flag sheet. Reissue of H-316 (1955).

H-350 KMS Bismarck   1963-80   1/570 $20-30
Gray plastic. Very detailed kit with 150 parts. Reissued as H-351 *Tirpitz* (1964).

H-351 KMS Tirpitz   1964-70   1/570 $20-30
Gray plastic. Part of the Commander series in 1964. Reissue of H-350 *Bismarck* (1963) with some alternate detail parts. Reissued as H-351 (1973).

H-352 USS Wisconsin   1968-80   1/535 $20-30
Gray plastic. Reissue of H-301 *Missouri* (1953).

H-359 USS Independence   1966-79   1/542 $35-45
Gray plastic. Reissue of H-339 *Forrestal* (1957).

H-360 USS Ranger   1962-70   1/542 $35-45
Gray plastic. Reissue of H-339 *Forrestal* (1957).

H-368 USS Long Beach   1960-61   1/508 $40-50
Gray plastic. Decals. Paper flag sheet. Superstructure lifts off to show nuclear reactor. Nuclear-powered guided missile cruiser. Part of the Nuclear Fleet

series in 1961. Reissued as: H-424 (1962); H-460 (1968).

H-369 USS Iowa   1960-78 1/535 $35-45
Gray plastic. Part of the Picture Fleet series. Reissue of H-316 *New Jersey* (1955).

H-370 USS Helena   1960-67 1/481 $35-45
Gray plastic. Part of the Picture Fleet series in 1960 and Commander series in 1964. Reissue of H-306 *Los Angeles* (1954).

H-370 USS Oriskany   1968-74 1/538 $60-80
Gray plastic. Reissue of H-353 *Essex* (1958).

H-371 USS Fletcher   1960-69 1/301 $20-30
Gray plastic. This model is the H-305 *Sullivans* (1954) with optional parts to replace three original parts: An anti-submarine rocket launcher can replace the second 5" turret, and two gun direction finders can replace two 40mm guns on the lower bridge deck. Part of the Picture Fleet series in 1960 and later the Flanker series. Steel box art. Reissued as: H-429 *Radford* (1962); H-458 *Fletcher* (1977).

H-372 USS Canberra   1960-67 1/481 $30-50
Gray plastic. In Picture Fleet series and Commander series. Reissue of the H-334 *Boston* (1956).

H-373 USS Midway   1960-70 1/547 $40-60
Gray plastic. Part of the Picture Fleet series in 1960. Reissue of H-307 *F. D. Roosevelt* (1954).

H-374 USS Coral Sea   1966-74 1/547 $45-65
Gray plastic. Leynnwood box art. Reissue of H-307 *F. D. Roosevelt* (1954).

H-375 USS Buchanan   1960-65 1/240 $35-45
Gray plastic. Part of the Picture Fleet series in 1960. Reissued as: H-427 *Aaron Ward* (1962); H-450 *Campbeltown* (1972); 2502 *Campbeltown* (1979) Advent.

H-375 USS Wasp   1968-80 1/538 $30-40
Gray plastic. Decals. Paper flag sheet. "Prime recovery vessel for Gemini." Includes S-2s, A-4s, A-6s, Sea Kings, and a tiny Gemini capsule. Reissue of H-353 *Essex* (1958).

H-376 SS Oriana   1961-65 1/493 $40-60
Light tan plastic! British luxury liner. Reissued as H-401 motorized (1961).

H-376 USS Hornet (Doolittle Raid) 1968-72 1/485 $20-30
Gray plastic. Decals. B-25 bombers on deck. Reissue of H-378 *Enterprise* (1967).

H-378 USS Enterprise "Big E"   1967-72 1/485 $20-30
Gray plastic. Decals. Includes twenty SBD dive bombers. *Scale Modeler* (March 1968, 63) declared that the model did not do justice to this important subject. It faulted the kit for poor detail and part fit. Reissued as: H-376 *Hornet* (1968); H-383 *Yorktown* (1968); H-501 Midway Carrier (1976); 2556 *Enterprise* (1979) Advent.

H-379 USS Burton Island   1960-65 1/292 $20-30
Gray plastic. Part of the Picture Fleet series in 1960. Reissue of H-337 *Eastwind* (1957).

H-380 USS Montrose Transport   1960-65 1/376 $20-30
Gray plastic. PA 212 decal. Part of the Picture Fleet series in 1960. This World War II attack transport was re-activated for the Korean War. Reissue of H-329 *Randall* (1956).

H-381 Hospital Ship Repose   1960-65 1/480 $25-35
White plastic. Decals. Part of the Picture Fleet series. Reissue of H-320 *Haven* (1956).

H-383 USS Yorktown   1968-74 1/485 $20-30
Gray plastic. Reissue of H-378 *Enterprise* (1967).

H-384 USS Bon Homme Richard   1961-70 1/538 $45-60
Gray plastic. Part of the Picture Fleet series in 1961. Reissue of H-353 *Essex* (1958).

H-385 USS Saratoga   1961-70 1/542 $30-45
Gray plastic. Part of the Picture Fleet series in 1961. Reissue of H-339 *Forrestal* (1957).

H-386 USS Currituck (Picture Fleet) 1961-65 1/431 $30-40
Gray plastic. Decal. Part of the Picture Fleet series. Reissue of H-362 *Pine Island* (1958).

H-387 Balboa Marlin Fishing Boat 1961-68 1/56 $20-30
White plastic. This is the H-302 Flying Bridge Cruiser (1954) with added fishing gear and fisherman figure produced from a separate auxiliary mold. Part of the Coastal series in 1964. Reissued in motorized version H-400 (1961).

H-388 SS Hope Hospital Ship   1964-65 1/480 $20-30
White plastic. Floating medical clinic of the People to People Health Foundation. Part of the Commander series in 1964. Reissue of H-388 *Haven* (1956).

H-389 Fire Fighter   1962-67 1/82 $40-50
Brown, tan, white, brass plated plastic. Model of a New York City fire boat launched in 1938. Elevating tower. Includes five figures. Campbell primary model sculptor.

H-396 Motorized PT-212   1961-65 1/98 $60-80
Gray plastic. Part of the Picture Fleet in 1961. Reissue of H-304 (1954).

H-397 Motorized Long Beach Tug 1961-65 1/113 $40-50
Light gray plastic. Part of the Picture Fleet series. Steel box art. Reissue of H-314 (1956).

H-398 Motorized USS Arizona   1961-65 1/429 $60-80
Gray plastic. Steel box art. Part of the Picture Fleet in 1961. Reissue of H-348 (1958).

H-399 Motorized USS Coral Sea 1961-65 1/547 $60-80
Gray plastic. Part of the Picture Fleet in 1961. Reissue of H-307 *F. D. Roosevelt* (1954).

H-400 Motorized Sport Fishing Boat 1961-65 1/56 $30-50
White plastic. Steel box art. Also issued as H-387 (1961).

H-401 Motorized SS Oriana   1961-65 1/493 $50-60
Light tan plastic. Also issued as H-376 (1961).

H-402 Motorized Robert E. Lee 1961-65 1/271 $50-60
White plastic. Decals. Paper flag sheet. John Steel box art. Reissue of H-328 (1956).

H-404 Ship Motorizing Kit   1963 $10-15
Gray plastic. Japanese-made electric motor and wiring. Requires two D batteries. This ten-inch cigar-shaped unit could be attached to the underside of any model ship.

H-421 PT-212   1962-70 1/99 $20-30
Gray plastic. Part of the Sea Power series in 1962.

H-422 USS Pennsylvania   1962-70 1/426 $30-50
Gray plastic. Part of the Sea Power series. Steel box art. Reissue of H-348 *Arizona* (1958).

H-423 USS Buckley   1962-67 1/249 $30-50
Gray plastic. Part of the Sea Power series and Commander series. Reissue of H-355 (1958).

H-424 USS Long Beach   1962-67 1/512 $30-50
Gray plastic. Nuclear guided missile cruiser. Part of the Sea Power series in 1962 and the Commander series in 1964. Reissue of H-368 (1960).

H-425 Polaris Submarine   1962-67 1/261 $50-60
Gray, light green, black plastic. Decals. George Washington Class. Part of the Sea Power series in 1962. Reissue of H-313 *Abraham Lincoln* (1961).

H-426 USS Lexington   1962-69 1/538 $30-40
Gray plastic. Part of the Sea Power series in 1962. Reissue of H-353 *Essex* (1958).

H-427 USS Aaron Ward   1962-67 1/240 $30-40
Gray plastic. Part of the Destroyer Collection series in 1962 and the Commander series in 1964. Launched in 1917, this ship was given to Great Britain in the early days of World War II and renamed HMS *Castleton*. *Scale Modeler* (June 1969, 10) judged it: "probably the best WW II domestic ship model ever released." Reissue of H-375 *Buchanan* (1960).

H-428 USS Blessman   1962-67 1/249 $30-40
Gray plastic. Decals. Paper flag sheet. Part of the Destroyer Collection series in 1962 and the Commander series in 1964. Reissue of the destroyer escort H-355 *Buckley* (1958).

H-429 USS Radford   1962-69 1/301 $30-40
Gray plastic. Part of the Destroyer Collection series in 1962 and the Flanker series in 1964. Reissue of H-371 *Fletcher* (1960).

H-430 USS Decatur   1962-67 1/319 $30-40
Gray plastic. Part of the Destroyer Collection series in 1962 and the Commander series in 1964. Reissue of H-353 *Forrest Sherman* (1958).

H-433 USS Patrick Henry   1968-72 1/255 $40-50
Gray, light green, black plastic. Decals. Reissue of H-313 *Abraham Lincoln* (1961). Leynnwood art.

H-452 USS Montrose   1968   1/376 $20-30
Gray plastic. Reissue of H-329 *Randall* (1956).

H-453 USCG Eastwind   1968-69 1/285 $20-30
White, brown, mustard plastic. Reissue of H-337 (1957).

H-454 USCG Campbell   1968-69 1/301 $20-30
Reissue of H-338 (1957).

H-455 USS Pine Island Seaplane Tender 1968 1/424 $30-40
Gray plastic. Reissue of H-362 (1958).

H-456 Frigate Tai Chao   1967-68 1/249 $20-30
Light gray plastic. Decals. Nationalist Chinese paper flag sheet. No changes in mold from H-355 *Buckley* (1958). This is the former USS *Carter*, sold to Taiwan in 1948.

H-457 USS Pittsburgh   1967-69, 72-80 1/480 $40-50
Black plastic. The *Pittsburgh* fought at Iwo Jima, then lost her bow in a storm but returned home for repairs. Reissue of H-306 *Los Angeles* (1954).

H-458 USS Repose   1967-68 1/500 $20-30
White plastic. Decals. Paper flag sheet. Reissue of H-320 (1956).

H-459 USS Forrest Sherman   1968-69 1/320 $20-30
Gray plastic. Decal. Paper flag sheet. Reissue of H-352 (1958). Leynnwood box art.

H-460 USS Long Beach   1968-70 1/508 $20-30
Gray plastic. Nuclear guided missile cruiser. Reissue of H-368 (1960).

H-461 USS Boston   1968   1/480 $20-30
Gray plastic. Reissue of H-334 (1956).

159

1/720 International Scale Models

This series of models was designed to be smaller, lower priced ($1.00), and closer in scale to the 1/700 scale Japanese kits and 1/600 Airfix kits. Their hulls snapped in two at the waterline so builders could make either full-hull models or waterline models.

H-481 KMS Prinz Eugen 1967-76 1/720 $15-25
Gray plastic. Reissued as: H-480 *Blucher* (1974); H-490 *Admiral Hipper* (1975).
H-482 USS Arizona 1967-80 1/720 $8-12
Gray plastic. Reissued as H-486 *Pennsylvania* (1969).
H-483 HMS Ark Royal & Tribal Class DE 1967-69 1/720 $20-30
Gray plastic. This kit includes two ship models, and cost $2.00. The destroyer escort is based on the HMCS *Haida*, preserved in Toronto.
H-484 USS Ben Franklin 1969-70 1/720 $20-30
Gray plastic. Reissued as: H-488 *Essex* (1969); H-462 *Intrepid* (1973); 2501 *Essex* (1979) Advent.
H-485 USS Massachusetts 1968-80 1/720 $8-12
Gray plastic. South Dakota Class battleship. Reissued as H-487 *Alabama* (1969).
H-486 USS Pennsylvania 1969-79 1/720 $8-12
Dark gray plastic. Reissue of H-482 *Arizona* (1967).
H-487 USS Alabama 1969-80 1/720 $8-12
Dark gray plastic. Reissue of H-485 *Massachusetts* (1968).
H-488 USS Essex 1969-71 1/720 $20-30
Gray plastic. Hull split CV 9 (Essex Class). This is a model of the World War II *Essex* before it was modified to have an angled deck. Reissue of H-484 *Ben Franklin* (1969).
H-489 USS Enterprise Nuclear Carrier 1969-80 1/720 $20-30
Gray plastic. Decal. With E-2 Hawkeyes, F-4 Phantoms, A-4 Skyhawks, A-5 Vigilantes, and A-6 Intruders.

H-1278 Go & Show Drag Boat & Trailer 1963-65 1/25 $60-80
White, chrome plastic. Vinyl tires. Wood-grain contact paper for deck. Racing decals. Motor is the Custom Car Parts Chrysler 413 V-8. Can be built stock, show, or racing, with customizing hints by Ed Roth. This aquatic dragster was issued along with Revell's popular drag and show cars. Reissued as H-1312 *Hemi-Hydro* (1971).

1960s Historic Sailing Ships

H-324 Golden Hind with sails 1965-71 1/96 $20-30
Brown plastic. Decals. Includes crew figures, rigging thread, cement, pallet of paints. Sir Francis Drake's ship. Steel box art. Reissued as: H-325 *Golden Hind* (1972); H-367 *Spanish Galleon* (1974); H-324 *Spanish Galleon* (1978); H-345 *Golden Hind* (1978); H-519 *Pirate Ghost Ship* (1978).
H-325 Stag Hound Clipper 1962-67 1/213 $25-35
Black, tan, white plastic. Hound figurehead. Preformed ratlines, black and tan thread, decal, paper flag sheet. Revell engineer Ernest Brown designed this model by copying the H-344 *Flying Cloud* (1955), making adjustments for the *Flying Cloud's* greater length. It uses the *Flying Cloud's* hull, and the new deck parts almost duplicate those of the Flying Cloud, but details of the deck layout are different. Reissued as: H-345 (1966); H-317 (1972); H-343 (1973); H-319 (1976) *Cutty Sark*; H-304 (1977) *Cutty Sark*; H-361 (1978).
H-326 HMS Bounty with furled sails 1961-70 1/110 $20-30
Brown plastic. Steel box art. Some issues of this kit have end panels announcing the new MGM movie starring Marlon Brando and Trevor Howard. Reissue of H-326 (1956).
H-327 Mayflower with sails 1966-71 1/83 $20-30
Tan plastic. Five crew figures, vacuum-formed sails, preformed string ratlines, two spools of rigging thread, paper flag sheet. Leynnwood box art. Reissued as: H-366 (1970); H-316 (1972); H-389 (1975) *Elizabethan Man-O-War*; H-307 (1977).
H-328 HMS Beagle with sails 1966-69 1/74 $30-40
Tan plastic. Steel box art. Reissue of H-330 (1961).
H-329 USS Constitution with sails 1966-68 1/192 $20-30
Black, tan plastic. Paper flag sheet. Cement. H-319 (1956) with sails added.
H-330 HMS Beagle with sails 1961-63 1/74 $30-40
Tan plastic. Includes preformed string ratlines, paper flag sheet, cement. This is a revised version of H-326 *Bounty* (1956) with three added lifeboats, revised deck, different rigging. Charles Darwin's ship. Steel box art. Reissued as H-328 (1966).
H-331 Seeadler with sails 1968-71 1/232 $20-30
Reissue of H-382 (1960) with sails added.
H-345 Stag Hound with sails 1966-71 1/213 $20-30
Black, tan, white plastic. Reissue of H-325 (1962) with sails added.
H-346 Charles W. Morgan with sails 1968-71 1/160 $40-50
Includes preformed string ratlines, paper flag sheet, cement. Whaling ship preserved at Mystic Seaport, Connecticut. Reissued as: H-330 (1972); 2653 (1979) Advent.
H-361 Yacht America with sails 1969-74 1/56 $80-90
Black, tan plastic. Paper flag sheet. Rigging thread. Flexible, tough paper sails that

allowed the model to be sailed on ponds. "Simplified" series. Two-feet long. Reissued as H-372 Blockader (1974).
H-362 USS Constitution without sails 1969-75 1/159 $20-30
Black, tan plastic. Two spools of thread. paper flag sheet. "Simplified series" with one-piece deck assembly, injection-molded ratlines. This twenty-two inch model is midway between the original small *Constitution* (H-319) and the large, three-foot *Constitution* (H-386). Leynnwood box art. Reissued as H-357 (1972) with sails added.
H-364 Walt Disney's Peter Pan Pirate Ship 1969-70 1/72 $50-70
Purple plastic. Reissue of H-377 *Jolly Roger* (1960).
H-368 Cutty Sark with sails 1968-79 1/144 $20-30
"Simplified" series. Molded plastic ratlines. Includes thread, paper flag sheet, cement. This was a smaller, two-foot version of the large *Cutty Sark* (H-394).
H-377 Peter Pan's Pirate Ship Jolly Roger "S" 1960 1/72 $90-100
Beige plastic. Paper flag sheet. Injection molded sails and ratlines. This is a model of the Peter Pan™ ship at Disneyland. Reissued as H-364 (1969).
H-382 Seeadler "S" 1960-67 1/232 $50-60
Light gray, tan, black plastic. Preformed string ratlines. Spool of thread, paper flag sheet. This is the H-347 *Eagle* (1958) with two added deck guns, different life boats. German World War I commerce raider. Reissued as H-331 (1968) with sails added.
H-386 USS Constitution 1965-76 1/108 $40-60
Black, brown, tan plastic. Twenty crew figures, pre-painted copper hull, pre-formed string ratlines. Clear gallery windows show bathtub in captain's quarters and pictures on the walls. Includes booklet on the story of "Old Ironsides." A three-foot long, $12 kit. Reissued as: H-398 (1968); H-396 (1977) *United States*; H-391 (1978).
H-390 Thermopylae "S" without sails 1960-78 1/70 $80-100
Green, tan, gray, white plastic. Pre-painted copper hull. Can be built square or bark rigged. This model used the same hull as the H-364 *Cutty Sark* (1959), with different deck and upper parts. $11.95 kit. Thirty-six inches long.
H-391 USS Kearsarge without sails 1961-74 1/96 $130-150
Molded in four colors. Prepainted hull. Includes preassembled string ratlines, rigging thread, anchor chain. Twenty crew figures. Three feet long. This model shares the same hull with the H-392 *Alabama* (1961). Differences include: raised foredeck with large cannon, cabin on deck. This is today's most sought-after Revell sailing ship.
H-392 CSS Alabama with sails 1961-78 1/96 $50-70
Molded in four colors. Prepainted hull. Includes preassembled string ratlines, rigging thread, anchor chain. Twenty crew figures. Differences from H-391 *Kearsarge* include: two cannon in bow, bridge amidships, window gallery in stern, winch for raising propeller.
H-393 Great Eastern with sails 1963-67 1/388 $90-110
Black, tan, white, dark red plastic. With cable-laying equipment and marker buoys. The largest ship afloat in the 1860s, this great iron ship laid the first trans-Atlantic telegraph cable. It had both side wheels and a screw propeller. Steel box art.
H-394 Cutty Sark without sails 1966-74 1/96 $40-60
Black, brown, white plastic. Pre-painted copper hull. Decal. Anchor chain. Paper flag sheet. Rigging thread. Twenty crew figures. Twenty-six page booklet on clipper ships. The Cutty Sark is preserved in Greenwich, England. Reissue of H-364 (1959).
H-395 Cutty Sark with sails 1966-73 1/96 $40-60
Black, brown, white plastic. Pre-painted copper hull. Decal. Anchor chain. Paper flag sheet. Rigging thread. Twenty crew figures. Reissue of H-364 (1959).
H-398 USS Constitution with sails 1967-80 1/108 $40-60
Black, brown, tan plastic. Reissue of H-386 (1965).
H-399 Pedro Nunes 1967-70 1/70 $70-80
White, gray, tan, black plastic. Pre-painted copper hull, preformed string ratlines, rigging thread, anchor chain. Paper flag sheet. This is Revell's H-390 *Thermopylae* (1960) model with a new name plate, decals, and rigging. The actual *Thermopylae* underwent the same transformation, being sold to the Portuguese and renamed the *Pedro Nunes*.

1960s Armor

H-542 Scissors Bridge with M-48 1960-63 1/40 $50-60
Bridge folds in half and then folds back on M-48 tank transporter. John Steel box art. Reissued as: H-545 (1961); H-558 (1968).
H-544 Sherman M4 Tank motorized 1960-63 1/40 $50-60
The original idea for motorizing the Sherman Tank came from salesman Dave Fisher, who custom-built one and showed it to Lew Glaser. However, it was several years before Revell introduced its motorized line of kits. Reissue of H-522 (1956).
H-545 Scissors Bridge with M-48 motorized 1961-63 1/40 $80-100
Reissue of H-542 (1960).
H-546 Russian T-34 Tank motorized 1961-63 1/40 $50-60
Dark olive green. Decals. Leynnwood box art. Reissue of H-538 (1958).
H-554 M4 Sherman Tank 1968-69 1/40 $35-45
Reissue of H-522 (1956).

H-555 105mm Howitzer	1968	1/40	$15-25
Reissue of H-539 (1958).			
H-556 M-56 Self-Propelled Gun	1968	1/40	$15-25
Reissue of H-540 (1958).			
H-557 M-35 Army Truck	1968-69	1/40	$15-20
Reissue of H-537 (1958).			
H-558 Scissors Bridge with M-48	1968-69	1/40	$35-45
Reissue of H-542 (1960).			

1960s Cars

H-1553 Chrysler Slant 6 Engine	1961-62	1/4	$150-175

Black, gray, red, silver plastic. Decal. Stand. Screw assembly. With electric motor, screwdriver, wiring. Side of engine removes to show working pistons, turning crankshaft, and lighting spark plugs. The engine can be disassembled and reassembled—just like a real engine. With booklet by Chrysler, *The Story of the Internal Combustion Engine.* Ron Campbell primary sculptor. Reissued as H-1555 (1963).

H-1555 Chrysler Slant 6 Engine	1963	1/4	$150-175

Reissue of H-1553 with clear plastic see-through engine panel.

Cadet Series

These small scale models were developed by Revell Great Britain and first sold there in 1959. The tooling was then shipped to the United States for a brief production run. They sold at 49 and 59 cents, and were Revell's attempt to compete at the lowest end of the model car market. These kits had metal axles and "chrome" plated parts, but used sheets of clear acetate for windows, rather than clear injection-molded parts.

H-900 Rover 3 Litre Saloon	1962	1/40	$30-40
Black, silver plastic. Reissued as H-956.			
H-901 Volkswagen Karman-Ghia	1962	1/41	$20-30
Red plastic. Reissued as H-957.			
H-902 Jaguar Mk II	1962	1/46	$20-30
Blue gray plastic. Reissued as H-958.			
H-903 Ford Consul	1962	1/45	$20-30
Light green plastic. Reissued as H-959.			
H-950 Vauxhall Cresta	1963	1/42	$20-30
Yellow plastic.			
H-951 Triumph TR-3	1963	1/44	$20-30
Red plastic.			
H-952 Volkswagen Deluxe Sedan	1963	1/40	$20-30
Light blue plastic. Classic beetle.			
H-953 Morris 1000 Traveller	1963	1/46	$20-30
Green plastic.			
H-956 Rover 3 Litre Saloon	1963	1/40	$30-40
Black plastic. Reissue of H-900.			
H-957 Volkswagen Karman-Ghia	1963	1/41	$20-30
Red, chrome plastic. Reissue of H-901.			
H-958 Jaguar Mk II	1963	1/46	$20-30
Blue plastic. Reissue of H-902.			
H-959 Ford Consul	1963	1/45	$20-30
Light green plastic. Reissue of H-903.			

Chrysler 1962 Annual Car Models

In 1962 Revell made an agreement with Chrysler Corporation to produce a line of models based on Chrysler's new cars for that year. The cars came in two versions: regular plastic and transparent "metalflake" plastic. Both versions had black vinyl tires and hoods that opened. Both versions could be motorized by installing Revell's Electric Power Kit . The metalflake versions came with extra chrome customizing parts and suspension parts that allowed the body to be assembled at "stock" or "lowered" height, and special speed equipment racing decals.

H-1250 1962 Plymouth Valiant V-200	1962	1/25	$70-90

Light green, chrome, transparent red, clear plastic. Black vinyl tires. Decals for whitewalls. Hood opens. Also issued in metalflake as H-1260.

H-1251 1962 Plymouth Fury	1962	1/25	$70-90

Black, chrome, clear plastic. Also issued in metalflake as H-1261.

H-1252 1962 Dodge Dart 400	1962	1/25	$70-90

Dark red, chrome, clear plastic. Also issued in metalflake as H-1262. Mold revised and reissued as H-1265 "Revellion" (1967).

H-1253 1962 Dodge Lancer GT	1962	1/25	$80-100

Light tan, clear, chrome plastic. Also issued in metalflake as H-1263.

H-1254 1962 Chrysler Newport Convertible	1962	1/25	$110-130

Light brown, chrome, clear plastic. Also issued in metalflake as H-1264.

H-1255 1962 Chrysler Imperial Crown	1962	1/25	$100-120

Maroon, chrome, clear plastic. Also issued in metalflake as H-1265.

H-1256 Go! Electric Power Kit	1962		$25-30

Contains electric motor, battery holders, gears, wires, and switch. "Everything you need to motorize your Revell Chrysler Corporation Model Cars and other 1/25 scale cars."

H-1260 Metalflake Plymouth Valiant V-200	1962	1/25	$70-90

Sparkling shamrock green metalflake, chrome, clear plastic. Black vinyl tires. Speed equipment decals. Hood opens. Also issued in solid plastic as H-1250.

H-1261 Metalflake Plymouth Fury	1962	1/25	$70-90
Also issued in solid plastic as H-1251.			
H-1262 Metalflake Dodge Dart 400	1962	1/25	$70-90
Also issued in solid plastic as H-1252.			
H-1263 Metalflake Dodge Lancer GT	1962	1/25	$80-100
Also issued in solid plastic as H-1253.			
H-1264 Metalflake Chrysler Newport Convertible	1962	1/25	$100-120
Purple metalflake, chrome, clear plastic. Also issued in solid plastic as H-1254.			
H-1265 Metalflake Chrysler Imperial	1962	1/25	$100-120
Also issued in solid plastic as H-1255.			

Ed Roth Show Rods

H-1240 Surfite with Tiki Hut	1965-66	1/25	$80-100

White plastic. Clear acetate sheet for windshield. Black vinyl tires. Hood lifts off to show Austin 850 motor. Includes three surfboards. It was planned as a 1/12 scale model because the real car was so small that a 1/25 model of it would not fill Revell's standard model car box. But it came out in 1/25 scale with the "Tiki Surf Club" hut added to fill the void. The real car appeared very briefly in the movie *Beach Blanket Bingo.*

H-1274 Road Agent	1964-68	1/25	$100-125

White, clear plastic. Black vinyl tires. Hinged bubble top. Includes Ed Roth and Rat Fink figures. The Corvair engine from this model was reused with later Corvair-powered models. Leynnwood box art.

H-1277 Mysterion	1964-68	1/25	$80-100

White, chrome, clear plastic. Black vinyl tires. Hinged bubble top. Two Ford 406 motors. Leynnwood box art. Reissued as: H-1329 Dual Jewel (1975); 3131 Double Trouble (1979) Advent.

H-1279 Beatnik Bandit	1963-68	1/25	$80-100

White, chrome, clear plastic. Black vinyl tires. Olds V-8 motor on a shortened Olds chassis.

H-1282 Outlaw	1962-68	1/25	$80-100

White, chrome plastic. Black vinyl tires. First issue decals were incorrect lime-green; later decals corrected to blue-green. Includes stanchions, silver thread, and sign to surround this "show car." 1950 Cadillac engine. Leynnwood box art. Reissued as: H-1270 Robin Hood Fink (1965); H-1448 Canned Heat (1973); 3132 Yellow Fever (1979).

H-1286 Tweedy-Pie	1963-66	1/25	$125-150

White, chrome, clear plastic. Black vinyl tires. Optional cycle fenders for wheels. A Chevy V-8 mill on a '32 Ford. Roth bought this car from Bob Johnson, repainted it purple and added chrome wheels and quad headlights. Reissued as: H-1271 Boss Fink (1965); H-1444 Rodfather (1973); 3133 Rodfather (1979) Advent.

Ed Roth Monsters

These models were sculpted by staff artist Harry Plummer. Most of the art was done by outside artists, but three were done by Jack Leynnwood. He didn't like doing them, but, according to art department head Howard Rieder: "I told him his preliminary paintings were no good—not humorous. This got him mad, and he went out and put some humor into them." All are molded in off-white plastic with red jewel eye pupils.

H-1270 Outlaw with Robin Hood Fink	1965	1/25	$125-150

Contains a copy of the *Outlaw* car and uses the same chrome tree as the *Outlaw* kit (H-1282). Distorted wheels and Fink figure added.

H-1271 Tweedy Pie with Boss Fink	1965	1/25	$430-450

White, black, chrome plastic. Figure of Roth himself in his H-1286 Tweedy Pie (1963). Extremely rare kit because it has never been reissued.

H-1301 Mr. Gasser	1963-65	1/25	$100-120

The first of the Roth Monsters. Rides a '57 Chevy Bel Air. Reissued as H-902 Heavy Head (1971).

H-1302 Mother's Worry	1963-65	1/25	$100-120

1923 Model T. Reissued as H-901 Shift Kicker (1971).

H-1303 Drag Nut with Rat Fink	1963-65	1/25	$100-120

Bantam dragster. Roth based this model on an old T-shirt design called "Race." Reissued as H-900 Korporal Amerika (1971).

H-1304 Brother Rat Fink	1964-65	1/25	$100-120

Reissued as H-903 Sleazy Rider (1971).

H-1305 Rat Fink	1963-65		$80-100

Six inch tall figure.

H-1306 Surfink	1964-65		$110-130

Fink catching a wave on surfboard.

H-1307 Angel Fink	1964-65		$90-110

Witch stirring up drum of nitro. Leynnwood box art.

H-1308 Super Fink   1964-65 $110-130
Fink on skateboard. Leynnwood box art.

H-1309 Scuz Fink with Dingbat   1965 $120-140
Creature from another planet. The name for this model came from a national
    Name the Monster Contest. First prize was a weekend with Ed Roth. Leyn-
    nwood box art.

H-1310 Fink-Eliminator   1965 $100-120
White plastic. Cyclops fink bashes cars with a mallet.

1960s 1/32 Scale Cars

In 1968 Revell introduced a new line of simple, snap-together kits aimed
at younger modelers. The kits featured one-piece bodies, detailed interiors,
and chrome plated parts. Most of these H-1200 series kits would be reissued
in 1975 in a H-1100 series.

H-1246 EMPI Imp Dune Buggy   1970-74   1/32 $25-35
Bronze, chrome, clear plastic. Model is a scaled-down H-1274 EMPI Imp
    (1969).

H-1247 VW Beetle   1970-74   1/32 $25-35
Yellow, chrome, clear plastic. Reissued as: H-950 (1974); H-1106 (1975).

H-1248 Opel GT   1970-74   1/32 $25-35
Metallic green, chrome, clear plastic. Reissued as H-1107 (1975).

H-1249 Ford Maverick   1970-74   1/32 $25-35
Yellow, chrome, clear plastic. Reissued as H-1108 (1975).

H-1250 1967 Mustang 2 + 2   1968-74   1/32 $25-35
Red, chrome, clear plastic. Reissued as H-1109 (1975).

H-1251 1967 Chevy Camaro SS 350   1968-74   1/32 $25-35
Blue, black, chrome, clear plastic. Reissued as H-1110 (1975).

H-1252 Pontiac Firebird "400"   1968-74   1/32 $25-35
Blue, chrome, clear plastic. Reissued as H-1111 (1975).

H-1253 1968 Mercury Cougar GT-E   1968-74   1/32 $30-40
Copper, chrome, clear plastic. Reissued as H-1112 (1975).

The following four kits were developed and the tooling produced in England.
They were regular cement-assembly, not snap kits.

H-1254 Triumph TR-4   1968-70   1/32 $25-35
Green, chrome, clear plastic. Hood opens to show engine. Left or right side drive.
    Reissued as 3001 (1979) Advent.

H-1255 Sunbeam Alpine Roadster   1968-70   1/32 $40-50
White, chrome, clear plastic. Hood opens to show engine. Left or right side drive.
    Reissued as 3004 (1979) Advent.

H-1256 Austin Healey 3000   1968-70   1/32 $20-30
Black, chrome, clear plastic. Hood opens to show engine. Left or right side drive.
    Reissued as 3002 (1979) Advent.

H-1257 MG-B Sports Car   1968-70   1/32 $20-30
Light blue, chrome, clear plastic. Hood opens to show engine. Left or right side
    drive. Reissued as 3003 (1979) Advent.

H-1290 '57 Ford T-bird   1969-70   1/32 $25-35
Black, chrome, clear plastic. Reissued as H-1104 (1975).

H-1291 '57 Corvette Hardtop/Convertible 1969-70 1/32 $15-25
White, chrome, clear plastic. Reissued as H-1102 (1975).

H-1292 '57 Ford Fairlane   1969-70   1/32 $20-30
Blue, chrome, clear plastic. Reissued as H-1103 (1975).

H-1293 '57 Chevy Bel Air   1969-70   1/32 $25-35
Orange, chrome, clear plastic. Reissued as H-1101 (1975).

H-1294 '69 AMC Javelin SST   1969-74   1/32 $30-40
Orange, chrome, clear plastic.

H-1295 '69 Plymouth Barracuda Formula S 1969-74 1/32 $30-40
Light metallic green, chrome, clear plastic.

H-1296 '69 AMC Javelin AMX "390" 1969-74   1/32 $30-40
Red, chrome, clear plastic.

H-1297 '69 Corvette Stingray   1969-74   1/32 $15-25
Silver, chrome, clear plastic. Reissued as: H-1105 (1975); H-1134 (1979).

1960s 1/25 Scale Cars

H-1212 '70 Mustang Grande   1969   1/25 $125-150
Green, chrome, clear plastic. Builds hardtop or convertible. This rare kit did
    not even make the 1970 Revell catalog. Model is a revision of the H-1261 '69
    Mustang (1968). It was then modified again to become the H-1209 Mustang
    Funny Car (1970).

H-1221 Fumin Fiat & Thunder Charger 1963   1/25 $125-150
"Double Car Kit" Altered Fiat and open-frame dragster. Chrysler Hemi and Buick
    V-8 engines. These double kits were created by combining pieces from seven
    "Custom Parts" to make two complete car models.
Fumin Fiat: white, black, gray, chrome plastic.

Thunder Charger: black, gray, chrome plastic.

H-1222 Scarlet Screamer & Bantam Bomber 1963 1/25 $125-150
"Double Car Kit" Includes Cadillac V-8 and small block Chevy engines.
Scarlet Screamer: red, black, gray, chrome plastic.
Bantam Bomber: white, black, gray, chrome plastic.

H-1223 Sanitary T & Mooneyes Dragster 1963 1/25 $125-150
Mooneyes Dragster: yellow, white, black, gray, chrome plastic. With parts from
    two earlier Chevy V-8 Parts Pack engines to create the correct Mooneyes motor.
    The Mooneyes is today on display at the Don Garlits Museum of Drag Racing in
    Ocala, Florida. Sanitary T: white, black, gray, chrome plastic.

H-1224 Tony Nancy's Roadster and Dragster 1963-66 1/25 $40-60
This kit includes model of two different cars belonging to drag racer Tony
    Nancy.
Red, chrome, clear plastic. Decals. Nancy's '23 T roadster/dragster.
Silver, chrome, clear plastic. Decals. Nancy's "22 Jr." dragster.

H-1232 1959 Chevy Corvette Convertible 1960-61 1/25 $40-60
Red, chrome, clear plastic. Hood opens. Reissued as: H-1242 (1961); H-1243
    (1961); H-1203 (1977); 3104 (1979) Advent.

H-1240 1957 Ford Ranchero   1960-63   1/25 $80-100
Blue, clear plastic. Customizing kit. This kit was manufactured from the modified
    mold of the H-1220 Country Squire (1957). The top remains unchopped. Reis-
    sued as: H-1241 (1960); H-1332 (1976); 3111 (1979) Advent.

H-1241 1957 Ford Ranchero with motor 1960-63   1/25 $100-120
Blue, clear plastic. Reissued as: H-1240 (1960); H-1332 (1976).

H-1242 1959 Competition Corvette Convertible 1961-63 1/25 $60-80
Blue, chrome, clear plastic. This model is a revised issue of H-1232, with new
    racing decals, an added roll bar, and a cut-down racing windshield. Reissue of
    H-1232 (1960).

H-1243 Motorized Competition Corvette 1961-63 1/25 $65-85
Blue, chrome, clear plastic. Motorized issue of H-1242. Reissue of H-1232
    (1960).

H-1244 Competition Austin-Healey   1961-63 1/25 $40-60
Green, chrome, clear plastic. This model is a revised issue of H-1217, with new
    racing decals, an added roll bar, and a cut-down racing windscreen. Reissue of
    H-1217 (1959).

H-1245 Motorized Competition Austin-Healey 1961-63 1/25 $50-70
Green, chrome, clear plastic. Motorized issue of H-1244. Reissue of H-1217
    (1959).

H-1246 Competition 1958 Porsche 1500 1961-63 1/25 $55-65
Silver, chrome, clear plastic. This model is a revised issue of the original 1959 model
    with new racing decals, an added roll bar, and a cut-down racing windscreen.
    Reissue of H-1238 (1959).

H-1247 Motorized Competition 1958 Porsche 1961-63 1/25 $65-85
Silver, chrome, clear plastic. Motorized issue of H-1246. Reissue of H-1238
    (1959).

H-1260 1957 Chevy Nomad Station Wagon 1968-73 1/25 $40-60
Creamy white, chrome, tinted clear plastic. Vinyl tires, red clear taillights. Doors,
    windows, tailgate open; front wheels steer. Body can be attached to the chassis
    at three different heights: raised, stock, lowered. Reissued as: H-1372 (1974);
    H-1390 (1979).

H-1261 '69 Ford Mustang Hardtop/Convertible 1968-69 1/25 $110-130
White, chrome, clear plastic. Decals. Vinyl tires with optional slicks. Doors, hood,
    trunk open; front wheels steer. 428 Cobra engine. Build stock, street modified,
    or drag. Revell received advanced information from Ford so the kit could be
    out in the fall of 1968. The tops of the model's rear fenders are flat, not slightly
    rounded—an error corrected in Revell's new '70 Mustang model (H-1212).
    Much of the tooling for this kit was used in creating the H-1209 Mustang Funny
    Car (1970).

H-1262 '51 Henry J Drag Coupe   1969-72   1/25 $60-80
Lime green, chrome plastic. Orange sheet acetate windshield. Racing decals. Reis-
    sued as: H-1315 (1973); H-1328 (1977); H-1432 (1978).

H-1263 1963 Volkswagen Herbie The Love Bug™ 1969-70 1/25 $60-80
White, clear plastic. Black vinyl tires. Decal. Licensed Walt Disney product based on
    the movie of the same name. A good selling model. Reissue of H-1264 (1969).

H-1264 VW 3 in 1 Kit!   1969-72   1/25 $35-50
Orange, chrome, clear plastic. "Inch Pincher Too." EMPI and Revell decals. Can be
    built to three versions. 1964 Volkswagen. This is a model of the actual car driven
    in the 1967 Baja 1,000 off-road race by Revell executive Don Ernst. Chassis used
    in H-1341 Baja Chopper (1971). Reissued as: H-1263 (1969); H-1326 (1974);
    H-1409 (1976); 3142 (1979) Advent.

H-1265 Dodge "Revellion" Funny Car   1967-70   1/25 $90-120
Metallic gold, chrome plastic. Sheet acetate windshield. Metal axles. Decals.
    Removable hood shows Dodge V-8 engine. Modified H-1252 Dart (1962)
    body riding on chassis of H –1224 "22 Jr." dragster (1964). Reissued as H-1217
    "Revellion" (1971).

H-1266 "Miss Deal" Funny Car   1967-71   1/25 $30-50
Light blue or blue-gray, chrome, plastic. Metal axles. Sheet of blue tinted acetate for
    windshield. Vinyl tires. Body hinged at the rear to lift up and show drag interior

and Chrysler V-8 engine. The body is from an abandoned 1953 Studebaker model project. Reissued by AHM in the 1970s in same box art as Revell issue.

H-1267 Deluxe Volkswagen Station Wagon 1967-68   1/25 $70-90
White, clear plastic. Vinyl tires. Removable sun roof, engine door opens, tailgate and doors open. Modified from H-1228 (1959) issue by changing the shape of the rear window and updating the headlights, taillights, and blinker lights.

H-1268 '51 Thames Drag Panel Delivery Truck 1968-70   1/25 $30-50
Metallic green, chrome plastic. Amber-tinted sheet acetate windshield. Decals. Metal axles. Narrow vinyl tires in front, wide slicks in back. "Simple Simon Pie Wagon" decals. Hood tilts forward to open; side and rear doors open; front wheels steer. Olds V-8 engine. Model developed from H-1269 Anglia and uses many of the same mold blocks. Reissued as: H-1344 (1971); 3115 "Jungle Fever" (1979) Advent.

H-1269 '51 Ford Anglia "Skipper's Critter" 1967-70   1/25 $50-60
Dark metallic red, chrome, plastic. Sheet acetate windshield. Racing decals. Hood tilts forward to open to show Olds V-8; doors and trunk open; front wheels steer. The H-1268 Thames Panel Truck was developed from this model and uses many of the same mold blocks. Reissued as: H-1281 (1971); 3116 (1979) Advent.

H-1270 1953 Chevy Panel Delivery Van 1969-70   1/25 $40-50
Dark metallic red, clear, chrome plastic. Hood, doors open. Alternate bumpers and grills for '53 or '54 versions. Reissued as: H-1219 (1971); H-1376 (1974).

H-1272 1929 Ford Model A Roadster/Pickup 1965-70   1/25 $40-50
White, chrome plastic. Sheet acetate windshield. Doors, hood, tailgate open. Reissued as: H-1327 (1975); 3124 (1979) Advent.

H-1273 '56 Chevy Bel Air 1963-70   1/25 $50-70
White, black, chrome, clear plastic. Metal axles. Doors, hood, trunk open. Front wheels steer. Builds either 150 or 210 models. Can be built stock, custom, or competition. Includes optional upholstered or metal door panels. Includes mounts to convert to a slot car racer. The H-1276 '55 Chevy (1964) uses the same underbody parts. Reissued as: H-1385 (1971); H-1373 (1974); H-1319 (1977); H-1391 (1979).

H-1274 EMPI Imp Dune Buggy 1969-71   1/25 $40-60
Red, chrome, clear plastic. Includes optional VW or Corvair engines, optional hardtop. This model was scaled-down to make the H-1246 1/32 EMPI Imp (1970). The real car was a grand prize in the 1970 Revell Sweepstakes. The H-1278 Safari Dune Buggy (1969) and H-1214 Gypsy Dune Buggy (1970) use the same underbody components.

H-1275 '31 Ford "Woody" or Tudor Sedan 1964-66   1/25 $65-85
White, chrome plastic. Clear acetate window sheet. Can be built either as a stock Model A Tudor sedan or "Woody" station wagon. Doors, tailgate open. Includes two surfboards. The mold was later modified so that the Tudor sedan could no longer be released. Reissued as: H-1204 (1970) '31 Delivery; H-1324 (1974) '30 "Woodstock;" H-1323 (1974) '31 Panel; 3123 (1979) '29 Ford Panel.

H-1276 '55 Chevy Bel Air 1965-70   1/25 $40-50
White, black, chrome, clear plastic. Metal axles. Vinyl tires. Racing slick rear tires. Racing decals. First issue decals have the names of the R & D department: "Keeler, Paeth, Jones." Doors, trunk, hood open. Can be built either stock V-8 or "blown" 409. The H-1273 '54 Chevy (1965) uses the same underbody parts. Reissued as: H-1343 (1971); H-1374 (1974); H-1392 (1979).

H-1278 Super Safari Dune Buggy 1969-71   1/25 $30-40
Metallic gold, chrome, clear plastic. Two sets of vinyl tires. The H-1274 EMPI Dune Buggy (1969) and H-1214 Gypsy Dune Buggy (1970) use the same underbody.

H-1280 1963 XK-E Jaguar 1963-71   1/25 $25-35
White, chrome, clear plastic. Metal axles. Hood opens. Snap-on hardtop or convertible parts; right or left side drive. Model designed and mold produced by Revell, Great Britain. Reissued as 3102 (1979) Advent.

H-1281 Mickey Thompson's Challenger I 1962-66   1/25 $50-70
Light blue, silver, chrome, clear plastic. Decals. Body lifts off to show interior and four chrome Pontiac V-8 engines. Each engine was a model in itself, with twenty-eight parts. This car debuted in 1959 at the Bonneville Salt Flats. In 1960 it set an unofficial world speed best of 406.6 miles per hour for a one-way run over a measured mile. Leynnwood box art.

H-1283 '56 Ford F-100 Pickup 1962-68   1/25 $50-70
White, chrome, clear plastic. Decals. Includes two chromed V-8 engines: '57 T-bird and '60 Pontiac. Includes surfboard. Doors, hood, and tailgate open. Reissued as: H-1325 (1974); H-1320 (1977); H-1378 (1979); H-1388 (1979).

H-1284 1957 Chevy Bel Air 1963-70   1/25 $40-50
Creamy white, black, chrome, clear plastic. Metal axles. Doors, trunk, hood open; windows raise and lower. Chevy 283 engine. First issue has delicate door hinges replaced on later reissues. Box art by Tom Daniel, later model designer for Monogram. Reissued as: H-1277 (1971); H-1371 (1974); H-1314 (1976); H-1389 (1979).

H-1285 Tommy Ivo's "Show Boat" Dragster 1963-66   1/25 $40-60
Red, black, chrome plastic. Four Buick 454 engines and racing slicks on all four wheels. Ivo was a star of ABC-TV's "Margie" series.

H-1287 1941 Willys Coupe "Swindler II" 1963-70   1/25 $40-60
Light blue, chrome, clear plastic. Metal axles. Doors, trunk open. 1960 Olds V-8 engine. This is a model of the Stone-Woods-Cook dragster that had many

highly publicized races with "Big John" Mazmanian's red '41 Willys. Reissued as H-1283 (1971).

H-1288 Mickey Thompson's Attempt I 1963-66   1/25 $50-70
Light blue, chrome, clear plastic. Includes transport trailer and vacuum formed drag chute. Canopy and body remove to show modified Pontiac Tempest engine. Not as popular a model as Thompson's H-1281 Challenger I. Leynnwood box art.

H-1289 '32 Ford Bob Tindle's "Orange Crate" 1963-70   1/25 $70-85
Orange, black, chrome, clear plastic. Hood removes, doors open, hinged body tilts up. Chopped-top '32 Ford Sedan. Blown Olds V-8 engine. Reissued as H-1282 (1971).

1960s Motorcycles

Revell's first motorcycle kits appeared in the early 1960s. Jim Keeler wanted to keep cycle models on the same 1/25 scale as car models. That made them too small for standard individual kits, but fine as items in the Custom Car Parts line.

C-1161 Triumph 650cc Cycle   1963   1/25 $25-35
Chrome plastic. Vinyl tires.
C-1162 BSA 650cc Cycle   1963   1/25 $25-35
Chrome plastic. Vinyl tires.
C-1163 Harley-Davidson Custom Cycle   1963   1/25 $25-35
Chrome plastic. Vinyl tires.
C-1164 '63 Honda Motorcycle   1963   1/25 $25-35
Chrome plastic. Vinyl tires.

Revell's cycle kits caught the American public's late 1960s fascination with freedom on the road. These models were very finely detailed and featured chromed parts, real rubber tires, and even flexible plastic tubing for fuel lines and brake cables.

H-1223 Triumphant Trike   1969-70   1/8 $100-125
Tomato red, chrome plastic. Clear red taillights. Flower decals. Custom show three-wheeler designed by Revell staffer Bob Paeth. Vacuum formed body shell. Reissued as H-1222 (1970) Tric-Up Trike.

H-1225 Yamaha Grand Prix 350   1969-73   1/8 $25-35
Blue, chrome, clear plastic. Red plastic taillight. International road and track racer. Reissued with modifications as: H-1220 Scrambler (1970); H-1226 Dirt Racer (1971).

H-1227 Harley Davidson Police Bike   1969-73   1/8 $25-35
Black, chrome, clear plastic. Vinyl tires. Highway Patrol decal. *Scale Modeler* (January 1971, 30): "The craftsmanship built into this series is truly superb." Modified reissue of H-1237 Chopped Hog (1968).

H-1230 Triumph Custom Show Bike   1966-71   1/8 $25-35
White, chrome, clear plastic. Red taillight. Decals for speedometer and tachometer. Vinyl tires. Includes wiring for fuel line, control cables. Two options for handle bars.

H-1231 Triumph Tiger 100 Motorcycle   1964-71   1/8 $25-35
Black, chrome, clear plastic. Red taillight. Decal for speedometer. Revell's first motor bike. Leynnwood box art. Reissued as: H-1232 (1965); H-1230 (1966).

H-1232 Triumph 650cc Drag Bike   1965-71   1/8 $50-60
White, chrome plastic. Vinyl tires. Modified reissue of H-1231 (1964).

H-1233 Honda Super Hawk   1967-71   1/8 $25-35
Red, chrome, clear plastic. Red taillight. Decals for speedometer and tachometer. Also issued as H-1234 and H-1235 (1967).

H-1234 Honda Racing Bike   1967-71   1/8 $25-35
Black, chrome, clear plastic. Reissue of H-1233 (1967).

H-1235 Honda Scrambler   1967-73   1/8 $25-35
Blue, chrome, clear plastic. Red taillight. 250cc trail bike. Steerable front wheel. Reissue of H-1233 (1967).

H-1236 Honda Drag/Custom   1968-71   1/8 $100-120
White pearl, chrome, clear plastic. Red taillight. Steerable front wheel. Reissue of H-1235 (1967).

H-1237 Harley-Davidson Hog   1968-73   1/8 $25-35
Lime green, chrome, clear plastic. "Chopped Hog." Steerable front wheel. Reissued as: H-1227 Police Bike (1969); H-1224 Electra Glide (1970).

1960s Figure Kits

H-1350 Paul McCartney   1964   1/8 $325-350
White plastic. Sculpted by Tony Bulone. Box art by Don Putman.
H-1351 Ringo Starr   1964   1/8 $325-350
White plastic. Sculpted by Magda Kopek. Box art by Don Putman.
H-1352 John Lennon   1964   1/8 $325-350
White plastic. Sculpted by Magda Kopek. Box art by Don Putman.
H-1353 George Harrison   1964   1/8 $325-350
White plastic. Sculpted by Magda Kopek. Box art by Don Putman.
H-1450 Flash Gordon & the Martian   1965-66   1/8 $100-120
White, clear plastic. Based on the comic strip character. Sculpted by Magda Kopek.

H-1451 The Phantom & Voodoo Witch Doctor 1965-66 1/8 $120-140
White plastic. Based on the comic strip character. Sculpted by Magda Kopek.

H-1554 Chicken Little 1961-62 1.5/1 $50-60
Blue, yellow, white, clear plastic. Vacuum-formed, pre-painted embryo parts. Snap to assemble and disassemble. Five clear plastic eggs, hatching egg, and newly-hatched chick show the development of a chicken embryo. Includes booklet *Miracle in an Eggshell* by a science teacher. This was the first of what was to have been a science series. Frog Life with Aquarium (H-1555) and Fish with Lighted Aquarium (H-1556) were developed and shown at the 1962 Toy Fair, but never went into production due to lack of interest from potential buyers. Plummer model sculptor. Box art by Leynnwood.

H-1920 Blaze King 1962-65 1/10 $50-60
Brown plastic. Just seven parts to this model. "Pre-waved saran mane and tail." With English riding saddle, real cloth riding blanket, halter, brush, pail, trophy. From the NBC-TV show "National Velvet." Reissued as: H-1921 (1963); H-1923 (1963); H-961 (1972, 1975); H-962 (1972, 1975).

H-1921 Golden Palomino 1963-66 1/10 $45-55
"Genuine palomino color" plastic. White saran mane and tail. Black parade saddle, cloth blanket, halter. Silver paper peel-n-stick saddle decorations. Reissued as: H-1920 (1962); H-1923 (1963); H-961 (1972, 1975); H-962 (1972, 1975).

H-1922 Quarter Horse 1963-66 1/10 $45-55
Buff, dark brown plastic. Black saran mane and tail. Western saddle, string lariat, green felt blanket. Reissued as: H-1924 (1963); H-960 (1972, 1975); H-963 (1972).

H-1923 American Saddlebred 1963-66 1/10 $45-55
Light brown plastic. Dark brown hair. English saddle, cloth blanket. Reissued as:H-1920 (1962); H-1921 (1963); H-961 (1972, 1975); H-962 (1972, 1975).

H-1924 Appaloosa 1963-66 1/10 $45-55
Brown plastic. Peel-n-stick spots to place on rump of horse, paint over, and peel off to create a dappled look. Reissued as: H-1922 (1963); H-960 (1972, 1975); H-963 (1972).

H-1930 "Flipper" and Pal Sandy 1965-66 1/12 $330-350
Off white plastic. Snap assembly kit. From the TV series and movie.

H-1931 Bonanza 1966 1/7 $80-90
White plastic. Hoss™, Little John™, and Ben™ from the TV series. Sculpted by Magda Kopek.

1970s Kits

1970s Aircraft

Dave Deal's Insane Planes

H-190 The Baron & His Fundecker Fokker 1970-72 $70-80
Red, chrome plastic. Five-wing Fokker with radial engine and optional Chrysler dragster motor. Peel-n-stick markings. Box shows "Slopwith Pup House" going down while its canine pilot parachutes to safety—a parody of Monogram's Snoopy™ and the Red Baron.

H-191 Lucky Pierre of the Lafayette Escadrille 1972 $70-80
Metallic greenish-gold, chrome plastic. Peel-n-stick markings. Pierre fires his machine gun over the top wing of his "Newport." This kit was reissued with modifications as 8104 Incredible Flying Machine (1980).

H-192 Flt. Lft. Rif Raf & His Spitfire 1972 $70-80
Light blue, clear plastic. Peel-n-stick markings.

H-193 Messa-Schnitzel 109 1972 $70-80
Metallic greenish-gold, clear plastic. Peel-n-stick markings. "Dimmler-Bent" engine with "GMC blower." Deal, a pilot himself, wanted the model without the car engine and blower—like the Spitsfire—so Revell made the kit with the option of building without the engine. Includes figure of pilot Weiner Moldy.

1970s Various Scale Aircraft

H-118 DC-10 Delta Airbus 1972-75 1/144 $20-30
White, clear plastic. Decals. Reissued as: H-141 (1974); H-157 (1975); H-271 (1979); 3401 (1979) Advent.

H-124 Lockheed L-1011 Eastern 1973-75 1/144 $20-30
White, clear plastic. Reissue of H-196 (1973) without interior. Reissued as: H-143 (1974); 3403 (1979) Advent.

H-136 Boeing 747 TWA 1975-77 1/144 $20-30
White, clear plastic. Reissue of H-197 (1974).

H-141 Western Airlines DC-10 Spaceship 1974-75 1/144 $20-30
White, clear plastic. Western decals. Reissue of H-118 (1972).

H-143 Delta Lockheed L-1011 Jetliner 1974-76 1/144 $20-30
White, clear plastic. Delta decals. Reissue of H-196 (1973) without interior.

H-148 "Blue Angels" KC-130F 1974-75 1/140 $15-25
White, clear plastic. Blue Angels decals. The support plane for the Navy's Blue Angels. Can also be built as KC-130B "Herky Bird." Reissue of H-247 (1957).

H-157 Douglas DC-10 United 1975-77 1/144 $20-30
White, clear plastic. United decals. Reissue of H-118 (1972).

H-159 Boeing B-29 Superfortress 1974-78 1/135 $15-25
Silver, clear plastic. Decals. Reissue of H-208 (1954).

H-163 Lockheed P-3A Orion 1974-76 1/115 $10-15
Gray, clear plastic. Reissue of H-163 (1965).

H-166 Republic F-105 "Thud" 1977-78 1/75 $8-12
Tan, clear plastic. Photo box art. Reissue of H-285 (1958).

H-167 Lockheed L-1049 Super G TWA 1975-77 1/128 $25-35
White plastic. (No clear parts.) TWA decals. Reissued as a collectors' model from the fifties. Reissue of H-245 (1957).

H-168 Douglas DC-7 United 1975-78 1/122 $25-35
Silver plastic (no clear parts). Passenger windows represented by black squares on decals. Pilot waving out cockpit window, passenger loading ramp. Reissue of H-219 (1955).

H-173 Sikorsky H-19 Rescue 1974-80 1/49 $10-15
Silver, clear plastic. Reissue of H-214 (1954).

H-196 Lockheed L-1011 TWA 1973-75 1/144 $30-40
White, clear plastic. TWA decals. "Show Off" model with cut-outs in left side panel to show interior. Includes five crew figures and stand. Reissued as H-124 (1973).

H-197 Boeing 747 United 1974-75 1/144 $30-40
White, clear plastic. United decals. "Show Off" model with cut-outs in left side panel. Crew figures. Reissued as: H-136 (1975); H-177 (1978); 3402 (1979) Advent.

H-233 Fokker Dr-1 Triplane 1976-78 1/27 $20-25
Red plastic. Von Richthofen decals. Pilot and two crew figures. Reissue of H-270 (1957).

H-234 Sopwith Camel 1976-78 1/28 $20-25
Olive plastic. Roy Brown decals. Pilot and one mechanic. Reissue of H-197 (1959).

H-235 Spad XIII 1976-78 1/27 $20-25
Green plastic. Rickenbacker decals. Pilot and crew figures. Reissue of H-256 (1957).

H-260 Douglas A-1H Skyraider "Sandy" 1974-76 1/40 $25-35
Tan, clear plastic. Air Force decals. Three ground crew figures. The original 500 pound bomb and underwing rockets are deleted and replaced by ten rocket launchers, two underwing gun pods, and a belly fuel tank. Reissue of H-169 (1959).

H-270 Douglas DC-8 Super 61 United 1970-72 1/144 $30-40
White (no clear) plastic. United decals. Reissue of H-248 (1959).

H-271 Sir Freddie Laker's Skytrain 1979-80 1/144 $20-30
White, clear plastic. Decals. Laker was a popular figure in England for his cut-rate air flights from Heathrow to JFK. To appeal to the British market Revell gave its DC-10 model new decals and a new package. Reissue of H-118 (1972).

H-910 "The Great Waldo Pepper" Camel 1976 1/28 $30-40
Green plastic. Came in two box styles, both with photographs of actor Robert Redford, star of the Universal Pictures movie *The Great Waldo Pepper*. Reissue of H-197 (1959).

H-999 Goodyear Blimp 1977-79 1/169 $30-40
Gray, white plastic. Snap-together construction. Peel-and-stick details. Introduced in Goodyear stores in late 1975 and in hobby shops in 1977. Features a lighted, rotating cylinder into which paper sheets with messages could be inserted. Comes with four colored pens for writing messages. Revell's best selling model at the time. Its success led to the issuing of other "Electronic Action" models.

1/72 Scale 1970s Aircraft

Fighting Deuces Series
Each kit contains two models of planes that faced each other in combat.

H-220 A5M5 Zero & F4F-4 Wildcat 1970-72 1/72 $10-15
Includes H-617 (1963) and H-639 (1965).

H-221 Spitfire Mk II & Messerschmitt Me-262 1970-72 1/72 $10-15
Includes H-611 (1963)and H-624 (1965).

H-222 P-51D Mustang & Ki-84 Hayate 1970-72 1/72 $10-15
Includes H-619 (1963) Mustang and the Ki-84 Hayate (not issued separately in USA).

H-223 Bf-109E & Hawker Tempest 1970-72 1/72 $10-15
Includes H-612 (1963) and H-620 (1963).

H-224 P-47 Thunderbolt & Ki-61 Hein Tony 1971-72 1/72 $10-15
Includes H-613 (1963) and H-621 (1963).

H-225 F4U Corsair & Ki-43 Oscar 1971-72 1/72 $10-15
Includes H-625 (1965) and H-641 (1965).

H-226 Hawker Hurricane & Fw-190 1971-72 1/72 $10-15
Includes H-616 (1963) and H-615 (1963).

Collector's Choice Series

Each kit came with parts and decals to make three different versions.

H-60 Curtiss P-40E Warhawk   1974-77   1/72 $5-8
Dark green, clear plastic. Decals for Chinese or two Army Air Corps versions.
  Reissue of H-623 (1964).

H-61 F4U-1D Corsair   1974-77   1/72 $5-8
Blue, clear plastic. Navy decals. Rockets, bombs, belly tank. Reissue of H-625
  (1965).

H-62 Focke Wulf FW-190A   1974-76   1/72 $5-8
Green, clear plastic. Decals. Reissue of H-615 (1963).

H-63 Messerschmitt Bf-109E   1974-77   1/72 $5-8
Light blue, clear plastic. Decals. Kit makes E-3, E-4, or E-7. Reissue of H-612
  (1963).

H-64 Sopwith Camel   1975-77   1/72 $5-8
Tan plastic. Four bombs added to the original model. Reissue of H-628 (1963).

H-65 Fokker Dr-1   1975-77   1/72 $5-8
Red plastic. Reissue of H-652 (1966).

H-66 Republic P-47D Thunderbolt 1975-77   1/72 $5-8
Green, clear plastic. Decals. Reissue of H-613 (1963).

H-67 Bell P-39 Aircobra   1975-77   1/72 $5-8
Olive, clear plastic. Decal. Reissue of H-640 (1967).

H-68 Spad XIII   1975-77   1/72 $5-8
Olive plastic. Reissue of H-627 (1963).

H-69 SE-5   1975-76   1/72 $5-8
Olive plastic. New four-blade prop, cowl, custom spinner for James McCudden's
  plane. Reissue of H-633 (1964).

H-70 Nieuport 28   1975-76   1/72 $5-8
Tan plastic. Reissue of H-653 (1967).

H-71 Fokker D-7   1975-76   1/72 $5-8
White plastic. Reissue of H-632 (1964).

H-72 North American P-51D Mustang 1976-77   1/72 $5-8
Silver, clear plastic. Decals. Reissue of H-619 (1963).

H-73 Grumman F4F-4 Wildcat   1976   1/72 $5-8
Blue-gray, clear plastic. Reissue of H-639 (1965).

H-74 Albatros D-III   1976   1/72 $5-8
Light brown plastic. Reissue of H-629 (1963).

H-75 Sopwith Triplane   1976   1/72 $5-8
Olive plastic. Reissue of H-654 (1966).

Air Battle & Air Show Scenes

These diorama kits packaged two 1/72 scale models together with cardboard
parts that could be cut out and glued to the kit box to form a "scene." One clear
plastic stand was included for one of the models, while the other rested on the
diorama base.

H-661 Battle of Berlin   1976   1/72 $20-25
A P-47D (H-613) swoops over a FW-190A (H-615) downed in a snowy landscape.

H-662 Battle of Midway   1976   1/72 $20-25
A A6M5 Zero (H-617) flies over a carrier deck where a F4F-4 (H-639) Wildcat
  taxies.

H-663 Battle of Britain   1976   1/72 $20-25
Diorama base has an aircraft bunker. Bf-109 (H-612) and Spitfire (H-611).

H-664 Air Racers!   1976   1/72 $20-25
Thompson Trophy pylon air racers. Includes: P-51D (H-619) and P-39 (H-640).

H-665 Fly-In   1976   1/72 $20-25
Includes Fokker Dr-1 (H-652) in red plastic and Spad XIII (H-627) in olive plastic.
  Two mechanic figures included. Doors slide open on hanger.

H-666 Barnstormers   1976   1/72 $20-25
Includes Bob Hoover's P-51D (H-619) and Joe Hughes's Super Stearman (H-650,
  Great Britain) in light blue plastic. Wing walker on the Stearman.

1/72 Aircraft Models 1970s in No Series

H-45 Vought F4U-1 Corsair   1978-80   1/72 $5-8
Blue, clear plastic. Decals. Reissue of H-625 (1965).

H-46 Curtiss P-40E   1978-80   1/72 $5-8
Olive green, clear plastic. Reissue of H-623 (1964).

H-47 North American P-51D Mustang 1978-80   1/72 $5-8
Silver, clear plastic. Reissue of H-619 (1963).

H-48 Republic P-47D Thunderbolt 1978-80   1/72 $5-8
Light gray, clear plastic. Reissue of H-613 (1963).

H-49 Messerschmitt Bf-109 E   1978-80   1/72 $5-8
Reissue of H-612 (1963).

H-50 Supermarine Spitfire   1978-80   1/72 $5-8
Olive green, clear plastic. RAF decals. Reissue of H-611 (1963).

H-51 Sopwith Camel   1978-80   1/72 $5-8

Olive plastic. Decals for Roy Brown's plane. Reissue of H-628 (1963).

H-52 Fokker Dr-1   1978-80   1/72 $5-8
Red plastic. Decals for Manfred von Richthofen's plane. Reissue of H-652 (1966).

H-56 Messerschmitt Me-262   1978-80   1/72 $5-8
Olive green, clear plastic. Decals. Reissue of H-624 (1965).

H-95 Messerschmitt Me-110   1978-80   1/72 $7-9
Gray, clear plastic. Decals. Ex-Frog mold. After the English company Frog went out
  of business, most of its molds were purchased by a Russian company, but these
  three German aircraft molds were not wanted by the Russians.

H-96 Dornier Do-335A   1978-80   1/72 $7-9
Dark green, clear plastic. Decals. Ex-Frog mold.

H-97 Messerschmitt Me-410 "Hornet" 1978-80   1/72 $7-9
Olive green, clear plastic. Decals. Flight surfaces move. Ex-Frog mold.

H-142 Junkers Ju-87 Tank Buster 1976-80   1/72 $5-8
Olive green, clear plastic. Builds either the D-5 version with five bombs or the
  G-2 version with 37mm underwing gun pods. Cowl removes to show engine.
  Leynnwood art.

H-144 Sikorsky HH-3E Jolly Green Giant 1970-80   1/72 $8-10
Green, clear plastic. Air Force decals. Rear loading ramp lowers. *Scale Modeler*
  (March 1972, 6) rated Revell's model better than Aurora's.

H-145 North American OV-10A Bronco 1970-77   1/72 $8-10
Olive green, clear plastic. Marine Corps decals.

H-147 Martin B-26 Marauder "Flak Bait" 1974-78   1/72 $8-10
Olive, clear plastic. Army Air Force decals. Reissue of H-111 (1966).

H-156 Douglas A-20C Havoc/Boston 1974-77   1/72 $8-10
Gray, clear plastic. US/RAF decals. Builds into either the US Air Force Havoc or the
  RAF Boston III. Has glazed nose, bombardier figure, and left and right fuselage
  gun pods that are not included in the H-232 Nightfighter reissue (1975). Reissue
  of H-115 (1968).

H-160 Heinkel He-219 Owl   1974-77   1/72 $5-8
Light gray, clear plastic. Decals. Reissue of H-112 (1967).

H-165 Junkers Ju-88C-6C Nachtjager 1975-77   1/72 $8-10
Light blue, clear plastic. Decals. Nightfighter. Reissue of H-113 (1968).

H-179 F4E Phantom II   1977-78   1/72 $6-9
Dark tan, clear plastic. Air Force decals. Makes three versions. Reissue of H-110
  (1965).

H-186 Blue Angels F4J Phantoms   1972-79   1/72 $25-35
Blue, clear plastic. Navy Blue Angels decals. Four planes mounted on a yellow
  four-spoke, lightning bolt stand. Uses the H-110 F4 Phantom mold.

H-195 Thunderbirds F4E Phantoms 1974   1/72 $20-30
White, clear plastic. Blue plastic stand. Air Force Thunderbirds decals. Mounted on
  the same stand as the Blue Angels (H-186). Uses the H-110 F4 Phantom mold.

H-202 Avro "Dam Buster" Lancaster 1972-73   1/72 $15-20
Black, clear plastic. RAF decals. Wheel struts are longer in this kit than in H-207 version to accommodate the externally carried skip bomb. Reissue of H-202 (1964).

H-204 Focke Wulf FW-200C Condor 1972   1/72 $15-20
Light gray-blue, clear plastic. Decals. Reissue of H-204 (1966).

H-205 Consolidated PB4Y-1   1974-75   1/72 $15-20
Blue, clear plastic. Decals. Navy version of H-203 B-24 (1964). Reissue of H-205
  (1965).

H-220 Lockheed P-38J/M   1977-80   1/72 $6-9
Gray plastic. Builds either the J version or the M two-seat nightfighter version.

H-222 General Dynamics F-16A   1977-80   1/72 $15-20
White, clear plastic. Decals for both of the first two prototypes. Ground equipment, engine, engine carriage, tow tractor, underwing ECM pods, Sidewinder
  missiles, bombs, fuel tanks. *Scale Modeler* (March 1977, 54) judged Hasegawa's
  kit more delicately detailed.

H-225 Dassault Mirage IIIE/R   1977-80   1/72 $15-20
Olive brown, clear plastic. French/Swiss decals. Optional nose parts for fighter-
  bomber or reconnaissance versions. Many underwing bombs and fuel tanks.

H-228 Boeing B-17E "Peggy"   1974-77   1/72 $18-22
Olive, clear plastic. Army Air Force decals. Reissue of H-201 (1962).

H-229 McDonald F4C Phantom II   1972-76   1/72 $6-9
Gray, clear plastic. Decals. This is a new Phantom mold, not a reissue of H-110
  (1965). Reissued as: H-179 (1977); H-186 (1972); H-195 (1974).

H-232 Douglas P-70 Nightfighter 1976-77   1/72 $10-15
Black, clear plastic. Army Air Force decals. This is the nightfighter version of the
  H-156 A-20 Havoc (1974). This issue has a solid nose, radar antennae array,
  and belly gun pod. Ground crewman and maintenance scaffold added. Reissue
  of H-115 (1968).

H-254 McDonnell F-15 Eagle   1975-80   1/72 $10-15
Light blue, clear plastic. Permanent mold changes from the previous year's H-257
  issue: square wing tips changed to rounded, underwing ordinance racks added
  with four sidewinders and twelve Mark 82 bombs. *Scale Modeler* (August 1977,
  15) thought Revell's model was better than Monogram's or Hasegawa's.

H-257 McDonnell F-15 "Eagle"   1974   1/72 $10-15
Light blue, clear plastic. Air Force decals. Canopy hinged to open. Engine may be
  removed. Four sparrow missiles. Reissued as H-254 (1975).

165

H-277 PBY-5 Catalina Flying Boat   1972-73   1/72 $12-18
White, clear plastic. Coast Guard decals. Wing-tip floats fold up. Landing gear deleted from this version of H-211 PBY-5A (1968); so model includes snap-on wheels for hauling on shore. Box art by Leynnwood.

H-576 Cousteau's PBY-6A   1977-78   1/72 $30-35
Off-white, clear plastic. "Calypso" decals. Underwater explorer Jacques Cousteau's plane. Taller tail fin, enclosed nose with diving platforms, Zodiac boat, and two skin-diver figures. This kit is the mate to the *Calypso* ship (H-575). Cousteau's son Philippe died in the crash of this plane. Reissue of H-211 (1968).

H-611 Spitfire Mk II   1972-73   1/72 $5-8
Brown, clear plastic. Reissue of H-611 (1963).

H-612 Messerschmitt Bf-109E   1972-73   1/72 $5-8
Light gray, clear plastic. Reissue of H-612 (1963).

H-617 A6M5 Mitsubishi Zero   1972-73   1/72 $5-8
Light gray, clear plastic. Reissue of H-617 (1963).

H-620 Hawker Tempest V   1972-73   1/72 $5-8
Olive green, clear plastic. Reissue of H-620 (1963).

H-623 Curtiss P-40E Warhawk   1972-73   1/72 $5-8
Silver, clear plastic. Reissue of H-623 (1966).

H-624 Messerschmitt Me-262A-1a   1972-73   1/72 $5-8
Light gray, clear plastic. Reissue of H-624 (1965).

H-627 Spad XIII   1972-73   1/72 $5-8
Tan plastic. Reissue of H-627 (1963).

H-628 Sopwith Camel   1972-73   1/72 $5-8
Tan plastic. Reissue of H-628 (1963).

H-639 Grumman F4F-4 Wildcat   1972-73   1/72 $5-8
Blue gray, clear plastic. Reissue of H-639 (1966).

H-652 Fokker Dr-1   1972-73   1/72 $5-8
Light blue plastic. Reissue of H-652 (1966).

H-656 Boeing P-26A Peashooter   1972-73   1/72 $5-8
Yellow, clear plastic. Pre-war Army Air Force decals. *Scale Modeler* (March 1968, 15) deemed the model "remarkable in its detail, accuracy, and quality." The lower wing part extends across the fuselage to insure proper dihedral. Reissued as 3308 (1979) Advent.

H-657 Macchi MC 200 Saetta   1972-73   1/72 $6-9
Light gray plastic. Fascist decals.

H-658 Curtiss 75/P-36A Hawk   1972-73   1/72 $6-9
Light gray plastic. Finnish decals.

1/48 Scale 1970s Aircraft

H-30 Curtiss P-40E Flying Tiger   1978-80   1/48 $10-12
Olive brown, clear plastic. Army Air Corps decals.

H-31 North American P-51D   1978-80   1/48 $10-12
Gray, clear plastic. "Man O' War" Army Air Force decals.

H-32 Spitfire Mk II   1978-80   1/48 $10-12
Green, clear plastic. East India squadron decals.

H-33 Messerschmitt Bf-109   1979-80   1/48 $8-10
Light gray, clear plastic. Decals.

H-197 Boeing B-17F "Memphis Belle"   1978-79   1/48 $15-20
Olive brown, clear plastic.

H-236 Lockheed F-104 Starfighter   1977-78   1/48 $10-12
Gray, clear plastic. USAF and German decals. F-104C with wingtip tanks or F-104G with sidewinder missiles. Fuselage panel can be built open to show Vulcan cannon.

H-237 MiG 21 PF   1977-80   1/48 $10-15
Gray, clear plastic. Russian aerobatic team/Syrian decals. Builds "early" or "late" variant.

H-285 North American B-25B/C   1977-80   1/48 $15-20
Olive brown, clear plastic. Army Air Force decals. Reissue of H 285 (1968).

H-288 McDonnell F-15A Streak Eagle   1977-80   1/48 $10-12
Gray plastic. Air Force decals. Makes two versions. With sidewinder missiles.

H-289 F-4E Phantom II   1977-80   1/48 $10-12
Olive, clear plastic. Luftwaffe/USAF decals. Builds E or F versions.

H-290 MiG-25 Foxbat   1979   1/48 $20-25
Light gray, clear plastic. Russian decals. With four underwing air-to-air missiles.

H-291 Grumman F-14A Tomcat   1979-80   1/48 $10-12
Gray, clear plastic. Jolly Roger Navy decals.

1/32 Scale 1970s Aircraft

H-146 Hughes OH-6A Cayuse   1970-78   1/32 $15-20
Olive, clear plastic. Army/civilian decals. Builds either a civilian version or a military version with an added gun pod. *Scale Modeler* (March 1971, 13) praised the model for its good part fit and "superb detailing." Reissued as H-161 (1978).

H-151 Republic P-47D RAF   1972-73   1/32 $25-35
Gray plastic. British Royal Air Force decals. "Razorback" canopy replaces the first edition's bubble canopy. Reissue of H-296 (1969).

H-152 North American P-51 RAF   1972-73   1/32 $20-30
Gray, clear plastic. Mold from H-295 P-51B changed to include a new fuselage insert changing the shape of the upper fuselage from a razorback shape to a bubble canopy shape. New "Malcolm Hood" replaces earlier B version canopy. Reissue of H-295 (1969).

H-153 Junkers Ju-87B   1972-73   1/32 $30-35
Dark green, clear plastic. Hungarian Air Force decals. Reissue of H-298 (1969).

H-155 Israeli Mirage 5J   1976-79   1/32 $35-45
Mustard yellow, clear plastic. Israeli and French decals. Builds two versions. Reissue of H-185 (1973).

H-161 SWAT Police Helicopter   1978-79   1/32 $20-25
Black, clear plastic. Decals. Pilot figure. Hughes OH-6J Reissue of H-146 (1970).

H-180 DeHavilland Mosquito IV   1973-74   1/32 $25-35
Light gray plastic. *Scale Modeler* (December 1972, 44) liked the model, but questioned the shape of the tail. This model was developed by Revell, GB.

H-182 McDonnell F-4E Phantom II   1977-79   1/32 $25-35
Green, clear plastic. Air Force decals. This model comes with lots of "stores:" three fuel tanks, six bombs, four Sidewinders, and four Sparrows. Nose cone detaches to show radar dish. Canopies hinged to open and close. Removable J-79 engine. Two crew figures. Reissue of H-188 (1972).

H-185 Dassault Mirage III   1973-76   1/32 $25-35
Dark green plastic. Decals for French E, R, and RS versions. Swiss decals for S version. Reissued as H-155 (1976).

H-188 McDonnell F4J Phantom II   1972-79   1/32 $15-20
Gray, clear plastic. Navy decals. Hinged canopies, two crew figures. Removable GE engine. Nose cone removes to show radar dish. Four Sparrow missiles. This kit was first proposed as a Blue Angels model with battery power to taxi down the runway, flash lights, and create engine roar. This concept was rejected as too expensive. Reissued as H-198 (1974) and H-182 (1977).

H-194 Hawker-Siddeley Harrier V/STOL   1974-76   1/32 $25-35
Olive, clear plastic. US Marines/RAF decals. Model developed by Revell, GB. Side panel removes to show engine. Canopy slides open.

H-198 McDonnell F4J Phantom   1974-76   1/32 $20-25
Olive green, clear plastic. US Air Force decals. Reissue of H-188 (1972).

H-215 Focke Wulf Fw-190D-9   1974-76   1/32 $25-35
Light blue-gray, clear plastic. Decals. "Long Nose Fw-190." Panel removes to show engine. Canopy slides open. *Scale Modeler* (January 1973, 24) welcomed this unusual model, but was "disappointed" in the lack of detail and accuracy.

H-217 Hawker Hurricane I   1971-72   1/32 $20-25
Olive, clear plastic. Sliding canopy. Developed in Europe. *Scale Modeler* (July 1971, 35) declared this: "probably the best kit Revell has ever produced."

H-218 Messerschmitt Me-262 A-1A   1973-74   1/32 $20-25
Light gray, clear plastic. Decals. "World's First Jet Fighter." Canopy hinged to open. Reissued as H-275 (1976).

H-250 Messerschmitt Bf-110-G-4 "Destroyer" 1974-75   1/32 $25-35
Light gray, clear plastic. Nightfighter version.

H-251 Bristol Beaufighter Mk 1F   1974-75   1/32 $20-25
Black, clear plastic. RAF decals. Cowls remove to show engines. Nightfighter of John Cunningham. *Scale Modeler* (September 1974, 8) liked the detail and accuracy, but condemned the part fit. "All-in-all, rather a poor kit." This model was developed by Revell staffer Ron Campbell, who had flown one in the RAF, but it was tooled in England and came out less well than expected, much to Campbell's disappointment.

H-262 Lockheed P-38J "Droop"   1976   1/32 $25-35
Light gray or olive, clear plastic. Decals. Panels remove to show highly-detailed engines, cockpit door opens. Big 20" wingspan. Reissue of H-280 (1970).

H-264 Nakajima Ki-43 Oscar   1974   1/32 $40-50
Dark green plastic. Decals.

H-265 Mitsubishi A6M5 Zero   1972   1/32 $25-35
Green, clear plastic. Decals. Reissue of H-265 (1968).

H-266 Hawker Typhoon IB   1973-75   1/32 $20-30
Dark green, clear plastic. RAF decals. Cockpit door hinged to open. Panel removes to show engine. This is a model of "Bea" Beaumont's plane from Squadron 609. Beaumont was a consultant on the model. *Scale Modeler* (January 1974, 23; April 1974, 17) labeled the kit "superb," but noted that some seams needed putty. Model developed by Revell, Japan.

H-267 MiG 21 PF/PFM   1975-80   1/32 $25-35
Gray, clear plastic. Russian and North Vietnamese AF decals. Parts for two versions.

H-271 Curtiss P-40E Aleutian Tiger   1970-73   1/32 $25-35
Olive, clear plastic. Reissue of H-283 (1967).

H-272 P-51 Bob Hoover Aerobatic Mustang 1974-76   1/32 $25-35
Yellow, clear plastic. Decal. Model of Bob Hoover's plane. Reissue of H-274 (1973).

H-274 P-51D "Miss America"   1973-75   1/32 $25-35
White plastic. Tinted clear canopy. Paper mask for painting stars and stripes paint scheme. Model of Howie Keefe's air show plane. Mold of H-295 P-51B (1969) changed to include a new fuselage insert altering the shape of the upper fuselage

from a razorback shape to a bubble canopy shape. New low-profile racing canopy, clipped wing tips, and reshaped wing leading edges. Revell was a sponsor of the real plane. Box photo is Lloyd Jones's prototype model built from Revell and Monogram "Phantom Mustang" parts.

H-274 Bell Huey Police Helicopter   1979   1/32 $20-25
White, clear plastic. Two crew figures. Decals for the Los Angeles Police Department. Bell UH-1D. Reissue of H-259 (1968).

H-275 Night Fighter Me-262 B-1a/U1   1975-76   1/32 $25-35
Gray, clear plastic. Decals. Leynnwood box art. Reissue of H-218 (1973).

H-276 Kawasaki Ki-61-I Hein "Tony"   1973   1/32 $70-80
Silver, clear plastic. Panel removes to show engine. Other than "too much flash," *Scale Modeler* (December 1972, 47) loved the model. Mold developed in Japan.

H-278 F4U-1D Corsair   1970-80   1/32 $18-25
Dark blue, clear plastic. US Navy decals. Reissued as: H-297 (1973); H-580 (1977).

H-279 Messerschmitt Bf-109G "Gustav"   1970-76   1/32 $25-35
Olive green, clear plastic. Revell's F version was modified with the addition of bulges on the engine compartment for cannon. Belly fuel tank added. Reissue of H-284 (1967).

H-280 Lockheed P-38J/L   1970-75   1/32 $25-35
Light gray, clear plastic. Decals for Richard Bong's plane, including portrait of his ex-wife on plane's nose. The former Mrs. Bong contacted Revell and asked that her picture be removed from the box art and decals, but Revell said the picture was part of history. Reissued as H-262 (1976).

H-281 Spitfire Mk5c USAAF   1976-78   1/32 $20-25
Tan, clear plastic. Decals for a plane used by the US Army Air Force. *IPMS Journal* (May 1991, 38) rates this the best of Revell's 1/32 scale kits. Reissue of H-282 (1967).

H-282 Spitfire MK-I   1972-76   1/32 $10-15
Light gray, clear plastic. Decals. Reissue of H-282 (1966).

H-284 Messerschmitt Bf-109F   1972-74   1/32 $25-35
Light blue, clear plastic. Decals. Reissue of H-284 (1967).

H-288 Mitsubishi J2M3 Raiden "Jack"   1972-73   1/32 $90-100
Dark green, clear plastic. Based on information gathered by Revell R & D staff from the only surviving example of this plane, preserved in a Southern California museum. This was the first mold developed in Japan.

H-294 Supermarine Seafire IB   1970-71   1/32 $20-30
Light gray, clear plastic. Royal Navy decals. Reissue of H-282 (1967) with modifications.

H-297 Royal Navy Corsair II   1973-74   1/32 $25-35
Gray, clear plastic. British Royal Navy decals. Vought F4U-1. The mold for this kit included "change block" inserts for the outer wing in order to mold parts that are shorter than in the US Navy version of this model (H-278). The actual Royal Navy Corsairs had wings six inches shorter than US planes due to the lower overheads in British carrier hanger decks. Reissue of H-278 (1970).

H-580 Baa Baa Black Sheep Corsair   1977-80   1/32 $25-35
Blue-gray, clear plastic. Navy decals. This kit tied-in with NBC-TV's "Black Sheep Squadron" show. Star Robert Conrad played the role of Gregory "Pappy" Boyington™. Only the decals were changed for this issue of the Corsair. Reissue of H-278 (1970).

H-581 Baa Baa Black Sheep Japanese Zero   1978-80   1/32 $25-35
Gray, clear plastic. Decals. Reissue of H-265 (1968).

H-801 Police Chase Chopper   1978-79   1/32 $25-35
Blue, clear plastic. Police decals. "Electronic Action" kit on a black base. Battery-powered landing lights, cockpit lights, spinning rotor, and motor noise. Bell UH-1D. Reissue of H-259 (1968).

H-801 Coast Guard Rescue Chopper   1979   1/32 $25-35
White, clear plastic. "Lights, Action, Sound! Electronic Action" kit on a black base. Battery-powered landing lights, cockpit lights, spinning rotor, and motor noise. Bell UH-1D. Reissue of H-259 (1968).

1970s Missiles and Space Models

H-177 Boeing 747 with Shuttle Enterprise   1978-79   1/144 $25-35
White, clear plastic. NASA decals. This is the Boeing 747 airliner (H-136) modified to carry the Space Shuttle *Enterprise* (H-194, H-200). *Scale Modeler* (May 1978, 8) rated the model "good," not "excellent." Leynnwood box art.

H-194 Shuttle Enterprise with Booster Rockets   1979   1/144 $25-35
White plastic. NASA decals. Seventeen inches tall. *Enterprise* was used in H-177 and H-200.

H-200 Shuttle Enterprise with Space Lab   1978-79   1/144 $20-30
White plastic. NASA decals. Cargo bay doors open to show Space Lab inside. Robot arm moves. The *Enterprise* is included with H-177 and H-194.

H-560 V-2 World's First Ballistic Missile   1973-76   1/69 $15-20
Gray plastic. Includes launch trailer, hinged to raise rocket, launch platform, and three ground crew figures. Hull half removes to show interior. Reissue of H-1830 (1960).

H-1800 Apollo/Soyuz   1976-77   1/96 $30-40
White plastic. Decals. Mounted on a clear display stand. Instructions in English and Russian. Includes astronaut and cosmonaut figures. The first issue (H-1800-380 on the instruction sheet) has part #21, the descent vehicle bulkhead in the wrong place and at the wrong angle. This was corrected in a revised issue (H-1800-380-A).

H-1855 Adventure in Space: Apollo & Gemini   1970-71 $125-145
H-1835 Gemini Space Capsule; H-1837 Gemini Astronaut; H-1838 Apollo Spacecraft; H-1861 Apollo 11 Tranquility Base.

H-1860 Apollo Astronaut on the Moon   1970   1/7 $35-45
White, clear plastic. Ten inch high model of an Apollo astronaut, Neil Armstrong, stepping onto the Moon's surface in 1969. Lunar base reads: "That's one small step for a man; one giant leap for mankind."

H-1861 Tranquility Base and Lunar Module   1970-73, 76-77   1/48 $25-35
Gray, clear plastic. Gold foil. NASA decals. The Apollo 11 lunar module resting on a crater-marked moon base. One astronaut on the stairs, another holds an American flag. Also issued as H-1861 (1969).

H-1862 Columbia and Eagle   1976-77   1/96 $25-35
Silver plastic. NASA decals. Gold foil covering for service module. Three astronaut figures. The Eagle rests on a moon base, and a clear plastic stand supports the Columbia command ship overhead. This kit is a reissue of H-1836 from 1968. Detaches into three sections. Reissue of H-1862 (1969).

1970s Ships

1970s Modern Ships

H-301 USS Missouri   1974-80   1/535 $10-15
Reissue of H-301 (1953).

H-302 USS Arizona   1975-80   1/426 $10-15
Reissue of H-348 (1958).

H-309 USS John Paul Jones   1972-80   1/320 $20-25
Dark gray plastic. Decal. Flag sheet. Reissue of H-352 *Forrest Sherman* (1958).

H-311 RMS Queen Mary   1972-78   1/568 $25-35
Reissue of H-311 (1961).

H-312 HMS Ark Royal & Ashanti   1973-76   1/720 $15-20
Gray plastic. Part of 1/720 "International Scale" series. Reissue of H-483 (1967).

H-314 Harbor Tug "Taurus"   1974-75   1/108 $15-20
Light tan plastic. Decal. Reissue of H-314 *Long Beach* (1956).

H-332 SS United States   1973-76   1/602 $20-25
Reissue of H-312 (1955).

H-341 USS Pine Island   1973-75   1/424 $20-25
Reissue of H-362 (1958).

H-342 Torpedo Boat PT-167   1973-75   1/72 $25-35
Gray plastic. Decals. Directions for dazzle camouflage. Reissue of H-310 *PT-109* (1963).

H-351 KMS Tirpitz   1973-79   1/570 $20-25
Reissue of H-351 (1964).

H-354 USS Hornet +3   1970-79   1/538 $30-35
Includes Apollo command capsule, Grumman S-2s, E-1 Trackers, Sikorsky Sea Kings. "Apollo 11 Moon Mission Recovery Vessel." Reissue of H-353 *Essex* (1958).

H-360 USS Ranger   1972-75   1/542 $25-35
Reissue of H-339 *Forrestal* (1957).

H-379 Russian Spy Fishing Trawler Volga   1971-72   1/142 $20-25
White plastic. Russian paper flag sheet. Box art by Ken Rush. US issue of Revell, Britain's North Sea Fishing Trawler. Reissued as 2554 (1979) Advent.

H-380 HMS King George V   1975-77   1/570 $20-25
Gray plastic. Decal. Paper flag sheet. *Scale Modeler* (October 1975, 9) rated it just a good, not excellent, model. Reissued as H-388 *Prince of Wales* (1976).

H-384 German Sub U-47   1975-80   1/125 $20-30
Dark gray plastic. Includes fifteen crew figures. Twenty-one inches long. A mark VII-B U-boat. "Show Off' model with cutaway side to show interior. Model of the submarine that sank the HMS *Royal Oak* at anchor in Scapa Flow fleet base in October 1939. Reissued as: H-408 U-99 (1978); 2553 U-99 (1979) Advent.

H-388 HMS Prince of Wales   1976-77   1/570 $20-25
Reissue of H-380 *King George V* (1975).

H-401 USS Washington   1971-75   1/570 $20-25
Reissue of H-313 *North Carolina* (1969).

H-402 KMS Scharnhorst   1976-77   1/570 $20-25
Dark gray. Decals. Paper flag sheet. This battle cruiser sank the HMS *Glorious* in 1940 and was herself sunk by the HMS *Duke of York* in 1943.

H-405 USCG Cutter Roger B. Taney   1976-77   1/302 $15-20
Cream plastic. Paper flag sheet. Reissue of H-337 *Campbell* (1957).

H-406 USS Tarawa Assault Ship   1977-80   1/720 $10-15
Light gray plastic. Navy carrier/amphibious assault ship. Includes helicopters, landing craft, tanks. Leynnwood box art.

H-408 German Type VII-B U-Boat U-99   1978   1/125 $25-35
Gray plastic. Reissue of H-384 U-47 (1975) without interior. Leynnwood box art.

H-421 PT-212   1972   1/99 $25-35
Reissue of H-304 (1954).

H-431 USS Flasher   1971-72   1/178 $25-35
Gray plastic. Decal. Paper flag sheet. Gato Class fleet submarine. This is a big, 21" long model. Leynnwood box art. Reissued as H-436 *Growler* (1973).

H-432 Jet-Powered Patrol Gunboat Tacoma 1971-72   1/130 $15-20
Gray plastic. Decals. Paper flag sheet. A 150-foot Asheville Class patrol boat designed for use on Vietnam's rivers and harbors. Powered by two conventional diesel engines and the same GE-79 jet engines that powered the McDonnell F-4 Phantom II aircraft. Revell R & D staffer Lloyd Jones's "research" included taking the *Tacoma* out for a spin in San Diego's harbor. *Scale Modeler* (January 1972, 44) praised Revell's model for its flawless molding and clean assembly. Leynnwood box art. Reissued as H-435 *Defiance* (1973).

H-435 USS Defiance   1973   1/130 $25-35
Gray plastic. Decals. Flag sheet. Leynnwood box art. Reissue of H-432 *Tacoma* (1971).

H-436 USS Growler   1973-74   1/185 $25-35
Gray plastic. Decal. Paper flag sheet. Wounded in an attack by a ship, Captain Howard Gilmore ordered his boat to submerge while he remained on deck. He posthumously was awarded the Medal of Honor. Leynnwood box art. Reissue of H-431 *Flasher* (1971).

H-437 Polaris Nuclear Submarine   1976-80   1/255 $45-55
Dark gray plastic. Decals. The right side hull part that was removable in earlier issues of this kit now has cut-away sections to show the interior. Markings for *Patrick Henry, George Washington, Abe Lincoln,* and *Theodore Roosevelt.* Reissue of H-313 (1961).

H-440 USS Coral Sea   1975-80   1/547 $35-45
Reissue of H-307 *F. D. Roosevelt* (1954).

H-441 USS Midway   1975-80   1/547 $35-45
Gray plastic. Decals. Reissue of H-307 *F. D. Roosevelt* (1954).

H-442 USS Bon Homme Richard   1975-77   1/538 $35-45
Reissue of H-353 *Essex* (1958).

H-443 USS Olympia   1975-77   1/232 $20-25
Reissue of H-367 (1960).

H-444 USS Lexington   1976-80   1/538 $20-25
Gray plastic. Decals. Essex Class carrier launched in 1942. Converted to angled deck in 1952—as represented in this model. Reissue of H-353 (1958).

H-445 RMS Titanic   1976-80   1/570 $10-15
White plastic. Decal. Revell thought a long time before making this model; after all, who would want to make a model of a ship that sank?

H-450 HMS Campbeltown   1972-75   1/240 $20-25
Gray plastic. An American Four-stacker destroyer traded to Great Britain that rammed Axis dry docks in France during World War II. Reissue of H-375 *Buchanan* (1960).

H-451 Icebreaker USS Burton Island 1972-73   1/285 $20-25
Gray plastic. Paper flag sheet. Reissue of H-337 *Eastwind* (1957).

H-452 USS Montrose   1972-73   1/376 $20-25
Reissue of H-329 *Randall* (1956).

H-457 USS Pittsburgh   1972-80   1/480 $20-25
Gray plastic. Paper flag sheet. Reissue of H-306 *Los Angeles* (1954).

H-458 USS Fletcher   1977-80   1/301 $20-25
Reissue of H-371 (1960).

H-461 USS Boston   1972-80   1/480 $25-35
Reissue of H-334 (1956).

H-462 USS Intrepid   1973-80   1/720 $15-20
Part of the "International Scale" 1/720 series. Reissue of H-488 *Essex* (1969).

H-463 USS Forrest Sherman   1973-79   1/320 $20-25
Reissue of H-352 (1958).

H-464 PT-211   1975-77   1/106 $25-35
Reissue of H-304 (1954).

H-480 KMS Blucher   1974-77   1/720 $10-12
German cruiser. "International Scale" series. Reissue of H-481 *Prinz Eugen* (1967).

H-490 KMS Admiral Hipper   1975-77   1/720 $10-12
German heavy cruiser. Part of Revell's 1/720 "International Scale" series. Reissue of H-481 *Prinz Eugen* (1967).

H-501 Battle of Midway Carrier   1978-80   1/485 $25-35
Gray plastic. Decals. Optional detail parts allow building of *Enterprise, Yorktown,* or *Hornet.* Plaques for each ship. Leynnwood box art. Reissue of H-378 *Enterprise* (1967).

H-520 USS Andrew Jackson   1978-79   1/200 $20-30
Gray plastic. Ex-Renwal kit. This Renwal model is slightly larger than Revell's Polaris sub model H-313 *Abraham Lincoln* (1961). Spring-loaded missile fires from rear tube. Also issued as H-521 *George Washington* (1978).

H-521 USS George Washington   1978-79   1/200 $20-30
Gray plastic. Ex-Renwal kit. Also issued as H-520 *Andrew Jackson* (1978).

H-575 Jacques-Yves Cousteau's Calypso 1977-80   1/125 $40-50
White plastic. Includes two diving saucers, anti-shark cage, two sharks, two diver figures, Zodiac boat, and a Hughes 330C helicopter. Twelve page booklet on Cousteau's adventures. Ocean research ship. Paired with Cousteau's PBY (H-576).

H-1312 Hemi-Hydro Speedboat   1971   1/25 $30-40
Blue, chrome plastic. Decal. Chrysler hemi V-8 engine. Includes water skis. Reissue of H-1278 Drag Boat (1963).

1970s Historic Sailing Ships

H-303 Constitution (Quick Build) with sails 1977-79   1/192 $15-20
Black, brown plastic. Molded ratlines, paper flag sheet, string. The "Quick Build" series of models featured one-piece decks, injection-molded ratlines, and snap-on yardarms. Reissue of H-319 (1956).

H-304 Cutty Sark (Quick Build) with sails 1977-79   1/216 $15-20
Black, brown, white plastic. Three-piece hull-deck assembly. Molded ratlines. This is a reworking of the old H-325 *Stag Hound* (H-1962).

H-307 Mayflower (Quick Build) with sails 1977-78   1/83 $15-20
Reissue of H-327 (1966).

H-316 Mayflower with sails   1972-77   1/83 $15-20
Molded ratlines. Reissue of H-327 (1966).

H-317 Stag Hound with sails   1972-76   1/213 $15-20
Tan plastic. Vacuum-formed sails, black, tan and silver thread, decal, paper flag sheet. Injection-molded ratlines replace the earlier string ratlines. Reissue of H-344 (1957).

H-318 Bounty with sails   1972-76   1/170 $15-20
Brown plastic. Molded ratlines. Reissue of H-327 (1956).

H-319 Cutty Sark without sails   1976   1/216 $15-20
This is a reworking of the old H-325 *Stag Hound* (1962).

H-320 USS Constitution with sails   1973   1/192 $15-20
Black, Tan plastic. Molded ratlines replace preformed string ratlines of H-329. Reissue of H-319 (1956).

H-322 Santa Maria with sails   1972-77   1/90 $15-20
Molded ratlines. Reissue of H-336 (1957).

H-323 Robert E. Lee   1973-77   1/275 $15-20
White plastic. Decal, flag sheet. Reissue of H-328 (1956).

H-324 Spanish Galleon with sails (Quick Build) 1978-79   1/96 $20-25
Brown plastic. Molded ratlines. Reissue of H-367 (1974).

H-325 Golden Hind with sails   1972-77   1/96 $15-20
Brown plastic. Molded ratlines. String, flag sheet, decals. Reissue of H-324 (1965).

H-326 Viking Ship (Quick Build) with sail 1977-79   1/63 $25-30
Brown plastic. Falcon decal for sail, insignia for shields. String for rigging. Model of a replica Viking ship in Lincoln Park, Chicago. This model is the last new sailing ship released by Revell—everything since then has been just reissues from existing molds.

H-327 Santa Maria with sails (Quick Build) 1978-79   1/90 $15-20
Reissue of H-336 (1957).

H-330 Charles W. Morgan with sails   1972-77   1/160 $25-35
White, black plastic. Molded ratlines. String, flag sheet. Reissue of H-346 (1968).

H-338 Bounty (Low Cost)   1978-79   1/110 $15-20
The "Low Cost" series launched in 1978 was aimed at "first time ship builders." Reissue of H-327 (1956).

H-343 Yankee Clipper with sails   1973-74   1/232 $15-20
Black plastic. Molded ratlines. Flag sheet, string. This is the H-344 *Flying Cloud* (1957).

H-344 Flying Cloud with sails   1975-77   1/232 $15-20
Brown plastic. Paper flag sheet. Reissue of H-344 (1957).

H-345 Golden Hind (Low Cost)   1978-79   1/96 $15-20
Reissue of H-325 (1972).

H-347 USS Eagle with sails   1976-77   1/254 $20-25
The *Eagle* was one of the tall ships that sailed in the Bicentennial celebration in New York harbor. Reissue of H-347 (1958).

H-357 Old Ironsides with sails   1972-79   1/159 $15-20
Black, tan plastic. Paper flag sheet, cement. USS Constitution. "Simplified series." Reissue of H-362 (1969) with sails added.

H-361 Stag Hound (Low Cost)   1978-79   1/213 $15-20
Gray plastic. Reissue of H-344 (1957).

H-363 HMS Victory with sails   1972-74   1/146 $15-20
Tan, brown plastic. Molded ratlines. Reissue of H-363 (1959).

H-365 Thermopylae with sails   1970-74, 76-77   1/120 $20-25
"Simplified series" with one-piece deck and injection-molded ratlines. A smaller twenty-four inch model of the *Thermopylae.* Reissue of H-368 *Cutty Sark* (1968).

H-366 Mayflower with sails   1970-79   1/83 $12-15
"Simplified series" with one-piece deck and injection-molded ratlines. Leynnwood box art. Reissue of H-327 (1966).

H-367 Spanish Galleon with sails   1974-76   1/96 $20-25
Brown plastic. Modified H-325 *Golden Hind* (1972) with new figurehead, row of shields added to sides, two lanterns on stern, and new stern carving. Cross, saint decals for sails.

H-372 Civil War Blockader with sails   1974-76   1/56 $60-80
Black, brown plastic. Rigging thread. Paper flag sheet. This is a reissue of the H-361 Yacht *America* (1969) with three swivel cannon added to the ship's railings. Foremast and bowsprit are lengthened from the original issue. A "Simplified Assembly" kit. This kit was released in the "Bicentennial Series."

H-389 Elizabethan Man-O-War with sails   1975-77   1/83 $30-40
Rust brown, dark brown plastic. Injection-molded ratlines. "E. R" decals for sails. String for rigging. This is the *Mayflower* without its lifeboat and with twelve cannon added. Reissue of H-327 (1966).

H-391 USS Constitution (Museum Classics)   1978-80   1/108 $40-50
Black, tan, ivory plastic. Philippine mahogany base with brass-plated pedestals. Cloth flags. Reissue of H-386 (1965).

H-393 Cutty Sark with sails (Museum Classics)1978-80   1/96 $40-50
Black, brown, white plastic. String ratlines. Cloth flag sheet. Pre-painted hull. Philippine mahogany base with brass-plated pedestals. Reissue of H-364 (1959).

H-396 USS United States with sails   1977-80   1/108 $60-70
Black, brown, tan plastic. String ratlines. Paper flag sheet. Made from the H-386 USS *Constitution* (1965) mold with a raised poop deck and changes in the stern cabin area.

H-397 English Man O' War with sails   1972-79   1/65 $60-70
Black, brown, white plastic. Big thirty-inch model. White vacuum-formed sails. "E. R." decals for sails. Paper flag sheet. Molded ratlines. Differences from H-400 Spanish Galleon are lion figurehead, absence of shields along sides, extra poop deck and fourth mast. This kit was designed to look like a traditional old-fashioned wooden ship model.

H-399 Cutty Sark with sails   1974-80   1/96 $30-40
Black, brown, white plastic. Reissue of H-364 (1959).

H-400 Spanish Galleon with sails   1970-78   1/65 $60-70
Brown, tan plastic. Yellow vacuum-formed sails. Crosses and eagles decals for sails. Molded ratlines. Crew figures. A robust, twenty-five inch long model. Eagle figurehead, three masts, lower poop deck, row of shields along sides are major differences from H-397 English Man-O-War (1972). Lloyd Jones researched his model at the reference library of MGM movie studio.

H-519 Pirate Ghost Ship   1978   1/96 $20-25
Black plastic. Skull-and-crossbones decals for sails. Glow in the dark paint. This is the H-324 *Golden Hind* (1965).

H-801 USS Constitution wall plaque   1972-75 $15-20
Brown plastic. Includes bottle of gold antiquing wax, thread for rigging. These three wall plaques were based on development materials used for the old full-hull models, but were completely new molds. They are not just half-hulls, but project out from the plaque slightly. Authentic old maps for the backgrounds. Based on H-319 Old Ironsides.

H-802 Cutty Sark wall plaque   1972-75 $15-20
Black plastic. Based on H-317 *Stag Hound*.

H-803 Spanish Galleon wall plaque   1972-75 $25-35
Brown plastic. Based on H-400.

1970s Armor

H-554 M-4 Sherman Tank   1972-76   1/40 $30-35
Tank commander and five foot soldiers. Reissue of H-522 (1956).

H-555 105mm Howitzer   1972   1/40 $10-15
Includes four soldiers. Reissue of H-539 (1958).

H-556 M-56 90mm Self-Propelled Gun   1972-74   1/40 $20-30
Includes four soldiers. Reissue of H-540 (1958).

H-557 M-35 Military Truck   1972   1/40 $10-15
Includes seven soldiers. Reissue of H-537 (1958).

H-559 PYCCKNN T-34 TAHK   1973, 75-76   1/40 $20-25
Olive green plastic. Decals. Russian T-34 Tank. Reissue of H-538 (1958).

H-1117 Panzer Tank   1977-79   1/48 $10-15
Olive green plastic. Decals. Panzerkampfer IV. H-1126 with a different turret.

H-1118 M4A3 Sherman Tank   1977-79   1/48 $10-15
Snap kit. Same kit as H-1125 without the rocket launcher.

H-1125 Sherman Tank with Rocket Launcher1977-79   1/48 $10-15
Snap kit. Same kit as H-1117 with added rocket launcher.

H-1126 Flak Panzer IV   1977-79   1/48 $10-15
Snap kit. Same kit as H-1117 with different turret.

1970s Cars

H-902 Visible V-8 Engine   1977-80   1/4 $50-70
Red, silver, black, clear plastic. This model was manufactured from a mold purchased from Renwal. It was molded in four colors of plastic, including clear pieces that showed the action of the internal working parts. This kit was also sold by J. C. Penny (HS-902).

H-906 Visible 2.3 Litre Turbo   1979   1/3 $30-40
Clear plastic. Motorized and powered by two C batteries.

Freaky Riders

These are reissues of Ed Roth monsters from the 1960s with new names and no mention of Roth.

H-900 Korporal Amerika & Road Freak   1971 $30-40
Light tan plastic. Red eyes. This is a reissue of H-1303 Drag Nut (1963), including "Rat-Type accomplice"—the small Rat Fink included with the original kit.

H-901 Shift Kicker   1971 $30-40
Light blue plastic. Red eyes. This is a reissue of H-1303 Mother's Worry (1963).

H-902 Heavy Head   1971 $30-40
Flamingo pink plastic. Red eyes and headlights. Reissue of H-1301 Mr. Gasser (1963).

H-903 Sleazy Rider   1971 $35-45
Lime green plastic. Red eyes. This is a reissue of H-1304 Brother Rat Fink (1964).

Deal's Wheels

All these kits, except two, were developed by Dave Deal himself. Box art also by Deal. Instruction sheets feature a Deal cartoon and story line directions by Deal's artist friend Don Mackie. Early editions had "Good-Boot" tires with a Playboy Bunny emblem on them. This was removed from later issues to avoid controversy. If you didn't want to build the model with the driver's head, you could use the substitute steering wheel part.

H-1351 Bug Bomb/Bug Out   1971-72 $50-60
Metallic orange, chrome, clear plastic. Peace sign where VW emblem should be. First editions of this VW came out under the name "Bug Bomb," but later issues were changed to "Bug Out"—because some company with the "bug bomb" trademark wrote a letter of protest to Revell. Same chassis as H-1361 Baja Humbug. The mold for this kit was modified and used to produce H-950 Li'l Herbie (1974).

H-1352 Glitter Bug   1971-72 $60-70
Lime green, clear plastic. Dune buggy. Also issued with turret as H-1356 Swine Hunt.

H-1353 ZZZZZZ-28   1971-72 $30-40
Orange plastic. Racing stripe decal. Camaro. Uses same underbody components as H-1357 Trans-Um.

H-1354 Stink Ray   1971-72 $50-60
Metallic purple, clear plastic. Uses same underbody components as H-1359 McLapper.

H-1355 '57 cHEVY   1971-72 $50-60
Yellow, chrome, clear plastic. 1957 Chevy Bel Air.

H-1356 Swine Hunt   1971 $70-80
Light brown plastic. German armored car. Pay phone on rear of vehicle, peace sign gun sight. Also issued without turret as H-1352 Glitter Bug.

H-1357 Trans Um Tirebird   1971-72 $60-70
White, chrome, green-tinted clear plastic. "Trans Um" decal. Pontiac Trans Am. Uses same underbody components as H-1353 ZZZ-28.

H-1359 McLapper Mk. V8   1971-72 $60-70
Orange, green-tinted clear plastic. McLaren "Can't-Am" racer with spoiler. Uses same underbody components as H-1354 Stink Ray.

H-1361 Baja Humbug   1971-73 $60-70
Dark metallic blue, clear plastic. "61 Revell" decals. Same chassis as H-1351 Bug Out.

H-1362 Van   1971-73 $60-70
Brown, clear plastic. Rear engine lid opens to show tiny 3.5 hp motor. Large Mercedes emblem on front where VW insignia should be. Surf van with two boards on top.

H-1363 Ferd Phony Car   1971-73 $60-70
Orange, chrome, clear plastic. Decals. Body hinged at rear to lift up. No driver because, as the box tells us, he fell out. Body sculpted by Darrell Zipp.

H-1364 Go-Mad Nomad   1971-73 $60-70
Metallic green, clear plastic. 1957 Chevy Nomad with surf board in back.

H-1365 Super Spurt   1972-73 $60-70
Metallic green, clear plastic. Body raises to show interior and engine. Chassis is same as H-1363 Phony Car. No driver in this Chevy Chevelle because, as the box says, he was too fat to fit in. Body sculpted by Dennis Rich.

Classic Jewel 1/48 Scale Cars

These four small scale kits were made from tooling purchased from Renwal, which had originally issued them in 1966. Although Revell listed nine more ex-Renwal models in its 1978 catalog, only these four were actually released.

H-1266 1930 Packard Victoria   1978   1/48 $10-15
Dark green, chrome, clear plastic.

H-1268 1934 Duesenberg SJ   1978   1/48 $10-15
Red, black, chrome, clear plastic.

H-1269 1939 Mercedes Benz 540K   1978   1/48 $10-15
Red, black, chrome, clear plastic.

H-1272 1931 Cadillac Phaeton   1978   1/48 $10-15
Olive green, black, chrome, clear plastic.

1970s 1/32 Scale Cars

H-950 Li'l Herbie   1974-75   1/32 $40-50
White, chrome, clear plastic. Vinyl tires. "53" racing decals. From the Disney movie *Herbie the Love Bug Rides Again*. Revell advertised this model as an easy-to-build kit designed for children ages 7-12. This model was made from the modified mold for the Deal's Wheels H-1351 Bug Out (1971) with a cut-out sunroof and smaller tires.

In 1975 Revell reissued its H-1200 series kits and changed the numbering to H-1100.

H-1101 1957 Chevrolet Bel Air   1975-80   1/32 $10-15
Yellow, chrome, clear plastic. Reissue of H-1293 (1969).
H-1102 '56 Chevrolet Corvette   1975-80   1/32 $10-15
Red, chrome, clear plastic. Reissue of H-1291 (1969).
H-1103 '57 Ford Fairlane   1975-80   1/32 $10-15
Light green, silver, clear plastic. Reissue of H-1292 (1969).
H-1104 '57 Ford T-Bird Hardtop/convertible 1975-80   1/32 $10-15
Red or blue, silver, clear plastic. Reissue of H-1290 (1969).
H-1105 1969 Corvette Stingray   1975-77   1/32 $10-15
Red, clear, chrome plastic. Reissue of H-1297 (1969).
H-1106 VW Bug   1975-77   1/32 $20-25
Red, chrome, clear plastic. Black vinyl tires. Reissue of H-1247 (1970).
H-1107 Opel GT   1975-78   1/32 $20-25
Metallic green, chrome, clear plastic. Reissue of H-1248 (1970).
H-1108 Ford Maverick   1975-78   1/32 $25-30
Yellow, chrome, clear plastic. Reissue of H-1249 (1970).
H-1109 Ford Mustang Fastback   1975-77   1/32 $10-15
Reissue of H-1250 (1968).
H-1110 Chevrolet Camaro SS350   1975-77   1/32 $10-15
Yellow, chrome, clear plastic. Reissue of H-1251 (1968).
H-1111 Pontiac Firebird 400   1975-78   1/32 $15-20
Red, chrome, clear plastic. Reissue of H-1252 (1968).
H-1112 1968 Mercury Cougar   1975-78   1/32 $20-25
Metallic green, black, chrome, clear plastic. Reissue of H-1253 (1968).
H-1115 "The Snake" '75 Vega Funny Car   1976-78   1/32 $40-50
Red, black, silver, clear plastic. Decals. Snap construction. Body hinged to lift up. Reissued as: H-1119; 2701 (1979) Advent.
H-1116 "Mongoose" Rail Dragster   1976-78   1/32 $30-40
Red, black, silver plastic. Decals. Snap construction. Removable body shell. Reissued as: H-1120; 2702 (1979) Advent.
H-1119 "Jungle Jim" '75 Vega Funny Car   1977-78   1/32 $45-55
Yellow, black, silver plastic. Decals. Snap construction. Reissued as: H-1115; 2703 (1979) Advent.
H-1120 "Jade Grenade" Rail Dragster   1977-78   1/32 $20-30
Yellow, black plastic. Decals. Snap. Reissued as: H-1116; 2704 (1979) Advent.
H-1121 SWAT Command Van   1977-80   1/32 $15-20
Black, silver, clear plastic. Decals. Red bar on decal sheet cut outs to fold inside clear emergency light on roof. Chevy van. Snap. Reissued as: H-1123; H-1127.
H-1122 SWAT Police Car   1977-80   1/32 $15-20
Black, silver, clear plastic. Decals. Snap. Hood opens. Reissued as: H-1124; H-1128.
H-1123 Paramedic Van   1977-80   1/32 $15-20
Red, silver, black, clear plastic. Decals. Snap. Reissued as: H-1121; H-1127.
H-1124 1969 Chevrolet Nova Stock Car   1977-80   1/32 $15-20
Red, black, silver, clear plastic. #23 decal and generic race products decal sheet. Roll cage, window net. Hood opens. Reissued as: H-1122; H-1128.
H-1127 Custom Chevy Van   1977-80   1/32 $15-20
Yellow, black, silver, smoked clear plastic, cycle decal. Reissued as: H-1121; H-1123.
H-1128 L. A. Street Machine   1977-80   1/32 $10-15
Yellow, silver, clear plastic. Flame decal. Hood opens. Reissued as: H-1122; H-1124.
H-1129 Chevrolet Custom Pick-Up   1978-80   1/32 $15-20
Red, black, silver, smoked clear plastic. Decal. Snap construction. Hood opens to show V-8 engine. With trail mini-bike.
H-1130 "Charlie's Angels" Chevy Custom Van 1978-79   1/32 $25-30
Red, silver, clear plastic. Decal. Snap construction.
H-1131 Z-28 Camaro   1979-80   1/32 $10-15
Blue plastic. Decal. Snap construction.
H-1132 Ford Boss 302 Mustang   1979-80   1/32 $10-15
Green or yellow, silver, black, clear plastic. Decals.
H-1133 Pontiac Firebird 400   1979-80   1/32 $15-20
Yellow, silver,, black, clear plastic. Decal. Reissue of H-1252 (1968).

H-1134 1969 Corvette Stingray   1979-80   1/32 $10-15
Orange, silver, clear plastic. Race stripe decals. Reissue of H-1297 (1969).

1970s 1/25 Scale Cars

Chevy Street Classics

H-1371 '57 Chevy Bel Air   1974-78   1/25 $20-25
Yellow, chrome, clear plastic. Reissue of H-1284 (1963).
H-1372 '57 Chevy Nomad   1974-78   1/25 $20-25
White, chrome, tinted clear plastic. Vinyl tires, red taillights. Reissue of H-1260 (1968).
H-1373 '56 Chevy Bel Air Sedan   1974-78   1/25 $20-25
White, chrome, clear plastic. Reissue of H-1273 (1965).
H-1374 '55 Chevy Bel Air   1974-78   1/25 $20-25
White, chrome, clear plastic. Reissue of H-1276 (1964).
H-1375 '54 Chevy "Highboy"   1974-80   1/25 $30-40
Neon orange, chrome, clear plastic. Racing decals. Reissue of H-1205 (1970).
H-1376 '53 Chevy Panel   1974-80   1/25 $25-30
White, chrome, clear plastic. Reissue of H-1270 (1969).
H-1377 '53 Chevy 210 Sedan   1977-80   1/25 $20-25
Baby blue, chrome, clear plastic. Trunk, hood open to show 409 engine. Cragar wheels.

California Classics

H-1389 '57 Chevy Bel Air   1979-80   1/25 $20-25
Red, chrome, clear plastic. Reissue of H-1284 (1963).
H-1390 '57 Chevy Nomad   1979-80   1/25 $20-25
Bronze, clear plastic. Reissue of H-1260 (1969).
H-1391 '56 Chevy Bel Air   1979-80   1/25 $20-25
Black, white, chrome, clear plastic. Reissue of H-1273 (1965).
H-1392 '55 Chevy Bel Air   1979-80   1/25 $20-25
Yellow, clear, chrome plastic. Vinyl tires. 409 V-8 engine with three variant building options. Reissue of H-1276 (1964).

Non-Series Cars

H-1201 1943 Willys Pickup   1971-72   1/25 $30-40
Yellow, black, chrome plastic. Sheet acetate windshield. Vinyl tires. Based on a World War II vintage US Navy Willys pickup—turned into a dragster model by Revell's shop. Reissued as H-1336 (1976) and H-1433 (1978).
H-1202 Austin Healey 100-Six   1977-79   1/25 $20-30
Red, chrome, clear plastic. Hood, trunk open. This is a reissue of the H-1217 Austin Healey first issued back in 1959.
H-1203 "Bed Bug" Panel Van   1970-71   1/25 $35-45
Orange, clear plastic. Vinyl tires. Includes surfboards. Flower power decals. Reissue of H-1228 (1959) with side windows and sun roof removed. Stock tires replaced with Goodyear street tires and wheels are Porsche chromed rims. "VW" logo on front replaced with Peace Sign. Box art by Dave Deal.
H-1203 '60 Chevrolet Corvette Convertible 1977-79   1/25 $15-20
Dark blue, chrome, clear plastic. Vinyl tires. This is the original version of the H-1232 Corvette first issued in 1960.
H-1204 Porsche Speedster   1977-79   1/25 $25-35
Silver, chrome, clear plastic. Hood, trunk open. This is the 1961 racing version of the H-1246 Porsche with a new Tonneau cockpit cover.
H-1204 1931 Ford Model A Delivery   1970-71   1/25 $20-30
Blue, chrome plastic. Sheet acetate windshield. This delivery truck is a modified version of the H-1275 Model A Tudor Sedan (1964). Reissued as H-1323 (1974).
H-1205 1954 Chevrolet Highboy   1970-73   1/25 $40-50
Orange, chrome, clear plastic. This model uses the chassis of the H-1270 Chevy Panel (1969). Reissued as H-1375 (1974).
H-1207 Kookie Kar Meter Cheater   1970-71   1/25 $70-80
Light blue, clear plastic. Corvair engine. Part of the Kookie Kars series along with H-1210 and H-1213 designed by Revell staffer Bob Paeth. All three cars share common chassis/engine/wheels. Box art by Dave Deal.
H-1208 '50 Austin Drag Sedan   1971-72   1/25 $40-50
Maroon, black, chrome plastic. Sheet acetate windshield. Racing decals. Front end tilts up to show Ford 427 engine. Doors open. Reissued as: H-1316 (1973); H-1339 (1977); H-1428 (1978).
H-1209 Boss Mustang Funny Car   1970-74   1/25 $80-90
Metallic lime green, chrome, clear plastic. Racing decals. Body tilts up to show engine and interior. This model uses the same underbody parts as the H-1216, H-1342, and H-1440 Funny Cars. This model uses the body shell of the H-1261 '69 Mustang (1968). Reissued as 3114 (1979) Advent.
H-1210 Amazing Moon Mixer   1970-71   1/25 $60-80
Metallic burgundy, chrome, clear plastic. Vinyl tires. "Moon Cross-eyes" decal. Part of the Kookie Kars series with H-1207 and H-1213. Mold was modified to create

the H-1330 T-Bone Stake Pickup (1975). Box art by Dave Deal.

H-1213 Der Guber Wagen 1970-71 1/25 $45-55
Red-orange, chrome, clear plastic. Popcorn truck decals. Part of the Kookie Kars series with H-1207 and H-1210. This mold was modified to create the H-1338 "Patent Pending" C-Cab Rod (1976). Box art by Dave Deal.

H-1214 Cushenberry's "Gypsy" Dune Buggy 1970-71 1/25 $20-30
Orange, chrome, clear plastic. Bill Cushenberry design.

H-1215 Porsche 911 1970-72 1/25 $20-25
Blue, black, chrome, clear plastic. Reissued as: H-1400 (1972); 3103 (1979) Advent.

H-1216 Ford Maverick Funny Car 1971-73 1/25 $40-50
Red, chrome, clear plastic. Black plastic rear slicks, vinyl front tires. Decals of various speed products companies. "Stretched" body lifts up to show interior. 427 SOHC engine. This is the only time this model was issued. This model uses the same underbody parts as the H-1209, H-1342, and H-1440 Funny Cars.

H-1217 '62 Dodge Dart "Revellion" Funny Car 1971 1/25 $80-90
Metallic gold, chrome plastic. Sheet acetate windshield. AA/G 1962 Dodge Dart funny car. Also issued as H-1252 Dart (1962) and H-1265 Revellion (1967).

H-1219 1953 Chevy Panel Delivery 1971-73 1/25 $30-40
Metallic red plastic. Reissue of H-1270 (1969).

H-1260 Custom Parts for Vans 1977 1/25 $15-20
White, chrome, clear plastic. Vinyl tires. Includes fender flares, three sets of wheels, custom grills, six different shaped side windows, refrigerator, TV, and more. For customizing vans from Revell or other model companies.

H-1261 Custom Parts for Pick-ups 1977 1/25 $15-20
White, chrome plastic. Accessories, step side beds for full-size and mini-pickups.

H-1277 1957 Chevy Bel Air 1971-73 1/25 $20-25
White, clear plastic. Leynnwood box art. Reissue of H-1284 (1963).

H-1281 1951 Ford Anglia "Skipper Critter" 1971-76 1/25 $40-50
Dark metallic red, chrome plastic. Sheet acetate windshield. Hood tilts forward to open to show Olds V-8; doors and trunk open; front wheels steer. Reissue of H-1269 (1968).

H-1282 Orange Crate Chopped '32 Ford Tudor 1971-76 1/25 $40-50
Orange, black, chrome plastic. Decals. Reissue of H-1289 (1963).

H-1283 1941 Willys "Swindler II" 1971-76 1/25 $40-50
Light blue, chrome plastic. Sheet acetate windshield. Racing decals. Reissue of H-1287.

H-1285 '56 Chevy Bel Air Sedan 1971-73 1/25 $25-35
White, chrome, clear plastic. Vinyl tires. Reissue of H-1273 (1965).

H-1300 1974 Chevrolet "LUV Machine" pickup 1977-80 1/25 $15-20
Yellow, chrome, smoked clear plastic. Decal. Hood lifts off. Custom street rod with sun roof, CB radio, Buttera suspension.

H-1301 1975 Datsun "Desert Rat" pickup 1977-80 1/25 $20-30
Tan, chrome, clear plastic. Decals. With Husqvarna off-road motorbike.

H-1302 Ford Fun Truckin' Courier 1977-80 1/25 $10-15
Black, chrome, clear plastic. Decals. Reissued as H-1386 (1978).

H-1310 VW Van "Rubber Duck" 1977-79 1/25 $30-40
Yellow, chrome, clear plastic. Vinyl tires. Decal. Flared fenders, two CB antennas, custom engine air scoops, two surfboards on top rack. "CB" emblem replaces "VW" on front. Modified reissue of H-1202 "Bed Bug" (1968).

H-1314 '57 Chevy Low Rider 1976-79 1/25 $20-30
Pink, chrome, clear plastic. Build as show car or street cruiser. Reissue of H-1284 (1963).

H-1315 '51 Henry J Gas Coupe 1973-75 1/25 $35-45
Red, black, chrome plastic. Acetate windshield. Race decals. Reissue of H-1262 (1969).

H-1316 1950 Austin Gasser 1973-75 1/25 $30-40
Yellow, black, chrome, tinted clear plastic. Race decals. Reissue of H-1208 (1971).

H-1317 Porsche 914 1972-73 1/25 $25-35
Blue, chrome, clear plastic. Reissued as H-1403 (1973) and 3141 (1979) Advent.

H-1318 Champion "Spark Bug" VW 1973-76 1/25 $30-35
White, chrome, clear plastic. Champion spark plugs and Revell decals. Model of the car built by Dave Deal and raced by Deal and Don Ernst in the Baja 1,000. Revell gave away the actual bob-fender VW in a sweepstakes. Reissue of H-1341 Baja Chopper (1971).

H-1319 1956 Chevy Bel Air "Bad Dreams" 1977-78 1/25 $20-30
Green, white, chrome, clear plastic. Lowrider street cruiser. Reissue of H-1273 (1965).

H-1320 1956 Ford F-100 "Big Ten-Ford" 1977-78 1/25 $15-20
Metallic brown, chrome, clear plastic. Vinyl tires. "Bear Bait" decal. CB antenna, "wood" side board parts for truck bed added. Cragar wheels. Reissue of H-1283 (1962).

H-1321 Gran Turismo 1973-74 1/25 $15-20
Blue, chrome, clear plastic. Optional VW or Corvair engines. Show Car.

H-1322 Barris' Kustom Rolls/VW 1973-75 1/25 $40-50
Black, clear, chrome plastic. This is Revell's standard H-1264 VW (1969) with added Rolls hood, grille, hood ornament, and oversize Lucas headlights. Rolls

trunk can be substituted for standard engine hood. All the regular parts for the standard model are also included.

H-1323 1931 Ford A "Mother's Cherry Pie" 1974-77 1/25 $30-40
Red, chrome plastic. Clear acetate windows. Panel Sedan. Reissue of H-1275 (1964).

H-1324 1930 Model A Ford "Woodstock" 1974-77 1/25 $20-30
Orange, chrome plastic. Clear acetate window sheet. Reissue of H-1275 (1964).

H-1325 '56 Ford Pick-Up "Super Trick Classic" 1974-78 1/25 $15-20
Blue, chrome, clear plastic. Reissue of H-1283 (1962).

H-1326 1963 VW "Herbie the Love Bug" 1974-75 1/25 $80-90
White, chrome, clear plastic. Decals. From the Disney movie *Herbie the Love Bug Rides Again*. Reissue of H-1263 (1969).

H-1327 '29 Ford Model A "Sundance Express" 1975-77 1/25 $25-35
Orange, chrome, clear plastic. Pickup rod. Hood, doors, tailgate open. Front wheels steer. Reissue of H-1272 (1965).

H-1328 1951 Henry J Dyno-Mite "J" 1977 1/25 $40-50
Yellow, red, chrome plastic. Acetate windshield. Decals. Reissue of H-1262 (1969).

H-1329 "Dual Jewel" Twin V-8 Roadster 1975-76 1/25 $40-50
Blue, chrome, clear plastic. This is the H-1277 Mysterion (1964) with its bubble top replaced by a low windscreen. Has a new roll bar and high spoiler wing added to the rear.

H-1330 T-Bone Stake Pickup 1975-76 1/25 $40-50
Yellow, chrome, clear plastic. This is a modified reissue of H-1210 Moon Mixer (1970). Reissued as H-1431 (1978).

H-1331 Buttera's '26 T Street Rod 1976-77 1/25 $15-20
Bronze, chrome, smoked clear plastic. Vinyl tires. "LIL J" decal for license plate. John Buttera Street Rod #1. Model of Buttera's real show rod, a "Tall T Tudor." Ford 289 Cobra V-8 engine, chrome spoke wheels. First Revell car model with air conditioning. This models shares many parts with the H-1334 T Touring (1977). Reissued as: H-1343 T Delivery (1977); H-1436 (1978); 3121 (1979) Advent.

H-1332 '57 Ford Ranchero Pickup 1976-78 1/25 $40-50
Light blue, clear plastic. This is the old H-1240 kit from 1960, now with a chopped top.

H-1333 '59 Ford Galaxie Skyliner 1976-77 1/25 $30-40
Yellow, chrome, clear plastic. Hardtop convertible. This is the old H-1227 kit from 1959.

H-1334 Buttera's '27 T Touring 1976-77 1/25 $15-20
Yellow, chrome, smoked clear plastic. John Buttera Street Rod #2. This kit shares parts with the H-1331 '26 T Street Rod (1976) except for a different body and interior. Reissued as 3122 (1979) Advent.

H-1335 '32 Ford Tudor "Chopped Deuce" 1976-78 1/25 $35-45
Blue, black, chrome, clear plastic. Darrell Zipp, reluctantly, supervised the conversion of Bob Tindle's "Orange Crate" into this generic '32 hot rod. Later this conversion was reversed. Modified reissue of H-1289 (1963).

H-1336 1941 Willys Pickup "Moving Violation" 1976-77 1/25 $20-30
Metallic purple, chrome plastic. Race decals. Although the model year is designated 1941, this is still the '43 Willys. Reissue of H-1201 (1971).

H-1337 Chopped '34 Ford Coupe 1977 1/29 $15-20
Red, chrome, clear plastic. Vinyl tires. "Lil John" Buttera's three-window coupe. Buttera Rod #3. This model rides on the chassis for the H-1331/1334 (1976) Model T Buttera cars. Since the T chassis was shorter than the actual '34 Ford chassis, the model's body had to be reduced in scale to 1/29 to fit the T chassis. Reissued as H-1427 (1978).

H-1338 C-Cab Rod "Patent Pending" 1976 1/25 $30-40
Red, chrome, clear plastic. This is a modified reissue of H-1213 Der Guber Wagon (1970). Reissued as 3134 "Medicine Man" (1979) Advent.

H-1339 1950 Austin "Wrench Connection" 1977 1/25 $40-50
Red, black, chrome plastic. Tinted acetate sheet window. Reissue of H-1208 (1971).

H-1340 Buttera '33 Ford 3-Window Coupe 1977 1/29 $15-20
Blue, chrome, clear plastic. Buttera Rod #4. This model rides on the chassis for the H-1331/1334 (1976) Model T Buttera cars. Reissued as H-1426 (1978).

H-1341 1968 VW "Baja Chopper" 1971-73 1/25 $25-35
Yellow, chrome, clear plastic. Race decals. Off road racer with cut-away fenders, running lights on front of roof, and air filers on back of roof. Rides on the chassis of the H-1264 VW Bug (1969). Reissued as: H-1318 Spark Bug (1973); H-1366 Valvoline (1976).

H-1342 Camaro "Heavy Hugger" Funny Car 1971-74 1/25 $30-40
Orange, chrome, clear plastic. "Heavy Hugger" decals. Z-28 funny car with body hinged to tilt up. This model uses the same underbody parts as the H-1209, H-1216, and H-1440 Funny Cars. Reissued as H-1440 (1972) and Advent 3113 Killer Camaro Z-28 (1979).

H-1343 1955 Chevy Bel Air 1971-73 1/25 $20-30
White, chrome, clear plastic. Reissue of H-1276 (1964).

H-1343 1926 Ford Model T Delivery Buttera 1977-78 1/25 $15-20
Olive green, chrome, clear plastic. "Lil' John's Delivery" decals. Buttera Rod #5. Includes alternate solid rear side windows of coupe version to create panel truck. Reissue of H-1331 (1976).

H-1344 1951 Thames Panel Delivery 1971-76 1/25 $25-35
Metallic green, chrome plastic. Orange sheet acetate windshield. Racing decals. Reissue of H-1268 (1968).

H-1345 Cobra Street Racer 1978-80 1/25 $15-25
Yellow, chrome, clear plastic. 1976 Ford Cobra Mustang II T-top.

H-1346 1978 Chevrolet Monza "Super Spyder" 1978-80 1/25 $15-25
Black, chrome, clear plastic. Spider decal. Front air dam and flared quarter panel farings.

H-1347 1978 Formula Sunbird IMSA 1978-80 1/25 $15-25
Red, chrome, clear plastic. Decals. Convertible.

H-1366 Baja Racer Valvoline VW 1976 1/25 $30-40
White, chrome, clear plastic. Valvoline decals. Revell co-sponsored the actual VW, driven by Gary Kohs and Revell's Don Ernst. Reissue of H-1341 Baja Chopper (1971).

H-1378 1956 Ford F-100 Pickup "Big Ten-Ford" 1979-80 1/25 $15-20
Metallic brown, chrome, clear plastic. Bear decals. Only the kit number was changed for this issue. Features are the same as H-1320 (1977). Reissue of H-1283 (1962).

H-1379 1977 Chevy Tow Truck "Sneaky Pete" 1977 1/25 $25-30
Bronze, chrome, clear plastic. Decal. Kit number changes to H-1380 in 1978.

H-1380 1977 Chevy Tow Truck "Sneaky Pete" 1978-80 1/25 $25-30
Bronze, chrome, clear plastic. Decal. First issued as H-1379.

H-1381 Datsun Pickup/Bikes "Rough Riders" 1978-80 1/25 $35-45
Yellow, chrome, clear plastic. Motocross decals. Pickup with trailer and two dirt bikes.

H-1382 Chevy Luv Pickup River Rat 1978-80 1/25 $15-25
Orange, black, smoked clear plastic. Decals. With trailer and speed boat.

H-1383 1978 Chevy Truck "Midnite Cowboy" 1978-80 1/25 $20-30
Black, chrome, clear plastic. Decals. Wrecker tow truck. Hood tilts forward.

H-1384 1977 Chevy Step Side Pickup/Snowmobile 1979-80 1/25 $40-50
Blue, chrome, clear plastic. "Ice Patrol" decal.

H-1385 Billy Carter's "Redneck Power" Pickup 1978-79 1/25 $35-45
White, chrome, clear plastic. Vinyl tires. "Billy Carter's Super Service" decal. Hood, tailgate open. Chevy 350 V-8 engine. Includes jack, two jerry cans, three batteries, case of oil, and case of "soft drinks."

H-1386 1978 Ford Courier "Coors" Pickup 1978-80 1/25 $15-20
Red, clear, chrome plastic. Licensed by the Adolph Coors Company. Includes chrome Coors medallion. Dennis Rich designed model. Reissue of H-1302 (1977).

H-1387 John Travolta's "Firebird Fever" 1979-80 1/25 $30-35
Silver, smoked clear plastic. "Travolta Fever" decal. 1979 Pontiac Firebird with flared fenders, opening shaker hood, and "whale" spoiler. Tinted t-top panels. Hood tilts to show motor. Model of actual car customized by George Barris.

H-1388 1956 Ford F-100 "California Pickup" 1979-80 1/25 $15-20
Blue, chrome, clear plastic. Reissue of H-1283 (1962).

H-1393 1977 Chevy "Mean Mudder" Van 1978-80 1/25 $25-35
Brown, clear plastic. Decals. Off-road van and motorcycle. Reissue of H-1395 (1977).

H-1394 1977 Chevy Van "Brute Force" 1978-80 1/25 $25-35
Dark brown, tan, chrome, clear plastic. "Big rig" vertical exhaust pipes. Model designed by Dennis Rich. Decal designed by Kenny Youngblood. Reissue of H-1395 (1977).

H-1395 1977 Chevy Van "California Cruiser" 1977 1/25 $20-30
Yellow, brown, chrome, smoked clear plastic. Decal. Roof lifts off to show interior with bed, TV, stereo. Model of the *Car Craft* magazine custom van given away in Revell's 1976 Van-Tastic Sweepstakes. Reissued as: H-1396 (1977); H-1397 (1977); H-1393 (1978); H-1394 (1978); H-1398 (1978).

H-1396 1977 Chevy Van "Convoy" 1977-79 1/25 $30-40
Blue, red, chrome, smoked clear plastic. Decal. Reissue of H-1395 (1977).

H-1397 1977 Chevy "Charlie's Angels" Van 1977-79 1/25 $30-40
Pink, black, smoked clear plastic. Decals. Licensed from the *Charlie's Angels* TV series, although no such vehicle appeared in the show. Reissue of H-1395 (1977) with added CB radio and side mirror antennae.

H-1398 1978 GMC Hardy Boys' Van 1978-79 1/25 $30-40
Butterscotch brown, dark tan, black, smoked clear plastic. Decals. Customized 1978 GMC van. Licensed from the *Hardy Boys Mysteries* TV show. Reissue of H-1395 (1977).

H-1400 Racing Porsche 911 1972-73 1/25 $20-30
Red, chrome, clear plastic. Reissue of H-1215 (1970).

H-1401 Datsun 240Z 1972-74 1/25 $25-30
Orange, chrome, clear plastic. Hood opens. Reissued as: H-1402 (1972); H-1434 (1978); H-1410 (1976); 3101 (1979) Advent.

H-1402 1972 Pete Brock's BRE/Datsun 240Z 1972-74 1/25 $25-35
White, chrome, clear plastic. #46 racing decals. Car of Pete Brock and driver John Morton. Reissue of H-1401 (1972).

H-1403 Ritchie Ginther's Porsche 914/6 1973-74 1/25 $25-35
Orange, chrome, clear plastic. Decals. Reissue of H-1317 (1972) with new lower racing windscreen. SCCA racer.

H-1404 1972 Datsun 510 1973-74 1/25 $25-35
White, chrome, clear plastic. #46 decal. Peter Brock's car. Reissued as H-1405 (1974) and 3143 (1979) Advent.

H-1405 1972 Datsun 510 "Brockbuster" 1974 1/25 $30-40
White, chrome, clear plastic. Decals. Peter Brock's car. Reissue of H-1404 (1973).

H-1407 Porsche Carrera RS 1977-79 1/25 $15-25
Yellow, chrome, clear plastic. Engine cover opens. Includes optional rally equipment.

H-1409 "The California Bug" 1976 1/25 $25-35
Orange, chrome, clear plastic. Volkswagen. Build either stock or competition. Air scoops over rear side windows, air scoop on engine hood. Reissue of H-1263 (1969).

H-1410 1972 Datsun 240Z "Giant Killer" 1976-77 1/25 $25-35
White, chrome, clear plastic. #45 race decals of Walt Maas. Reissue of H-1401 (1972).

H-1411 1979 Porsche 928 1979-80 1/25 $20-30
Orange, chrome, clear plastic.

H-1425 '75 Vega "Veney's Vega" Funny Car 1976-77 1/25 $50-70
Red, chrome, clear plastic. Decals. The second-issue '75 Vega body differs from the first-issue '72 Vega in having a louvered grill, prominent blisters above each front tire, a large bulge on the hood, and a larger rear spoiler. Ken Veney's car. Reissue of H-1453 (1975).

H-1426 '33 Ford 3-Window Coupe 1978-79 1/29 $15-20
Light blue, clear plastic. Low price edition of Buttera car. Reissue of H-1340 (1977).

H-1427 1934 Ford Chopped Coupe 1978-79 1/29 $15-20
Red, chrome, clear plastic. Vinyl tires. Low price edition. Reissue of H-1337 (1977).

H-1428 Austin Gas Coupe "Wrench Connection" 1978-79 1/25 $30-40
Red, black, chrome plastic. Sheet acetate windshield. Low price edition. Reissue of H-1208 (1971).

H-1429 '72 Demon "Revellution" Funny Car 1978-79 1/25 $70-80
Red, chrome, clear plastic. Unlike the first-issue '72 Dodge Demon/Plymouth Duster kit, this second-issue '72 Demon/Duster has glue-on blisters above each front tire. Ed McCulloch's car. Low price edition. Reissue of H-1465 (1976).

H-1430 Ford C-Cab Rod "Patent Pending" 1978-79 1/25 $30-40
Red, chrome, clear plastic. Low price edition. Reissue of H-1338 (1976).

H-1431 Ford "T-Bone Stake" 1978-79 1/25 $25-35
Yellow, clear, chrome plastic. Steerable front wheels. Corvair engine. Low price edition. Reissue of H-1330 (1975).

H-1432 '51 Henry J Dyno-Mite "J" 1978-79 1/25 $35-45
Yellow, black, chrome plastic. Sheet acetate windshield. Low price edition. Reissue of H-1262 (1969).

H-1433 '43 Willys Pickup "Moving Violation" 1978-79 1/25 $20-25
Metallic purple, clear, chrome plastic. Low price edition. Reissue of H-1201 (1971).

H-1434 '72 Datsun 240Z "Giant Killer" 1978-79 1/25 $25-35
White, chrome, clear plastic. Low price edition. Reissue of H-1401 (1972).

H-1435 "Cha Cha" Shirley Muldowney Rail 1978-79 1/25 $65-75
Pink, chrome plastic. Decals. Rear-engine. Low price edition. Reissue of H-1462 (1977).

H-1436 Buttera's 26 T Street Rod 1978-79 1/25 $15-20
Bronze, chrome, smoked clear plastic. Low price reissue of H-1331 (1976).

H-1437 '76 Monza "The Snake" Funny Car 1978-79 1/25 $20-25
White, chrome, clear plastic. "Army" decals. Don "The Snake" Prudhomme's car. Low price edition. Reissue of H-1467 (1976).

H-1440 '71 Camaro "Jungle Jim" Funny Car 1972-74 1/25 $125-135
Light blue, clear plastic. Decals. Jim Liberman's dragster. Model uses the same underbody as the H-1209, H-1216, and H-1342 Funny Cars. Reissue of H-1342 (1971).

H-1442 '72 Ford Pinto "Revellaser" Funny Car 1973-75 1/25 $70-80
Dark blue, chrome, clear plastic. Racing decals. Mickey Thompson's Revell-sponsored car. Reissued as H-1451 (1974).

H-1444 1923 Ford Model T "Rodfather" 1973-78 1/25 $40-50
Blue, chrome, clear plastic. Psychedelic decals. Blue felt floor carpet. Optional top. Chevy 327 V-8 engine. Wide racing slicks and chrome mag wheels. Modified reissue of H-1286 Ed Roth's Tweedy Pie (1963).

H-1445 '72 Vega Pisano/Matsubara Funny Car 1973-76 1/25 $70-80
Yellow, chrome, clear plastic. Decal. Reissued as H-1449 (1974) and H-1456 (1975).

H-1446 '72 Charger "Snowman" Funny Car 1973-75 1/25 $70-80
Red, chrome, clear plastic. Decal. Gene Snow's funny car. Reissued as H-1450 (1974) and H-1452 (1974).

H-1447 '72 Demon "Revellution" Funny Car 1973-75 1/25 $70-80
White, chrome, clear plastic. Decal. First-issue '72 Demon. Ed McCulloch's car. Reissued as H-1457 (1975).

H-1448 1926 Ford Model T "Canned Heat" 1973-76 1/25 $40-50
Yellow, chrome, clear plastic. Flame decal. Modified reissue of H-1282 Ed Roth's "Outlaw" (1962). New induction system and mag rear wheels.

H-1449 '73 Vega "Jungle Jim" Funny Car 1974-76 1/25 $60-80
Dark blue, chrome, clear plastic. "Jungle Jim" decals. 500 cc hemi elephant engine. Jim Liberman's car. Reissue of H-1445 (1973).

H-1450 '72 Charger "Wild Willie Borsch" 1974-76 1/25 $60-80
Orange, chrome, clear plastic. Car body art designed by Revell staff artist Clare Darden. Reissue of H-1446 (1973).

H-1451 '72 Pinto "Eastern Raider" Funny Car 1974-76 1/25 $60-70
Orange, chrome, clear plastic. Al Hanna's funny car. Reissue of H-1442 (1973).

H-1452 '72 Charger "Chi-Town Hustler" 1974-77 1/25 $60-80
Silver-gray, chrome, clear plastic. Farkonas/Coil/Minick car. Reissue of H-1446 (1973).

H-1453 '74 Chevy Vega Funny Car 1974-77 1/25 $40-50
Yellow, chrome, clear plastic. Don "Revell's Supershoe" Schumacher's car. Reissued as H-1456 (1975) and H-1459 (1976).

H-1455 '72 Demon "The Mongoose" Funny Car 1976-77 1/25 $80-90
White, chrome, clear plastic. "English Leather" decals. Second-issue '72 Demon. Tom McEwen's car. Reissued as H-1465 (1976) and H-1429 (1978).

H-1456 '72 Vega "Speed Equipment World" 1975 1/25 $70-80
Yellow, chrome, clear plastic. "Superman" decal. Chuck Tanko's funny car. Driven by Jim "Superman" Nicoll. Reissue of H-1453 (1973).

H-1457 '72 Demon "Custom Body" Funny Car 1975-77 1/25 $90-110
Black, chrome, clear plastic. Decal. First-issue '72 Demon. Phil Castronovo's car. Reissue of H-1447 (1973).

H-1458 Tony Nancy's "Revel-liner" Rail 1976-77 1/25 $30-40
Yellow, black, chrome plastic. Decals. Rear-engine dragster.

H-1459 '75 Vega "Snowman" Funny Car 1976-77 1/25 $50-60
Red, chrome, clear plastic. "Revell's Snowman" decals. Reissue of H-1453 (1974).

H-1460 Don Garlits' AA Fuel Dragster 1974-77 1/25 $40-60
Black, chrome plastic. Rear-engine rail dragster. "Revell" decal on wing. Uses Revell's first-issue generic rail mold with a standing figure of driver holding a trophy, spoked bicycle front wheels, Enderle intake, small rear wing. Model of "Swamp Rat" #19, now on display in the Museum of Drag Racing, Ocala, Florida. Reissued as: H-1461 (1975); H-1462 (1977); H-1435 (1978).

H-1461 Keelin & Clayton "California Charger" 1975-77 1/25 $70-80
Light blue, chrome plastic. Rear-engine rail dragster. "Revell" decal on wing. Reissue of H-1460 with front wheel fenders.

H-1462 Shirley Muldowney Rail 1977 1/25 $70-80
Pink, chrome plastic. "Revell" decal on wing. Top Fuel rear-engine rail dragster. Last of the dragster kits to be issued. Reissue of H-1460 (1974).

H-1463 Tom McEwen "The Mongoose" Rail 1975-76 1/25 $70-80
Red, chrome plastic. "Fly Navy" decal. Rear-engine dragster. Uses Revell's second-issue generic dragster mold with standing driver figure with separate helmet, solid front wheels, three-butterfly blower, larger rear wing. Reissued as H-1464 (1975).

H-1464 Don Prudhomme "The Snake" Rail 1975-76 1/25 $80-90
White, chrome plastic. "Army" decal. Rear-engine rail dragster. Reissue of H-1463.

H-1465 '72 Demon "Revellution" Funny Car 1976-77 1/25 $70-80
Red, chrome, clear plastic. "Revellution" decals. Second-issue '72 Demon. Ed McCulloch's car. Reissue of H-1455 (1976).

H-1466 Jeb Allen's "Praying Mantis" Rail 1976-77 1/25 $40-50
Red, chrome plastic. "Revell" decal on wing. Rear-engine rail dragster.

H-1467 '76 Monza "Army" Funny Car 1976-77 1/25 $50-60
White, chrome, clear plastic. "Army" decals. Don "The Snake" Prudhomme's car. Reissued as: H-1468 (1977); H-1469 (1977); H-1437 (1978).

H-1468 '76 Monza Pisano/Matsubara Funny Car 1977 1/25 $70-80
Yellow, chrome, clear plastic. "Piscan/Matsubara" decals. Reissue of H-1467 (1976).

H-1469 '76 Monza "Jungle Jim" Funny Car 1977 1/25 $50-60
Blue, chrome, clear plastic. Decals. Jim Liberman's car. Reissue of H-1467 (1976).

1/16 Scale 1970s Cars

H-800 Police Pursuit Van (Electronic Action) 1978 1/16 $25-30
Black, clear plastic. The model rests on a base that contains an electric motor, speaker, and four "C" batteries. Siren, flashing emergency lights, gear-shift noise. Reissued as H-800 Paramedic Van.

H-800 Paramedic Van (Electronic Action) 1979 1/16 $20-30
Red, black, clear plastic. The model rests on a base that contains an electric motor, speaker, and four "C" batteries. Siren, flashing emergency lights, gear-shift noise. Reissued of H-800 Police Pursuit Van.

H-1288 1934 Rolls Royce Continental 1979-80 1/16 $50-60
Brown, black, brass chrome, clear plastic. Rubber tires. Plastic tube for engine wiring. Hood, trunk, doors open. Canvas textured, adhesive-backed "cloth" for roof; wood grain textured, adhesive-backed "wood" for dash and interior

trim. Base, gold braided rope for stanchions that surround base. In 1980 the builder could mail in for a personalized "built by" nameplate. "Museum Classic." Reissue of H-1294 (1978).

H-1290 "Big Bad Van" Custom Chevy 1977-80 1/16 $40-50
Orange, brown, black, chrome, clear plastic. "Big rig" truck style vertical exhaust pipes. Includes bed, sink, refrigerator, tape deck.

H-1291 Chevy "Movin' Out" Custom Van 1978-80 1/16 $40-50
Brown, chrome, clear plastic. With "big rig" truck stack exhaust pipes.

H-1293 Chevy High Sierra Pickup/Camper 1979-80 1/16 $40-50
Dark brown, light brown, chrome, clear plastic. 4x4 pickup with camper shell on back.

H-1294 1934 Rolls Royce Phantom II 1978-80 1/16 $40-50
Brown, black, brass chrome, clear plastic. Vinyl tires. Plastic tube for engine wiring. Hood, trunk, doors open. Canvas textured, adhesive-backed "cloth" for roof; wood grain textured, adhesive-backed "wood" for dash and interior trim. Base, gold braided rope for stanchions that surround base. This mold was purchased from Entex. The original tooling was developed in Japan and revised by Revell. Reissued as H-1288 (1979).

The following "Signature Series" car kits were models of actual rail and funny car dragsters sponsored by Revell.

H-1480 Tony Nancy's "Loner" Rail Dragster 1972-74 1/16 $80-90
Orange, black, chrome, plastic. "Wynn's Sizzler" decals. Front-engine dragster.

H-1481 Dodge Charger "Snowman" Funny Car 1972-75 1/16 $100-120
Red, clear, chrome plastic. Decals. Gene Snow's car.

H-1482 Duster "Revellution" Funny Car 1972-76 1/16 $70-80
White, blue, chrome, clear plastic. Art Whipple, owner; Ed "Ace" McCulloch, driver.

H-1483 Keeling & Clayton Rail Dragster 1972-74 1/16 $90-110
Light blue, black, chrome plastic. "California Charger" decals. Front-engine dragster.

H-1484 "Praying Mantis" Rail Dragster 1973-77 1/16 $80-90
Blue, chrome, clear plastic. "Jeb Allen" decals. Rear-engine dragster. Standing driver figure holding gloves, molded in either blue or white plastic.

H-1485 Grand Am "Revelleader" Funny Car 1973-75 1/16 $70-80
Yellow, blue, chrome, clear plastic. Mickey Thompson's car. Reissued as H-1499 (1976).

H-1486 '72 Vega "Jungle Jim" Funny Car 1973-77 1/16 $80-100
Blue, chrome, clear plastic. Decals. Jim Liberman's car.

H-1487 "Revell Hawaiian" Funny Car 1974 1/16 $90-100
Metallic blue, chrome, clear plastic. Decals. Roland Leong's Dodge Charger.

H-1488 Kuhl & Olsen Rail Dragster 1974-75 1/16 $80-100
Yellow, chrome plastic. "Da Revell Fast Guys" decal. Rear-engine dragster.

H-1489 "The Snake" Rail Dragster "Army" 1974-77 1/16 $100-120
White, black, chrome plastic. Standing driver figure. "Army" decals. Don "The Snake" Prudhomme's 1974 rear-engine AA rail fueler.

H-1490 Tom "Mongoose" McEwen Rail "Navy" 1974-77 1/16 $110-130
Red, blue, chrome plastic. White plastic driver figure. "Fly Navy" decal. Rear-engine dragster.

H-1491 Don Garlits' "Swamp Rat" Rail 1975-77 1/16 $80-100
Black, chrome plastic. Standing driver figure holding helmet. Rear-engine dragster. Upscale version of H-1460.

H-1492 Duster "Revellation" Funny Car 1977 1/16 $90-110
Blue, chrome, clear plastic. Ed "The Ace" McCulloch's car.

H-1496 "The Snake" Vega "Army" Funny Car 1975-77 1/16 $100-115
White, black, chrome, clear plastic. "Army" decals. Don "The Snake" Prudhomme's car.

H-1497 Duster "English Leather" Funny Car 1975-77 1/16 $80-100
White, blue, chrome, clear plastic. Tom "The Mongoose" McEwen's car.

H-1498 Chevy Vega "Snowman" Funny Car 1976-77 1/16 $90-110
Red, black, chrome, clear plastic. Gene Snow's "Snowman." Also issued as H-1496 (1975).

H-1499 Grand Am "U. S. Marines" Funny Car 1976-77 1/16 $100-110
Blue, chrome, clear plastic. Decals. Mickey Thompson's car. Reissue of H-1485 with new decals and paint scheme.

1/12 Scale 1970s Cars
These are ex-Renwal models.

H-1285 1954 Mercedes-Benz 300 SL 1977-79 1/12 $50-60
Red, brown, black, chrome, clear plastic. Black vinyl tires. Fifteen inches long. This classic car with "gull-wing" doors, features a detailed engine, opening doors, hood, trunk. *Scale Modeler* (June 1978, 17) deemed it: "truly superb." Ex-Renwal.

H-1286 1965 Mustang 2 + 2 Fastback 1978-80 1/12 $80-90
Yellow, black, chrome, clear plastic. Ex-Renwal.

H-1287 1965 Ferrari 275 GTB 1979-80 1/12 $80-90
Red, chrome, clear plastic. Vinyl tires.

1970s Motorcycles

All have rubber tires and flexible plastic tubes for cables and fuel lines.

1/8 Scale Cycles

H-802 Police Bike (Electronic Action)   1978-79   1/8 $20-30
Black, chrome, clear plastic. Mounted on stand that holds electric batteries for siren, flashing lights, gear change noise. Also issued as H-1224 and H-1553.

H-1220 Yamaha Scrambler 350   1970-74   1/8 $30-40
Blue, chrome plastic. Red taillight. Modified reissue of H-1225 Grand Prix (1969).

H-1221 Corvair Six-Pack Trike   1971-73   1/8 $90-100
Metallic blue, chrome plastic. Leynnwood box art.

H-1222 Tric-Up 3-Wheeler Trike   1970-72   1/8 $90-100
Orange, chrome plastic. C-Cab body. Modified reissue of H-1223 (1969).

H-1224 Harley-Davidson Electra Glide   1970-73   1/8 $30-40
Dark red, gray, chrome, clear plastic. Reissue of H-1227 Police Bike (1969).

H-1226 Yamaha Dirt Cycle   1971-74   1/8 $25-35
Yellow, chrome plastic. "32" decal. Reissue of H-1225 Grand Prix (1969).

H-1228 Kawasaki 500 Mach III   1970-74   1/8 $50-60
Black, chrome, clear plastic. Red taillight. Reissued as H-1275 (1971).

H-1229 "Evil Iron" Trike   1971-80   1/8 $90-100
Red, chrome plastic. Triumph 650 engine. Designed by Darrell Zipp.

H-1240 Harley-Davidson L. A. Street Chopper 1971-80   1/8 $60-70
Red, chrome plastic. Harley 74 "Knucklehead" engine. Designed by Darrell Zipp.

H-1275 Kawasaki Drag Bike Mach III   1971-73   1/8 $70-80
Blue, chrome, red, clear plastic. Designed by Darrell Zipp. Reissue of H-1228 (1970).

H-1550 Harley-Davidson #1 Drag Bike   1972-73   1/8 $70-80
Metalflake blue, chrome plastic. Solid rubber rear tire. Harley 74 "Knucklehead" engine. Designed by Darrell Zipp.

H-1551 Midnight Rider   1972-74   1/8 $60-80
Purple, chrome plastic. Designed by Darrell Zipp. Long spokes in front.

H-1552 BMW R75-5 "Wunderbike"   1973-74   1/8 $40-50
Blue, chrome plastic. Vinyl tires.

H-1553 California Highway Patrol Bike   1977-80   1/8 $30-40
Black, white, chrome, clear plastic. Harley-Davidson 1200 Electra Glide. California Highway Patrol decals.

H-1554 Yamaha Dirt Bike   1979-80   1/8 $35-45
Yellow, black, chrome plastic. Rubber tires.

H-1560 Triumph Drag Bike   1973-75   1/8 $60-80
White, chrome plastic. 650cc engine, racing slick in back.

H-1590 "Dragonfire" Trike   1972-80   1/8 $80-90
Green, chrome plastic. Vinyl tires. Designed by Dennis Rich.

H-1591 Formula Fast Trike   1974-75   1/8 $80-90
White, chrome plastic. Racing slicks in back, rear airfoil spoiler. Corvair powered.

1970s 1/12 Scale Motorcycles

H-1500 Kawasaki Mach III   1972-73   1/12 $35-45
Blue, chrome, clear plastic. Model developed by Takara for Revell. 500 cc engine.

H-1501 Harley-Davidson Rough Rider   1972-75   1/12 $35-45
Gold metalflake, chrome plastic. Shovelhead engine. Designed by Darrell Zipp. Reissued as H-1514 (1976).

H-1502 Yamaha 250 DT-1 Enduro   1972-75   1/12 $20-30
Copper, clear, chrome plastic. Rubber tires. Model developed by Takara for Revell. Reissued as H-1513 (1976).

H-1503 Husqvarna 400cc Moto-Cross   1973-75   1/12 $35-45
Gray, chrome plastic. Vinyl tires. Racing decal. This is the bike of Malcolm Smith, star of the racing bike movie *On Any Sunday*. Model developed by Takara for Revell. Reissued as H-1519 (1976).

H-1504 Street L'Eagle Trike   1973-74   1/12 $60-80
Blue, chrome plastic. Harley with shovelhead engine and custom body with eagle motif.

H-1505 Kawasaki Street Racer Mach III   1973-74   1/12 $35-45
Red, chrome plastic. Model developed by Takara for Revell.

H-1506 Yamaha 250 MX   1973-75   1/12 $20-30
Copper, chrome plastic. Decals. Motocross racer. Model developed by Takara for Revell. Reissued as H-1518 (1976).

H-1507 Chain Gang Chopper   1974-75   1/12 $35-45

Purple, chrome plastic. Reissued as H-1515 (1976).

H-1508 Harley-Davidson Voodoo Trike   1974-75   1/12 $60-80
Brown, chrome plastic. "Head Hunter" bike with two tiki heads on the seat.

H-1509 Suzuki TM-400   1975   1/12 $35-45
Yellow, chrome plastic. Decals. Cyclone Dirt Racer. Reissued as H-1517 (1976).

H-1511 Husqvarna 400cc Baja Husky   1976-80   1/12 $30-40
Black, chrome plastic. "Desert Raider."

H-1512 Suzuki TM-400 Cyclone Dirt Racer 1977-80   1/12 $35-45
Yellow, chrome plastic.

H-1513 Yamaha 250 DT-1 Enduro   1976   1/12 $20-30
Yellow, chrome plastic. Reissue of H-1502 (1972).

H-1514 Harley-Davidson Rough Rider   1976-78   1/12 $35-45
Yellow, chrome plastic. '74 Shovelhead engine. Reissue of H-1501 (1972).

H-1515 Chain Gang Chopper   1976-80   1/12 $35-45
Purple, chrome plastic. Reissue of H-1507 (1974).

H-1516 Kawasaki Café Racer   1976   1/12 $35-45
Red, chrome plastic. Rubber tires.

H-1517 Roger DeCoster Suzuki Motocrosser 1976-80   1/12 $35-45
Yellow, chrome plastic. Goodyear knobby rubber tires. Reissue of H-1509 (1975).

H-1518 Yamaha 250 MX   1976-79   1/12 $20-30
Gray, chrome plastic. Decals. Reissue of H-1506 (1973).

H-1519 Baja Husky   1976   1/12 $35-45
Black, chrome plastic. "26" Decal. Husqvarna 400cc Moto-Cross. Reissue of H-1503 (1973).

H-1520 Kawasaki KZ900 LTD   1977-80   1/12 $35-45
Black, chrome plastic. Rubber tires.

1970s Figure Kits

Endangered Species Series

H-713 Endangered Species Set   1974-75 $150-170
Includes H-700, H-701, H-702, H-703. All of the Endangered Species models were sculpted by Chris Matson. They featured snap-together construction and moving parts.

H-700 White Rhino 1974-75   1/12 $30-50
Gray plastic. Legs, head, ears, tail move.

H-701 Komodo Dragon   1974-75   1/10 $40-50
Metallic yellow-green plastic.

H-702 California Condor   1974-75   1/8 $30-40
Black plastic.

H-703 Mountain Gorilla   1974-75   1/10 $40-60
Black plastic.

H-704 Polar Bear   1975   1/12 $40-50
White plastic.

H-705 Black Panther   1975   1/12 $50-60
Black plastic. Twist the panther's head, and his mouth opens.

H-900 Visible Man 1977-80   1/5 $15-20
Cream, clear plastic. Ex-Renwal mold.

H-901 Visible Woman   1977-80   1/5 $15-20
Cream, clear plastic. Ex-Renwal mold.

H-902 Human Skeleton   1977-80   1/5 $15-20
Glow-in-the-dark plastic. Ex-Renwal mold.

H-904 Human Skull 1977-80   1/1 $15-20
Glow-in-the-dark plastic. Ex-Renwal mold.

H-945 Robin Hood Set #1   1974-75 $50-70
Snap assembly. Little John™, Robin Hood™, Maid Marion™, Prince John™, Sir Hiss™. Includes: cardboard backdrop and cut-out figures on the box sides. Based on the Disney animated movie. Model department manager Ron Campbell judged the Robin Hood molds "a waste of money" since the kits didn't sell.

H-946 Robin Hood Set #2   1974-75 $50-70
Red, yellow plastic. Snap assembly. Royal Coach, Loyal Elephant, Prince John. Includes cardboard backdrop and cut-out figures on the box sides.

H-960 The Appaloosa   1972, 75-76   1/10 $35-45
Black plastic. Bronze vinyl western saddle and accessories. Brown cloth blanket and string rope. Reissue of H-1922 (1963).

H-961 The Jumper   1972, 75-76   1/10 $35-45
Brown plastic. Hair texture added to plastic surface. English saddle, cloth blanket. Reissue of H-1920 (1962).

H-962 The Palomino   1972, 75-76   1/10 $35-45
Palomino color plastic. Western show saddle. Reissue of H-1920 (1962).

MORE SCHIFFER TITLES

www.schifferbooks.com

Lesney's Matchbox® Toys The Superfast Years, 1969-1982. Revised 2nd Edition. Charlie Mack. The most popular die cast toys in the world, Matchbox metal vehicles took on a new look in 1969 with the introduction of the Superfast line, and this new book documents them all. The diversity of these tiny toys is truly amazing. Written as a sequel to this other popular volume, Lesney's Matchbox Toys, Regular Wheel Years, 1947-1969 (Schiffer, 1992), author Charlie Mack has compiled clear color illustrations of the toys and accurate text to identify all of the many variations in details which make each toy so recognizable and collectible today. This new edition features an updated Price Guide that is helpful to collectors who search for those elusive and rare models at today's swap meets, toy and antiques shows, or flea markets.

Size: 9" x 6"	160+ photos	128pp.
Price Guide		
ISBN: 0-7643-0772-X	soft cover	$19.95

Matchbox® Toys The Universal Years, 1982-1992. Revised 2nd Edition. Charlie Mack. In 1982, ownership of Matchbox die cast toys, the most popular metal vehicles in the world, passed from

Lesney to Universal. The toys produced under Universal's ownership are documented in this thorough text. It includes the vehicles and a wide variety of other toys manufactured under the Matchbox logo, including infants' educational toys, dolls, and puzzles. This is the third in a series (preceded by Lesney's Matchbox Toys: The Superfast years, 1969-1982 and Lesney's Matchbox toys, Regular Wheel Years, 1947-1969, published by Schiffer Publishing) of marvelous Matchbox books by Charlie Mack. In this revised edition, he has gathered fine color photographs of all the vehicles, their variations, and the other toys produced by Universal. Additional materials include lists of places of interest for the collector to visit and mail order sources.

Size: 9" x 6"	186 color photos	256pp.
Price Guide		
ISBN: 0-7643-0771-1	soft cover	$19.95

The Unauthorized Encyclopedia of Corgi Toys. Bill Manzke. Hop in for a complete tour of the tiny world this British toy maker created. Explore four decades of diecast production, following the route the industry took as it shed outdated techniques for state-of-the-art cars James Bond would have been proud of. Written from the unique perspective of an American collector, the book presents topics never before discussed in print, chronicling the rise, fall, and rebirth of Corgi Toys, all illustrated with hundreds of color photos of models and memorabilia never before seen in print. The smaller Husky and Corgi Juniors lines, often neglected in other books, are also covered. Other sections examine Corgi clubs, marketing, packaging, memorabilia, and special interest groupings. Most importantly, this encylopedia presents the most complete variation listing and value guide published to date, including sections covering Corgi, Husky, and Juniors models from their introduction through the present day.

Size: 8 1/2" x 11"	779 color photos	256pp.
Price Guide		
ISBN: 0-7643-0308-2	soft cover	$34.95

Collecting Matchbox™ Regular Wheels, 1953-1969. Charlie Mack. Matchbox vehicles, from cars and trucks to tractors and trailers, produced in series 1 through 75, from 1953 to 1969, are presented here in both detailed text listings and over 370 vivid color photographs. Variations of each vehicle manufactured are described, and

many are shown. Various box styles used throughout this period are presented. Prices for the Matchbox vehicles and their variations are listed in this easy-to-use text.

Size: 8 1/2" x 11"	373 photos	136pp.
Price Guide		
ISBN: 0-7643-1198-0	soft cover	$29.95